City of the
End of Things

Lectures on Civilization and Empire

Northrop Frye

J.Robert Oppenheimer

Edward Togo Salmon

Introduction by Jonathan Hart

OXFORD

UNIVERSITY PRESS

OXFORD
UNIVERSITY PRESS

70 Wynford Drive, Don Mills, Ontario M3C 1J9

www.oupcanada.com

Oxford University Press is a department of the University of Oxford.
It furthers the University's objective of excellence in research, scholarship,
and education by publishing worldwide in

Oxford   New York

Auckland   Cape Town   Dar es Salaam   Hong Kong   Karachi
Kuala Lumpur   Madrid   Melbourne   Mexico City   Nairobi
New Delhi   Shanghai   Taipei   Toronto

With offices in

Argentina   Austria   Brazil   Chile   Czech Republic   France   Greece
Guatemala   Hungary   Italy   Japan   Poland   Portugal   Singapore
South Korea   Switzerland   Thailand   Turkey   Ukraine   Vietnam

Oxford is a trade mark of Oxford University Press in the UK
and in certain other countries

Published in Canada by Oxford University Press

Library and Archives Canada Cataloguing in Publication

City of the end of things : lectures on science, civilization and empire / edited by Jonathan Hart.

Lectures from a series given at McMaster University from 1956 to thepresent.

Complete contents: The flying trapeze / J. Robert Oppenheimer — The modern century / Northrop Frye — The
nemesis of empire / Edward Togo Salmon.

ISBN 978-0-19-543005-9

I. Hart, Jonathan

CB5.C58 2008   081   C2008-903959-9

Cover image: "Urban Beauty" by Leslie Furness (2006)

1 2 3 4 — 12 11 10 09

Oxford University Press Canada is committed to our environment. This book is printed on Forest Stewardship
Council certified paper which contains 30% post-consumer waste.

Printed and bound in Canada.

Printed on 30% recycled paper

20
trees were saved
for our forests

Preserving our environment
Oxford University Press Canada chose to use recycled
paper to print this book and saved these resources[1]:

energy	water	greenhouse gases	solid waste
28 million BTUs	51,866L	1,911 kg	734 kg

Printed by **Webcom Inc.**
on Legacy TB Natural 30% post-consumer waste.

FSC

Mixed Sources
Product group from well-managed
forests, and recycled wood or fiber

Cert no. SW-COC-002358
www.fsc.org
© 1996 Forest Stewardship Council

[1]Estimates were made using the Environmental Defense Paper Calculator.

For George Edward Hart and Mary Alice Marshall

Contents

The City of the End of Things

Archibald Lampman

Beside the pounding cataracts
Of midnight streams unknown to us
'Tis builded in the leafless tracts
And valleys huge of Tartarus.
Lurid and lofty and vast it seems;
It hath no rounded name that rings,
But I have heard it called in dreams
The City of the End of Things.
Its roofs and iron towers have grown
None knoweth how high within the night,
But in its murky streets far down
A flaming terrible and bright
Shakes all the stalking shadows there,
Across the walls, across the floors,
And shifts upon the upper air
From out a thousand furnace doors;
And all the while an awful sound
Keeps roaring on continually,
And crashes in the ceaseless round
Of a gigantic harmony.
Through its grim depths re-echoing
And all its weary height of walls,
With measured roar and iron ring,
The inhuman music lifts and falls.
Where no thing rests and no man is,
And only fire and night hold sway;
The beat, the thunder and the hiss
Cease not, and change not, night nor day.

And moving at unheard commands,
The abysses and vast fires between,
Flit figures that with clanking hands
Obey a hideous routine;
They are not flesh, they are not bone,
They see not with the human eye,
And from their iron lips is blown
A dreadful and monotonous cry;
And whoso of our mortal race
Should find that city unaware,
Lean Death would smite him face to face,
And blanch him with its venomed air:
Or caught by the terrific spell,
Each thread of memory snapt and cut,
His soul would shrivel and its shell
Go rattling like an empty nut.

It was not always so, but once,
In days that no man thinks upon,
Fair voices echoed from its stones,
The light above it leaped and shone:
Once there were multitudes of men,
That built that city in their pride,
Until its might was made, and then
They withered age by age and died.
But now of that prodigious race,
Three only in an iron tower,
Set like carved idols face to face,
Remain the masters of its power;
And at the city gate a fourth,
Gigantic and with dreadful eyes,
Sits looking toward the lightless north,
Beyond the reach of memories;
Fast rooted to the lurid floor,
A bulk that never moves a jot,
In his pale body dwells no more,

Or mind or soul,—an idiot!
But sometime in the end those three
Shall perish and their hands be still,
And with the master's touch shall flee
Their incommunicable skill.
A stillness absolute as death
Along the slacking wheels shall lie,
And, flagging at a single breath,
The fires shall moulder out and die.
The roar shall vanish at its height,
And over that tremendous town
The silence of eternal night
Shall gather close and settle down.
All its grim grandeur, tower and hall,
Shall be abandoned utterly,
And into rust and dust shall fall
From century to century;
Nor ever living thing shall grow,
Nor trunk of tree, nor blade of grass;
No drop shall fall, no wind shall blow,
Nor sound of any foot shall pass:
Alone of its accursèd state,
One thing the hand of Time shall spare,
For the grim Idiot at the gate
Is deathless and eternal there.

Introduction

In his first Whidden Lecture of 1967, Northrop Frye echoes a line and title from Lampman (1861–99), one of the most evocative poets writing in English in the last part of the nineteenth century. The 1892 poem seems to represent a hellish or apocalyptic dream that begins in the Tartarus of classical mythology.[1] Frye names his first lecture after the poem in a book about Canada's first century, which also happens to be a modern century. This was a time of urbanization and change in which the community was threatened by the end of things in ways Lampman could not have imagined before the advent of the atomic bomb—although the wrath of God and nature on such a scale would have been part of his cultural heritage. The end that the bomb brought was human-made. The title of this volume, which comes from Lampman via Frye, suggests the precariousness of modernity in its cities in and against nature. This is a book of ends as aims and as the crisis that might bring an end with a finality of great brutality or suffering. These are the times of hope and despair. The years in and about 1967 have a good deal to say about what went before and came after.

This book brings together three lectures in the crucial time from 1962 to 1973, from the final tag-end of the dissolution of the Western European empires and in the shadow of the Cold War, to the Oil Crisis and one of the Arab-Israeli Wars. From the time that renowned physicist J. Robert Oppenheimer delivered his Whidden lecture on physics at McMaster University in 1962, through Northrop Frye's 1967 lecture, to Edward Togo Salmon's in 1973, much had happened to transform the world.

I remember this time well, one of my childhood and youth. Like anyone there then, I recall the day of Kennedy's assassination, not quite two years after the Oppenheimer lectures; the wars in the Middle East; and the Canadian Centennial that took place the year of the Frye lecture. There was further conflict in what was once called the Near East (or the *Proche Orient* to the French) and the Oil Crisis the year of Salmon's lectures. And Vietnam was first escalating and then casting its shadow through this period. The 1960s were a defining moment for so many in the West—the Baby Boomers, those born in around the Second World War, came of age in jobs or at university during this era. It was a time of flux in politics, economics, religion, and culture. In popular culture, music, fashion and drugs, and images in film, television, advertising, and propaganda all changed with a great pace and transformed mental, physical, emotional, and spiritual landscapes. It was a time of revolution. There were so many young people—and that was a great pressure on the less young. And, as Oppenheimer points out, the atomic bomb changed the world like nothing before it: all this flux was taking place in its shadow. *Dr Strangelove* was and was not fiction. The Cuban Missile Crisis and the arms race were not.

This was the world in which the organizers of the Whidden Lectures, a distinguished series at McMaster University, found themselves. The lectures were also established during the Cold War in 1954, the last year that Winston Churchill was Prime Minister of Britain (he resigned in 1955) and during Eisenhower's presidency. This was a time when the Second World War was still much on the minds and in the lives of many. It was also a time of great change: the first computer course was held at the University of Cambridge in 1953. From the first Whidden Lecture in 1956, the year of the Suez Crisis, the international and interdisciplinary nature of the speakers and the topics was apparent. When E.C. Fox, a member of the Board of Governors at McMaster, set up the lecture series to honour the remarkable Howard P. Whidden, churchman, one-time member of the Parliament of Canada, and Chancellor of McMaster, who had moved the entire University from Toronto to Hamilton in 1930, he did so to cross the thresholds between departments in the university.

The Whidden Lectures have been influential, and their association with Oxford University Press fruitful. McMaster University has distinguished itself in additional ways with foresight and excellence in the humanities and has, as part of that legacy, collected the papers of Bertrand Russell (the archive arriving in 1968). The three Whidden Lectures collected here are worthy of our attention because of the critical time in which they were delivered, the quality of their thought, and because they tell us something about the crisis of modernity, that prolonged phenomenon that developed with the age of exploration, the scientific revolution, and the Industrial Revolution, and has been prolonged in the never-ending technological revolution that science has unlocked. Oppenheimer, Frye, and Salmon discuss nothing less than the knowledge, culture, and history of the age that begot us and the one that we must try to survive and thrive in.

This was also an age of ideological conflict. Those caught between communism and capitalism were involved in a protracted conflict that had begun in earnest in the late eighteenth century. The origins of the conflict were in the French Revolution, in the workings of the Industrial Revolution, in the Russian Revolution of 1917, and even in the struggles in Europe in the wake of the First World War. Variations on the same conflict arguably continued through the Great Depression, the Second World War, and the Cold War. Karl Marx's *Das Kapital* was published in 1867, the year Canada was granted independence over its domestic affairs as a Dominion in the British Empire. Revolts and revolutions are means of violent struggle in human societies that have taken place at least since classical antiquity. The Dutch Revolt, the English Revolution, the American Revolution, the French Revolution, the Russian Revolution, and others from the sixteenth century onward have shaped our "modern" world.

In all this turmoil, Canada had been a cross-roads from the late fifteenth century. J. Robert Oppenheimer writes about three crises in physics; Northrop Frye about the modern (or twentieth) century, and E.T. Salmon about the relation between the British and Roman empires. Canada was part of the coming of age of the Americas, in which the balance of power in the world shifted westward. In the twentieth century, and especially the years surrounding the Second World War, Canada helped to mediate between Britain and the United States as it once had been a site of conflict between France and Britain, and then Britain and the United States. It was geographically caught between the United States and the Soviet Union in the missile and arms race. So it is fitting that the

Whidden Lectures collected here acknowledge this positioning, and explore pressing questions of the time that are still with us.

In this age of science, how much is science a power for good or ill? In this age of technology, can literature and culture play a vital role? In this age of nationalism, what is the ghost of empire? Are science, literature, and history used for ideological ends? People are still wondering whether they live in an age of decolonization, postcolonialism, or neo-imperialism. What has happened to the lasting peace that politicians like Woodrow Wilson, Franklin Roosevelt, Lester Pearson, and others advocated? It is no surprise that we may still find ourselves in a crisis of modernity in science, culture, and history; and that political and economic progress is halting, uneven, and disappointing, clearly unable to relieve significantly the suffering of the poor, sick, and disadvantaged in Canada and elsewhere.

More than 25 years before giving the Whidden Lectures, E.T. Salmon, Professor of Ancient History at McMaster University, speaking to the Empire Club in Toronto on 17 April 1947, reminded his audience at the opening of his speech—entitled "The Making of the Peace"—about what Roosevelt had said in Washington in 1940:

> Today we seek a moral basis for peace. It cannot be a real peace if it fails to recognize brotherhood. It cannot be a lasting peace if the fruits of it are oppression, starvation, or cruelty, or human life dominated by armed camps. It cannot be a sound peace if small nations must live in fear of powerful neighbours. It cannot be a moral peace if freedom from invasion is sold for tribute. It cannot be an intelligent peace if it denies free passage to that knowledge of those ideals which permit men to find common ground. It cannot be a righteous peace if worship of God is denied.[2]

The great theme of this collection is war and peace, and this complex topic takes on additional dimensions with the development of atomic power. How do history and culture make a difference in the age of science—when science itself evolved to become a great tool for both good and harm? Francis Bacon, discussing "natural philosophy" (what we now call science) in the early stages of what has been called modernity, as long ago as 1597, declared that knowledge is power.[3] Lord Acton also famously declared that "Power tends to corrupt and absolute power corrupts absolutely."[4] Logic might lead us to think that if knowledge is power and power tends to corrupt, then knowledge itself may also corrupt. That is the myth of the Fall, when Adam and Eve eat of the forbidden fruit of the Tree of the Knowledge of Good and Evil.

It also recalls the story of Dr Faustus or Faust that both Christopher Marlowe and Wolfgang von Goethe represented with such brilliance. The Faustian bargain is part of the alienation of nature and nurture, mind and body, the spiritual and physical worlds. But paradoxically, it may be knowledge that is the safeguard against its own abuses. Knowledge has the power to help and heal as well as the power to harm and kill. Its very ambivalence and tension is part of the scientific revolution and the so-called explosion of knowledge in the twentieth century. And of course this tension continues today. Oppenheimer, Frye, and Salmon focus on the knowledge of physics, literature, and empire as a means of understanding the present and the future they foresaw and that we, as readers, now inhabit.

Culture, science, and politics have never been easy bedfellows. Plato's Socrates would exile the poets who refused to sing the praises of the republic. Galileo was placed under house arrest for a science that challenged the religious belief and dogma of the time. In his famous discussion of "The Two Cultures," the Rede Lecture of 7 May 1959 given at the University of Cambridge (where Oppenheimer and Salmon had been students), British scientist and novelist C.P. Snow described how the lack of communication between the sciences and the humanities was an impediment to "progress," particularly in light of the complicated new world of atom bombs and alienation.[5] Snow's formulation proved controversial; it was attacked by F.R. Leavis, a Cambridge don in English literature.[6] Leavis thought that Snow's distinctions sounded primarily like public relations for science, trivializing culture (as embodied in the humanities) as a kind of relief or entertainment. Although this book explores knowledge and modernity, rather than the issue of a gulf between science and culture, we will see how this relationship continues to be a complicated one.

It is no wonder that G.H. Hardy's younger friend, C.P. Snow, who spoke so eloquently about science and the arts, was drawn to write an introduction to the new edition of Hardy's *A Mathematician's Apology* (1940) in 1967, long after Hardy, a brilliant mathematician who held fellowships at Cambridge and Oxford, was dead. This is a book that poets and mathematicians can both read to advantage. The reader, who has almost invariably been a student and has taught something to someone at some time, has scope to understand how Hardy embodies a respect and love for his subject. Horace spoke about poetry instructing and delighting, but it was Hardy who stressed that professors in all subjects had to embody the importance of their subject even to the point of slight exaggeration.[7] He is implying that there is a dramatic quality to teaching, whatever the subject, and I think he is right. Those who take the role of public intellectual, such as the Whidden or Rede lecturers, embody their subjects as a teacher would.

The three Whidden lecturers were university teachers. They use comparisons, contrasts, stories, illustrations, and anything else that allows for that embodiment and enables their audience to digest their argument. Hardy made an illuminating comparison between mathematics and poetry:

> The beauty of a mathematical theorem depends a great deal on its seriousness, as even in poetry the beauty of a line may depend to some extent on the significance of the ideas which it contains.[8]

For Hardy, mathematics is a creative art. He ends his wonderful, small book with the creations of mathematicians, "or of any of the artists, great or small, who have left some kind of memorial behind them."[9] There is a beauty to poetry and mathematics—the two underlying languages of culture past and present—that should move readers and students to love them, however complex and challenging they may be. The development of skills and techniques in these languages, the core of creativity in the science, arts, and humanities, are part of the creative process; they are the dialogue between author and reader, speaker and audience. We are all students talking to other students, learning as we teach, crossing disciplinary boundaries from the bounds of our own. That is where I start, and where, it seems the idea of the Whidden Lectures started.

These three Whidden Lectures are linked through their focus on the relation between order and liberty, nations and their international commitment, the past and the future, war and peace, the beauty of aesthetics and the truth of ethics, thinkers from the past and future knowledge, continuity and change, science and society, pastoralism and utopia, and the world and its representation in physics, literature, and histories. The movement of this book is from Oppenheimer in 1962, through Frye in 1967, to Salmon in 1973, from physics, through literature and culture, to historical views of empire. At a critical moment in history, in an age proclaiming its modernity, these important figures offer some key views on a world fraught with problems and the possibility of the good life; as Plato's central question in *Republic*, of finding some ways forward, perhaps even making progress.

I

In 1962, J. Robert Oppenheimer had a formidable task: to explain the contribution of physics to people both inside and outside of the field. He had accepted the invitation after Harry Thode, a leading scientist at McMaster, had assured him that a top physicist would edit the lectures for publication, given that Oppenheimer did not have the time to write them up himself.[10] In his lecture "The Flying Trapeze: Three Crises for Physicists," Oppenheimer sought to bridge the gap between mathematics and words in describing the advances in physics. But Oppenheimer did not speak only the language of science. In addition to science, he had studied Greek and other humanities in school and French and philosophy at Harvard. His delivery of the Whidden Lectures was dramatic. Oppenheimer paced before the audience with a stack of papers in one hand "and on each page were three or four words written in very large letters"; and "when he was finished with one page he would toss it on the floor and move on to the next with the flourish of an actor."[11]

He opens his lecture with the advances of science in this "great century" of physics, which have greatly changed "the condition of human life." Our understanding of natural science has developed significantly, and he considers the "changes in the human situation brought about by the developments in physics and other sciences" (43). Scientific knowledge is doubling at an ever more rapid rate— a fact that seems as true now as it was in 1965. But despite the swift evolution of science, Oppenheimer points out the need for balance in scientific advance: even if the science of the biological and human worlds catches up to that of the physical world, our knowledge will always be

> very very incomplete and partial, and that the sense of having to
> live and act in response to tradition, good judgement, and wisdom,
> which we have now, will not ever be alleviated by any development
> of the sciences (44).

Science needs ethics and wisdom, potential limits to its power. Coming from the so-called "father of the atomic bomb," this is an intriguing and suggestive statement.

Oppenheimer was a highly controversial figure. He had ultimately lost his security clearance given his earlier political views. He had also been suspended from his post at the Atomic Energy Commission as a security risk for having opposed the hydrogen bomb in 1949 on moral and technical grounds.[12] Like Albert Einstein, he believed that the world community would have to work together and limit nuclear arms if humanity was to survive.

And as a scientist, Oppenheimer shows humility:

> the deep things in science are not found because they are useful;
> they are found because it was possible to find them (45).

And in addition to the haphazard nature of scientific advance, we learn more than just physics:

this progress in learning about the world of nature has changed rather profoundly not only what we know about nature, but some of the things that we know about ourselves as knowers (46).

Oppenheimer extends this knowledge to learning about the difference and reality of other cultures. This opening up is salutary. For him, it involves the combination of adventure and an adherence to the existing order and clarity. That means using tradition as much as possible unless one has to make a break. And some discoveries may be unsettling: for instance, Kepler sought spheres and found ellipses; Max Planck was not satisfied with the discontinuity he found; Albert Einstein could not reconcile himself to quantum theory. Oppenheimer notes that *revolution* is not the right word for the radical alteration of the changes in the beliefs and experience of physicists, who are "both traditional and conservative and at the same time a little too adventurous" (47).

He has a poetic way of describing the role of mathematics in physics, whose discoveries "could probably not have been made without the mathematical forms which give a quick synoptic and luminous way of representing the order that inheres in nature" (6). Mathematics are involved in nature because nature is consistent. Although Oppenheimer has to address a general audience with a limited use of mathematics, he sees this kind of explication as still being useful. To achieve his ends, he calls on analogies—it is still worthwhile to read Hamlet even in the absence of seeing a performance, to read Pasternak in English if one cannot read Russian.

Time and space, the realm of Einstein, brought changes to our understanding of physics that, in this context, Oppenheimer does describe as "revolutionary." Einstein's work was made possible by his predecessors, such as the Paris school of natural philosophers in the thirteenth and fourteenth centuries (Buridan, Oresme), and their work on impetus or momentum, and later Galileo, who produced related work in the "causeless character of uniform motion" (49). And of course, there is Isaac Newton, whose first law is a theory of impetus. There is a beauty in these earlier systems, according to

Oppenheimer, "a magnificently precise and beautiful science involving the celestial mechanics of the solar system" (50).

But this perfect system soon began to unravel. With Galileo there was a small doubt about "transformation," and later there was misgiving in Newton's mechanics (noted briefly by Leonhard Euler, whose *Mechanica* was published in 1736–37). The study of light and electromagnetism, which Hans Christian Ørsted—a Danish physicist and chemist—discovered in 1821, raised further doubts. James Clerk Maxwell's explanation of the propagation of electromagnetic waves of light in the 1860s, and Michael Faraday's idea of space consisting of different "fields" were not consistent with Galileo's property of invariance. Faraday's discoveries in the 1830s and 1840s were not fully understood until Maxwell's work. If space is full of magnetic and electric fields, it can appear as different things when a body (say, a person) moves in relation to it. Einstein solved the dilemma with the special theory of relativity, which "predicts correctly the behaviour of rods and clocks under motion," a series of equations which are now used in nuclear, atomic, and particle physics (58).

This theory changed our understanding of natural science in a significant way. It has given coherence to the connection between these facts:

> light travels with a velocity that cannot be added to or subtracted from by moving the source of light, … objects do contract when they are in motion … processes are slowed down when they take place in motion, and very much so if they move with velocities comparable to the velocity of light (60).

The implications of Einstein's theory continue to unfold. One of his theories about gravity maintains "that gravitational forces are determined by matter and express themselves in the geometry of space and time" (65). Moreover, gravity determines the gravitational forces acting on bodies. Oppenheimer stresses the simplicity and elegance of Einstein's mathematics in expressing his theory, adding that whether or not experiments will prove the theory correct in all areas, no one today who tries to express it in more pedestrian ways "can fail to be overwhelmed by the imagination, the daring, and the beauty of what Einstein did" (66). This is the kind of beauty G.H. Hardy was talking about that joins the mathematician and poet through aesthetics and imaginative power. And poetry also reminds us of mystery: whether space is finite or infinite is something Oppenheimer says we may never know.

The atom and the "field" is the topic of the second lecture, which moves into the rarefied realm of quantum theory. One of the central ideas is the relationship between fields and the structure of atoms, "that a changing magnetic field makes an electric one, a changing electric one makes a magnetic one, and that this pumping cycle produces an electromagnetic wave" (68). Oppenheimer returns to the beauty of the explanation of light in terms of waves with his own elegance:

> a century of experimentation showed how beautiful is the phenomena of the propagation of light—its reflection, its passage through slits, its diffraction from gratings, its dispersion—could be explained in terms of these simple ideas of the interference of waves (71).

He adds, with his own kind of explanatory drama, that "this harmonious picture of the nature of electromagnetic radiation received a sharp jolt from which it has never recovered" (71).

This "sharp jolt" was brought by Max Planck, who derived a formula to reconcile the different equilibrium properties of radiation. He did this, as Oppenheimer explains, by making the assumption "that light was not emitted continuously as a wave should be, but only in energy packets, which correspond to a multiple of the frequency, viz. $h\nu$" (72). Planck himself struggled with this: it seemed wrong, so he tried "to get his formula without making this dreadful assumption which contradicted the whole idea of light as a wave" (72). Planck thought he had made a mistake, but he was wrong, for he was right (however reluctantly)—as Einstein later proved. Einstein's mathematics, in Oppenheimer's words, "beautifully confirmed" the formula and, as Einstein noted, "'This clinches it. Obviously there *are* units of energy in light'" (73).

Oppenheimer reminds us that this discovery did not supersede a century of the study of wave phenomena. Both came to co-exist: "Interferometers and prisms, microscopes and radio waves still studied light in terms of the propagation of waves" (73). What Planck and Einstein had introduced "was this discontinuous particle aspect, at least to phenomena in which light was absorbed or emitted" (73). In short, light had a dual nature.

Thomson's view of the negatively charged electron soon led to further discoveries. One of these, which Oppenheimer again describes as "beautiful" and as "a marvellous story," was Ernest Rutherford's discovery of "the atomic nucleus which has the positive charge which gives the atom its chemical and most of its physical properties" (75). But this did not solve the puzzle. More pieces were needed. The work of others (like Johann Balmer and Niels Bohr) recognized a full-blown crisis in quantum theory.

But human understanding of the atom and its behaviour continued to move forward, however slowly, with two related studies. First, there was the description of electromagnetic waves—light as a wave phenomenon that shows interference and gives diffraction patterns. However, these waves have a discrete character in their transactions with matter and behave like light quanta with definite energy and momentum. Oppenheimer says that these electromagnetic waves "negotiate with matter by giving up this energy, or by taking it from matter or by colliding with matter in an elastic collision" (78).

Second, a problem arose from Rutherford's discovery of the atomic nucleus: what happens when atoms are in the vicinity of the nucleus? Oppenheimer describes these electromagnetic waves as "a state of information" (rather than, say, magnetic or electric fields), adding that a "good, well-designed observation gives information" (83). Here is a new view of objectivity in which the physicist has "to take into account the relation between this object to the world of nature"—not to him or her "as a human being," but to him or her "as one of the many physicists who are in the game" (84). Objectivity is not in a book nor even necessarily a feature of the atom itself; rather, it is a way of talking among physicists. This way of talking depends on avoiding ambiguity and having reproducibility and verifiability. Quantum theory is not deterministic and is acausal—events happen with no precise and determined cause. Each event is unique, and different experiments will generally give different answers "because the connexion between the two experiments is a statistical one, not a necessary one" (85).

This is of course a very different outlook from Newton's universe. The world of physics builds on past discoveries—which are not "thrown out" unless completely wrong—adding new discoveries that can show, for instance, new ways of seeing (as in the case of atom and field).

Oppenheimer's third lecture, "War and the Nations," turns to complementarity, drawing on Bohr's connection between illuminating physics and "complementary aspects of human life" (86).[13] What is good for a person and what is just for a society involve complementarity, and in an ideal society, these two are not so far apart. Science, it turns out, is not a tidy, straightforward system; and here again we see a connection between the sciences and the humanities:

> Those who have lived through the unravelling of the heart of the atomic paradox as it existed twenty-five or thirty years ago believe that one has come to a vision of the physical world with far more room for the human spirit in it than could have been found in the great mechanism of Newton (87).

And complementarity takes him into the realm of politics.

The discoveries of the positron and the neutron and the designing and building of accelerators opened up the field. In 1939, fission occurred. During the 1920s, scientists from Russia, England, Germany, and Scandinavia worked together, but that stopped during the 1930s and many physicists left Germany for the United Kingdom and North America. Refugee scientists in England and the United States first interested their governments in making atomic explosives.

There was what Oppenheimer calls "an uneasy co-operation between the United Kingdom, Canada, and the United States" in this matter. On 16 July 1945, when Truman, Churchill, and Stalin were meeting at Potsdam, the first atomic bomb was exploded in the desert of the southwestern United States. According to Oppenheimer, "The bombs were used against Japan. That had been foreseen and in principle approved by Roosevelt and Churchill when they met in Canada and again at Hyde Park" (90).

As a key figure in the development of the bomb, what was Oppenheimer's view of it? He points out that we will never know if a political settlement would have ended the war in the Far East, and Stalin, followed by Truman, did not seem interested in an overture for peace from the dissident part of the Government of Japan. At their meeting in Potsdam, Stalin had told Truman about this overture to Moscow three weeks before the atomic bombs were dropped on Hiroshima and Nagasaki. The plans for conventional war involved estimates of half a million to a million Allied casualties, and twice the number of Japanese. At this point, according to Oppenheimer, there was no interest in seeking this peace with Japan; but he is not explicit about the reasons: perhaps the group that contacted the Russians did not have authority, or perhaps the leaders lacked the political will.

Oppenheimer does, however, speak explicitly about his personal view of events:

> Nevertheless, my own feeling is that if the bombs were to be used there could have been more effective warning and much less wanton killing than took place actually in the heat of battle and the confusion of the campaign (91).

A political settlement would have been the best solution; but if a bomb was necessary, it should have been employed as a demonstration rather than actually wiping out a population. The city should have been warned; even if the inhabitants had fled, they would still have seen the destructive potential of the bomb, Oppenheimer appears to be saying.

He is also careful to contrast this hindsight with the reality of the heat of battle in which terrible things are done:

> That is about all that I am clear about in hindsight. That, and one other thing: I am very glad that the bomb was not kept secret. I am glad that all of us knew, as a few of us already did, what was up and what readjustments in human life and in political institutions would be called for. Those are the days when we all drank one toast only: "No more wars" (91).

Oppenheimer also recalls the efforts of Einstein and Bohr after the war. When Roosevelt, Churchill, and General Marshall did not listen to Bohr, he spoke out to the public about ending the secrecy. Other politicians sought international government, atomic control, and peace, but Oppenheimer wryly observes this is not what Stalin wanted, nor even what those in other governments ultimately decided on.

All Oppenheimer can offer as counsel, he says, is sobriety and "some hope" (92). Now we are left with complicated decisions:

> But it is true that we have been marked by our deep implication in this development, by the obvious fact that without physics it could not have happened, and by the heavy weight which has been laid on so many members of this community in counselling their government, in speaking publicly and in trying above all in the early phases to find a healthy direction (92).

This meditation makes us think about the responsibility of physics and physicists. It might also suggest that we consider the bonds between Faust and Galileo and the ways they are represented and represent themselves. In a world of crisis or pressure, how do any of us, including the most brilliant of physicists, make a responsible choice? In beauty is there also a kind of seduction, even if that is the aesthetics of mathematics or poetry? Do we keep going for the mutual relation of Keat's beauty and truth? Is the power of knowledge a way to the knowledge of power? Will that power lead to a corrupt use of knowledge, even if not entirely by those who make the discoveries? Oppenheimer maintains that the time of the arms race, the Cold War, and obdurate political conflict—in which the world might be destroyed at any time—was an age without precedent.

Oppenheimer is also openly honest about science: "the community of physicists is certainly no more than any other free of evil, free of vanity, or free of their own glory; we must expect rather ugly things to happen and they do" (93). Although he describes himself at the outset of the lectures as a person of hope (and continues to look for "some hope" at the end), he is also delivering on sobriety. He advocates honesty, openness when possible, distinctions between knowledge and best guesses, differences between scientific knowledge and discussions of value, and contributions to an international community of knowledge and understanding. Oppenheimer speaks about sharing with "any community of interest, any community of professional, of human, or of political concern" (94). Concern, as we will see below, is also an important concept for Northrop Frye.

At the end, Oppenheimer shifts back to the discoveries of physicists that involve an "increasing understanding of the natural physical world," one full of wonder and unexpectedness (94). He ends by providing a place for physicists in a utopian view, a hope, a vision at the end of things:

> We think of this as our contribution to the making of a world which is varied and cherishes variety, which is free and cherishes freedom, and which is freely changing to adapt to the inevitable needs of change in the twentieth century and all centuries to come, but a world which, with all its variety, freedom, and change, is without nation states armed for war and above all, a world without war (94).

This, without Oppenheimer saying it, is the work for the public worldwide and not simply for the physicists among us.

II

Northrop Frye's lectures occurred during the centenary of Canada's Confederation, but Frye, who was always committed to Canadian literature and culture, decided to speak about a wider context: the modern century from the birth of Canada as a nation to the then present year of 1967. Even so, he cannot resist naming his three lectures after the titles of poems by Archibald Lampman, Irving Layton, and Émile Nelligan (thereby making a Trojan horse use of Canadian culture—smuggling Canadian examples into a more general discussion). Frye, with his usual sense of perspective, reminds his Canadian audience that the centenary "is a private celebration, a family party, in what is still a relatively small country in a very big world" (101).

Frye points out that there were more important events in 1867 for various majorities: the sale of Alaska for North Americans; the second Reform Bill for people in the orbit of British traditions; for those alive today, the publication of Marx's first volume of *Das Kapital*; and, for the dead, the publication of Thomas Hardy's poem "1967." He sets out to place Canadian culture in the context of the world of 1867 to 1967.

He also intends to dispel myths about Canada that were commonplace about the time of these lectures—in particular, that to be a colony is "mature" and to be a nation is to be "grown up," a kind of fallacy of composition from the individual to the group. This analogy may work as a figure of speech, but it fails as the basis of a coherent historical argument. And certainly it is not the foundation for judging the moral quality of Canadian civilization. He also urges caution about equating nation with identity, given that "we are moving towards a post-national world, and … Canada has moved further in that direction than most of the smaller nations" (103).

Thus, for Frye, the importance of the hundred years in question is that Canada has had time to move from the consciousness of pre-nation to that of post-nation. Canada has avoided the suddenness of becoming a nation in the post-war era or in "a vast imperial complex like the U.S.A. or the U.S.S.R." (103). The Canadian sense of proportion has helped, and Frye, with his own sense of proportion, discusses social contexts in a world in which the nation is ceasing to be what he calls "the real defining unit of society" (104).

The concept of the "modern," according to Frye, began about the time of the birth of Canada. In 1967, the real boundary is between the bourgeois world of Canada and the United States, and the communist world of the Soviet Union. The modern world, especially the Western and democratic part of it, has distinguished itself in history by trying to be objective and aware of "the presuppositions underlying its behaviour, to understand its relation to previous history and to see whether its future could in some measure be controlled by its own will" (104). Frye sees a cultural dialectic and intellectual antagonism between active and passive attitudes to the times, the world at large, and society in particular. For Frye, the creative arts are active, and he sees a passive and uncritical attitude as inherently dangerous. The communicating arts are a mixture of things and range from film and television through propaganda to public relations.

Frye, with his characteristic wit, describes the rate of change:

> In a world where dynasties rise and fall at much the same rate as women's hemlines, the dynasty and the hemline look much alike in importance, and get much the same amount of featuring in the news (106).

But he gives a more solemn warning in his analysis of changing trends in speech, fashion, and entertainment; that is "whatever is sufficiently formed to be recognized has already receded into the past" (106). This is "the panic of change," a sense that things are happening too fast for our minds to process them (106). (Frye died in 1991, about the time electronic mail was becoming popular; he might well have thought that this and other technologies of instant communication would have made his words in 1967 seem even more appropriate.) There is despair in "the alienation of progress" (107). Frye speaks of alienation as psychological in well-fed society—a kind of devil of boredom—and of the bomb, that, as in *Dr Strangelove*, means humans have lost control, if they ever had it, over their destiny in the shadow of the atomic bomb (108–109). Despite the claims on both sides of the Cold War, Frye maintains that neither the destruction of communism nor of "capitalist imperialism" would rid the world of alienation (109). In such a context, Frye argues that there is a pressure to be passive and give into frivolity, avoiding "genuine concern" (109). This effort to prevent anxiety leaves the mind on the edge of hysteria; critical intelligence thus becomes vulnerable to suggestion.

Satan's seduction of Eve in Milton's *Paradise Lost*, like advertising and propaganda, plays on this state of lacking inner resources. The frightened, credulous, or childish mind that does not want to deal with the world is most exposed (109). Advertising is ironic when the economy seems to be independent of politics and thereby "creates an illusion of detachment and mental superiority even when one is obeying its exhortations" (110). Propaganda, such as that surrounding the Vietnam War, involves a predicament between the passive and active in an attempt to navigate a world of created illusion. Even the concern of the engaged citizen who tries to respond critically can become a stock response.

Passive and active are two mental attitudes in the same person. Being self-aware, according to Frye, heightens a sense of responsibility while draining the will from expressing it. Science progresses unlike the arts, and this became especially apparent in the nineteenth-century sense of progress, intensifying the human sense of time as being "dragged backwards from a receding past into an unknown future" (112–113). Moreover, Frye emphasizes the underlying assumption of progress, "that the dynamic is better than the stable and unchanging" (114). Progress can sacrifice the present for an uncertain and unknown future. There is a tension between the utopian and dystopian; the one may end up being the other. Is progress a sinister force? Has progressiveness become progression? The individual's progress toward death becomes a source of alienation and anxiety.

A kind of mechanical uniformity, a "peneplain" as Frye calls it, is the sign of this progress. The city of the market and of community becomes the nightmare expressed in Baudelaire, Eliot, and Verhaeren, not to mention the one Lampman describes in "City of the End of Things" (117). Dickens, Morris, Ruskin, and others came to see the city in terms of disease or ugliness. It may be, as Frye suggests, that mass communication overwhelms the inner mind with prefabricated structures that erase privacy and communication.

Frye contrasts his interest in the free will of the individual with Marshall McLuhan's determinism in which mass media turn out to be an illusion of progress rather than an evolving mode of perception (118). In Frye's analysis of McLuhan, active and passive responses make all the difference in how we view technology and progress (118–119).

And here Frye comes to science. He sees as another illusion the notion that science, left to itself, will evolve more truth about the world because it is part of a society that directs its course. A free science is really unconsciously directed, so "the political power can hijack its technological by-products," by pressuring "science to develop in a direction useful to that power: target-knowledge, as the Nazis called it" (119–120). Human improvement, for Frye, can occur only when involving the human will to improve (120). Anxiety and alienation were once projected into the fear of hell, and since the First World War, the notion that cultures rise, grow, and fall, like that in Spengler, has qualified the view of progress. For Spengler, the decline after Alexander the Great or after Napoleon shows that technology and empire, to use George Grant's phrase, may lead as much to decline as to advance (120).

E.T. Salmon's Whidden Lecture later addresses some of these issues of empire in the typology of time. The nightmare of the future, or dystopia, lives side-by-side with the happy or no-place of tomorrow, or utopia. This perversion of science and technology into a dark politics is something George Orwell caught so well. The satiric visions of Jonathan Swift, Aldous Huxley, and William Golding are other examples. Frye provides recognitions of slavery as a part of human nature. People seek illusions or fictions as a form of a protected world. Nationalism is one such distraction. Perhaps, as Frye suggests, the world cannot get over compulsions to fight old battles and can see only the tyranny on the other side. Frye points to the importance and the difficulty of meeting the principle set out by the Nuremberg trials: that people are morally and legally responsible to resist orders that outrage human conscience.

Perhaps some reason can remain in an irrational world of tyranny and violence, and perhaps science can help. "Science," Frye says, "is a vision of nature which perceives the elements in nature that correspond to the reason and the sense of structure in the scientist's mind" (123). This view is not too different from Oppenheimer's presentation of physics. Frye takes a social view of science and thinks that as confidence in progress diminishes, people have separated the rational scientific view of nature from one that sees nature in emotional and imaginative terms as meaningless and absurd.

The same happens in separating reason and emotion in our vision of society. In literature, two plays—Becket's *Waiting for Godot* and Albee's *Who's Afraid of Virginia Woolf*—express this view of the alienation of progress. Art, imagination, and culture work for activity and reality even as they represent passivity and illusion. As long as our active selves recognize the passive version of ourselves in the mirror and are repulsed by it, we are, Frye maintains, more likely to be critical and to pass through it to a "genuine human destiny" rather than to identify with this image and thereby commit "the error of Narcissus" (125). Imagination and anxiety have, for Frye, genuine and parodic forms.

In his second lecture, "Improved Binoculars," Frye turns to the arts, especially literature, and he does so first by defining the "modern" in its various connotations—recent, mediocre, or of a given historical period, attitude, or style. The modern, according to Frye, began with the Industrial Revolution, the American Revolution, and the French Revolution, and involved the thought of French Encyclopaedists, the Romantics, and British Utilitarians. In its second and continuous phase, about 1867, it involved Darwin, Marx, Freud, Frazer, Rimbaud, Flaubert, Dostoevsky, Nietzsche, and the French impressionist painters. Frye argues that the arts "stir up guilt feelings, personal insecurities and class resentments"; so, for instance, the Nazis called modern art "Jewish art," and the Communists linked modern art's formalism with imperialism and bourgeois decadence (127).

The international and the local exist in tension in culture and in modernism, and theories can be dreams in relation to "cultural facts" (129). Although resistance to imperialism has been responsible for many of the world's great developments in culture, including the Greeks, Jews, English, Dutch, and German at key points, this "is not a social law" (130). Some of the very cultural seeds come from the imperial culture against which the local or peripheral culture is rebelling. Keeping Canada in mind, Frye adds, "Anything distinctive that develops within the Canadian environment can only grow out of participation" in the international style (131). The modern in culture is revolutionary: this can be seen in the changing forms of representing the human and the natural in painting, a dramatic feature of the shift from impressionism to Cézanne (132–134).

Even if the shifts are not progressive, those changes in the representation and expression of nature in the arts search for discoveries in new ways of seeing, in the same way as the sciences do. As we have less confidence about the idea of "progress," Frye notes that a "decline of admiration for continuity is one of the most striking differences between the Romantic and the modern feeling" (136). Modern poetry often tries for the discontinuous in order to disrupt a passive regime of predictable metre, narrative, and thought; the reader is expected to be creative in putting the fragments together in a continuous poem (136–137) Uncontrolled rhetorical babble is to poetry and the verbal arts what "stupid realism" is to the visual arts (137).

Wit and the oracular are two aspects of poetry. Modern poetry fights against "the anti-arts of passive impression"; or, in other words, "of persuasion and exhortation" (138, 142). Some writers, like Thoreau, withdraw from the social contract and search for a true society, in his case a genuine America "of those who will not throw all their energies into the endless vacuum suction of imperialist hysteria and of consuming consumer goods" (144). There are many kinds of withdrawals and oppositions. For some artists, their task is to explore "forbidden or disapproved modes of life in both imagination and experience" (145). Sometimes artists (or the characters they create who are like artists), are like criminals (Frye's main example is Jean Genet). Anti-social attitudes in modern culture can be reactionary. Society is, according to Frye, "a repressive anxiety-structure" and the creative power that resists it derives from a part of the mind that is neither moral nor rational.

Frye advocates an art that releases rather than represses wish-fulfillment, and he sees education and culture as a way of renewing the convention of worn-out creation, the "anti-art" of society, which is the subject of his third lecture, "Claire de lune intellectuel" (150).

Here, he examines the modern world in terms of recreation and leisure. The relation between economics and politics in light of the Industrial Revolution has changed, and now leisure is rivalling employment in importance. Genuine leisure is not something spare, but requires responsibility and discipline in order to acquire new skills. In other words, with patience a person takes time to develop thought and culture just as reading, writing, music, and mathematics take concentration over a long period to master. A liberal education depends on leisure time, and so leisure is not a matter of wasting time but making the most of it. Education depends a good deal on government, which is the source of revolution in our society, when it encourages freedom of movement. Training is, for Frye, not the real reason for universities and education but a pretext for fuller participation in society.

The university and cultural institutions now involve most creative artists in Canada and have a strong interest in contemporary culture; any "revolution" is now within the structures of government and education. Frye thinks that there is a shift from the individual art of poetry and fiction to the social art of drama and film—this reflects society's interest in funding the arts in Canada. Frye talks about three "estates"—economics, politics, and leisure—and sees that none can provide a complete or total social institution; rather, they need to provide checks and balances to one another. Although ideals are betrayed, democracy evolved alongside an idea of liberty; with industry evolved an idea of equality; and with leisure, fraternity. University education is liberal: "It emancipates, it is tolerant, it assimilates the learning process to a social idea" (162). Social context assimilates the attitudes of writers, and leisure is a structure of education. The end of teaching is a social education, and not simply an intellectual vision of society (163).

Every age has a mythology, which Frye defines as "a structure of ideas, images, beliefs, assumptions, anxieties, and hopes which express the view of man's situation and destiny generally held at that time" (163). The units of mythology are myths, which are expressions "of man's concern about himself, about his place in the scheme of things, about his relation to society and God, about the ultimate origin and ultimate fate, either of himself or of the human species generally" (163). Mythology, then, is about human concern about humanity and its place in the world. Myths began as mainly stories about the gods and developed into folktales and legends of heroes, and then the metaphors of poetry and the plots of fiction, or the principles of philosophical and historical thought.

Frye looks for two primary mythological constructions in Western culture. The Biblical-Aristotelian concentrated on the subject-object relation and on reason. This assumed that the rational approach to nature was better than experimental and empirical approaches and so the sciences most related to mathematics developed first. This construction involves the use of reason to discover rational design in nature, as opposed to the observing or testing of nature. The eighteenth century saw the development of a second construction that shifted the origins of society from God to the human. In this view, which is much influenced by scientists like Darwin, nature is not teleological but self-developing, not a matter of rational design but a product of error. Modern mythology, according to Frye, involves social mythology, which "is a faint parody of the Christian mythology which preceded it" (167).

Science plays an important role in the myth of concern because it has an ability to improve or destroy human existence. Frye discusses these matters in the context of an open or a liberal mythology found in democracy, which is a dialectic that contains its own opposite, which expands it through denial or qualification; a closed mythology, by contrast, is a structure of belief. The creed or theory of belief is not practical belief; this relates to an individual's conduct. A closed mythology has premises that trump scholarship and art. The open mythology of democracy caused a religious crisis in which the arts have taken on some of the religious prophetic functions in society and "poetry speaks the mythical language of religion" (173). Perhaps, religion—if taken to be mythical—would be an open mythology based on the limitlessness of human imagination. The fragility of humanity is that humans are much more destructive than they are creative, and so the world seems absurd and alien (174). In all this, Frye suggests that nations have "a buried or uncreated ideal" much like the innocence lost to experience in William Blake's lyrics (174). Before a Canadian audience in Canada's Centennial, Frye makes the bold Blakean suggestion: "The Canada to which we really do owe loyalty is the Canada that we have failed to create" (175). The uncreated identity that seeks genuine human life in freedom and criticism is a utopian vision worthy of Canadians and all peoples to unbury the best in their humanity.

This vision that Frye offers is explicitly for the next century after 1967, and it is for us to take up the challenge.

III

Both Oppenheimer and Frye talk about politics and empire as well as the social context of knowledge. In "The Nemesis of Empire," the Whidden Lecture of 1973, E.T. Salmon addresses the political and imperial head-on.

The first three Whidden lectures, by C.W. de Kiewiet on South Africa in 1956, Vijaya Lakshmi Pandit on India in 1957, and Ronald Syme on colonial elites in 1958, all dealt with colonization and decolonization in what might now be called the "postcolonial condition." Perhaps the hand of E.T. Salmon was behind this initial context for the lectures, and it is only fitting that he address empire as a nemesis in the after-shadow of empire in 1973, a time when Britain entered the European Common Market and was turning away from the empire it had relinquished (184).

As a classicist, Salmon, born in Britain and raised in Australia, chooses a typology between the Roman and British empires as a way into his subject. The first lecture, "A Fit of Absence of Mind," explores the British Empire that some thought had happened in a kind of absentmindedness, without a premeditated design. Salmon recalled his schooldays and "Rule, Britannia," on the eve of Empire Day; but five decades or so later that world "seems completely remote, if not more than a little incredible" (184). The Commonwealth remains, but many of the former colonies, including Canada, are on distinct paths. Salmon describes the sudden collapse of this empire: "The rapidity with which the British Empire crumbled seems all the more startling in that this has occurred so soon after it had reached its furthest territorial extension" (185).

Salmon correctly points out that every zenith is the beginning of decline. During the First World War and the 1920s, the British Empire was moving towards the British Commonwealth. Salmon considers this in terms of the Roman decline and fall. He agrees with those who see history as being affected by passion and coincidence, and as being too unpredictable to repeat itself; he does maintain, however, that there are analogies between these two empires. Both brought long periods of peace to large parts of their known world, and the British partly modelled themselves on the Romans.

He begins with differences. Rome had to fight to survive as a state in Italy, whereas England (later Britain) expanded with trading posts and settlements that were mainly private and barely official. The similarities are part of his thesis that

> Rome and British imperial power grew without premeditation, programme, or policy, and merely as events dictated, the Romans mostly for strategic reasons, the British mostly out of necessity to trade (187).

What Salmon calls "haphazard opportunism" led to long periods of inadequate administration in the annexed lands (187). The reforms of Augustus for the Romans, and the changes to politics and society and in moral and humanitarian standards for the British, led to solutions to this administrative problem.

The origin of imperial expansion is Salmon's main interest. The annexation of Sicily in the third century BCE, according to Salmon, is the starting point of the Roman Empire. The Romans soon took the position that no strong state could be its neighbour. The British, too, would not tolerate too potent a state on the Continent. According to Salmon, the Roman senate was not interested in conquest for the sake of conquest, but rather focused on conquest in terms of strategy and defence. Salmon also notes that the "priestly law of Rome forbade wars of aggression" (190). The Romans only accepted kingdoms that the Hellenistic or Greek monarch bequeathed to them when it was in their interest to do so, and similarly they seized territories by conquest when it was a matter of strategy. Salmon understands too well that a defensive war is "a highly subjective and very elastic concept" and so admits that the Romans had mixed motives (190). Roman generals could also have personal motives of triumph and its attendant benefits for their careers. Virgil and Pliny saw these wars as the duty of Rome, a duty to bring peace and civilization. The invasion of Britain seems to have had political and economic motives, but imperial defence, and not enrichment, was the primary goal of Roman expansion.

Salmon dates the origin of the British Empire with the settlement of Jamestown in 1607, and the motive here was the expansion of trade. The actual planting of a British flag often followed very slowly after trade had been established. The title of Salmon's lecture is an allusion to a lecture given by John Seeley in 1883, in which he claimed that the British Empire was acquired largely by absence of mind. Scientific, humanitarian, religious, and other motives mixed with trade, strategy, and politics in the expansion of England. Still, trade was uppermost. The scramble for Africa is, as Salmon says, notorious as "a race for materials, markets, and money" (195).

At the beginning of expansion, both the Romans and the British behaved as if empire were for the benefit of the imperial centre. Even if the Romans did not acquire their provinces for commerce, they eventually came to exploit and plunder them (195). Cicero, for instance, condemns excesses in the administration of the provinces under the Roman Republic (196). Unscrupulous governors of provinces could use the billeting of conscripted Roman citizens (Rome had no standing army) to exact payment for keeping these often ill-behaved men out of their houses. Unscrupulous governors often put plunder before the protection of their provinces from invasion. Private citizens, often aristocrats, also lobbied the senate in order to maximize their profits. Brutus, for example, used Roman troops to collect private debts. Salmon considers the administration of the provinces under the Roman Republic to be "often deplorable and scandalous" (198). He sees Augustus as rescuing Rome from the crisis caused by self-interest under Sulla, Pompey, and Julius Caesar, by reviving respect for authority; in this way he extended Roman authority. Salmon admits that this did not lead to liberty, but says that Augustus brought peace, stability, and Roman civilization to the world (198).

British colonies were founded on trade or on religious dissent, and the American colonies rebelled against British mercantilism, which was "designed to extract the maximum profit" from the colonies (24). In Africa, Britain came to monopolize the slave trade, and in India there was so much profiteering that Robert Clive was questioned by a committee of the House of Commons. Sheridan, as Salmon notes, characterized the greedy officials of the East India Company as "highwaymen in kid gloves" (199). Moreover, the British government taxed the profits of this company in its opium smuggling from India to China. The loss of the American colonies helped to reform the administration of empire. The French Revolution, the rise of humanitarian values, the Industrial Revolution and other influences helped to transform the British Empire, and there was hope that it might bring, as Augustan Rome had, a peace to the world. Whereas Rome was centrally located for such a task, Britain was not.

Salmon reminds us that Thucydides thought that fear, self-interest, and glory are the mainsprings that move humankind; glory and its attendant honour cannot be forgotten in the story of these two empires and indeed if they were simply engines of self-interest, they would by now be forgotten (200–201).

This observation leads Salmon to his second lecture, "Land of Hope and Glory," which echoes the famous lyrics Arthur Benson wrote to Edward Elgar's music in 1902—a celebration of Britain, its empire, and its rulers (202). Whereas the Roman Empire brought unity in peace to the ancient world, Britain saw its peace bring nationalism and independence to its colonies. The Romans allowed others to become Romans, whereas the British did not allow other subject peoples to become British. Roman provinces were geographical expressions and not political entities, and Rome granted self-government only at a local level.

Augustus created a small standing imperial army and established a peace, the *oikumene*, a civilized region of harmony, order, and rule of law (204–205). Still, abuses remained under this peace, such as in the area of provincial taxation. Money-grubbing procurators could help cause revolts like the one in Britain under Boudicca in CE 60–61 (206). Roman citizens held advantages; but unlike in the British Empire, citizenship could be gained, for instance by enlisting in the imperial army. Salmon also discusses the Roman class system in clear terms, including its inequality and its reliance on hierarchy despite its openness to talent and people of different racial backgrounds. Later on, emperors themselves did not have to be from Italy, or even Italian.

The British did not have a reverse flow of people to the imperial centre and certainly not a widespread assimilation in the upper reaches of society as in ancient Rome. Rome, like the United States, was a melting pot that depended on people adopting its outlook, manners, and language, although in the Roman Empire the aristocracy was probably the most cosmopolitan. The cities of the Roman Empire were spectacles and their engineering was a great achievement (213). Salmon shows the social mobility of the Romans in the unusual story of Marcius Agrippa, who started as a slave and ended up as a senator and governor (214). It is hard to think of such an example in the British Empire.

The Roman and British empires had different lifespans. The Roman Empire in the West endured for about 400 to 650 years, depending on when the counting starts. The barbarians who destroyed Rome (its final fall was 476 CE) proclaimed their own Roman emperors, and Rome persisted in the East until the fall of Constantinople in 1453; others tried to keep its idea alive until the death of the Holy Roman Empire in 1806 (215–216). The British Empire lasted less than two hundred years in the first American colonies, not much more in India and less than a hundred years in many of the African colonies (216). It is possible to look at the British Empire from the conquest of Ireland to the handover of Hong Kong, which could extend the expansion to a similar period to that of Rome. It is too early to judge how influential English will be in the American Empire and the globalized world in comparison to Latin and the Neo-Latin languages that persist even yet. Salmon's hypothesis is an interesting one that makes us think; counter-suggestions are only one way he has prompted debate.

In Salmon's comparison, the British revolutionize technology far more than even the Romans did with engineering. James Watt's steam engine in the 1760s and the Industrial Revolution were born in England and changed the per capita output of goods and services for the first time in almost 10,000 years of human settlement from the agricultural revolution. Industry and a strong navy extended Britain and its power (216–217). British technology was valued in the colonies because almost until the end of the nineteenth century, Britain had a monopoly on advanced technology, so that the British Empire was "dependent upon the land of hope and glory" (217). Even before the First World War, Germany and the United States had come to challenge Britain's industrial supremacy. Language kept ties between Britain and its colonies in an empire even more far-flung and diverse than the Roman Empire. As well, the British could learn about imperial administration from the Romans through classical education; but there was also a great deal of improvisation. Salmon sees the British as protecting indigenous peoples and, as trustees, encouraging responsible government until they could hand over the trust. He concludes that whatever one thinks of this controversy, "the British attempt to convert native peoples into modern nations ended as the Roman attempt to transform native peoples into Romans had ended, in the loss of empire" (222).

And so Salmon brings out some key points of debate with both these empires that provoke further debate. Both transformed the world and both continue to affect the present and so continue in the imagination and in cultural debates.

In "Westward the Course of Empire," the third lecture, whose title is taken from a poem from Bishop Berkeley on America, Salmon takes up the long debate over the dissolution of the Roman Empire. He also discusses the breaking up of the British Empire. Salmon suggests that the very success of Rome to assimilate foreigners to its governing class actually made the empire un-Roman, without a deep sense of Roman tradition and purpose. Recall the argument of Salmon's second lecture: even when new citizens thought or declared they were true Romans, they may have had little genuine sense of what this meant (223–224).

Salmon explores the difficult and fraught ground of the relation between intellectual, spiritual, and emotional orientation to practices and customs. He traces the separation of military and civilian functions. From 212 CE onward, all the inhabitants of the empire became Roman citizens, so that one of the great inducements of joining the army—citizenship—was taken away, and the army became increasingly barbarian. In about 250 CE, senatorials were not allowed to serve as officers, and emperors were being selected from the ranks of officers, who now did not have political experience. The draining of good local people to Rome meant that local administration slackened and the emperors sent out officials to collect taxes; this undermined local self-government, a mainstay of the Roman Empire.

Salmon believes that Roman religious attitudes were weakened, and discusses the auspices as an illustration of the Romans' relation with heaven, but also the connection of the auspices with the patricians, senate, and emperor in being go-betweens between the Roman people and their divinities. Constantine (312–37 CE) recognized Christianity as an official religion of the empire (233). From 235 to 285 CE, the senate recognized at least 15 emperors, the so-called "barrack emperors" (234). The barbarians assailed the borders of the empire, and the emperors claimed to be Roman, but even the restoration of a certain amount of peace did not hide the fact that (in Salmon's estimation) the empire was no longer Roman (235). For this reason, then, the Roman empire did not survive the third century CE. The united empire was divided in two first in 285 and permanently after 395 (236–237). Salmon states his thesis briefly: "The imprudent prodigality with which the citizenship was bestowed proved to be the nemesis of empire" (237). And here is the title of his Whidden Lecture.

Salmon also addresses the question of the disintegration of the British Empire. After 1800, the British made public declarations that the welfare of the governed was the first consideration; this took place around the time that Macaulay claimed freedom and civilization as something that should be available to any part of humanity (238). Nationalism in the wake of the French Revolution reinforced this movement. This also applied to the territories of the empire, and self-government came to reinforce this in the "white dominions," like Canada (238). The idea of imperial federation never made much headway after its launch in New Zealand in 1852 (239). Trade preferences never really bound the British Empire together, and by 1932, when they were agreed upon in Ottawa, it was too late (240). As W.E. Forster had predicted in 1875, association had replaced dependence (240).

Salmon thinks that the paradoxical nature of the British Empire itself was the reason it ended: the regional attachments it promoted trumped empire. Of Britain, Salmon argues, "Nemesis overtook the Empire because liberalism could not be reconciled with imperial rule" (241). So it seems that the most praiseworthy features of Rome and Britain led to their demise as empires. The human attempt to reconcile liberty and order lies at the heart of these stories of empire, and, as Salmon remarks, in the westward course of empire, the sun is ever the same even as it sets (242). And Salmon also finds interest in the association of Europe that Britain joined in the year of his lecture, as a free association of states. He does not predict the future but he sees in the study of the past some hope in facing what challenges may arise in the future (242–243).

* * *

We are that future. J. Robert Oppenheimer, Northrop Frye, and E. T. Salmon explore science, literature, and history, which were key concerns of the 1960s and 1970s when they lectured and wrote, and they do so by considering themes that are still very much with us: power, knowledge, empire, and modernity. Each of these distinguished professors and public figures, deliberating on crises and critical aspects of culture and thought, explains changes in context and with active engagement. They challenge us to understand and not to stand idly by. They challenge us to think more clearly and try to make sense of scientific, cultural, and historical change in a social context.

Oppenheimer explains the developments in physics that led up to the making of the atomic bomb and describes the test scientists and members of society face in creating ways to control these arms—including genuine international bodies and government to end war. Frye discusses literature, culture, and education in order to set out a way in which we can think more lucidly and actively. The goal here is to resist being passive consumers of advertising and propaganda in this world of technical revolution; instead we should ever aim to create our ideal society, the one we have yet failed to achieve. Salmon tries to make sense of a Britain that has moved from the great empire to another nation joining a new experiment in co-operation in Europe. In this critical change, he seeks a comparison with Rome and its decline and fall to help think about what the breakup of the British Empire might mean for the world.

These lectures see war and the breakdown of peace as great threats, past, present, and future, and consider the role of liberty, knowledge, and critical thought in the advancement of humanity. What city can we build that endures and is full of light rather a dark apocalyptic end to civility or even to all things? All three of these Whidden Lecturers, in Oppenheimer's words, seek to work for an "international community of knowledge and understanding" (94).

That is our challenge, too.

Notes

1 See D.M.R. Bentley, *The Gay]Grey Moose: Essays on Ecologies and Mythologies of Canadian Poetry 1690–1990* (Ottawa: University of Ottawa Press, 1992), p. 187.

2 Quoted in E.T. Salmon, "The Making of the Peace," *The Empire Club of Canada Speeches 1946–1947* (Toronto: The Empire Club Foundation, 1947), p. 316, see 316–330.

3 See Francis Bacon, *Meditationes Sacrae* (1597). The Latin phrase is *scientia potentia est*.

4 Lord Acton Letter to Mandell Creighton, April 5, 1887, quoted in Jim Powell, Lord Acton, *Political Power Corrupts: The Freeman: Ideas on Liberty* 46.6 (1996); online at http://www.fee.org/publications/the-freeman/article.asp?aid=3794. The context of the quotation is about papal power at around the time of the debate over the doctrine of papal infallibility, but there is a historical dimension that relates to power as Bacon and Oppenheimer discuss them: "I cannot accept your canon that we are to judge Pope and King unlike other men, with a favourable presumption that they did no wrong. If there is any presumption it is the other way against holders of power, increasing as power increases. Historic responsibility has to make up for the want of legal responsibility. Power tends to corrupt and absolute power corrupts absolutely."

5 C.P. Snow, *The Two Cultures* (Cambridge: Cambridge University Press, 1998, rpt. 2003), esp. p. 3. Snow first published his book in 1959 and Part 2 was added in 1964. He used the phrase in "The Two Cultures," *New Statesman* (6 October 1956), 413.

6 F.R. Leavis gave the Richmond Lecture at Downing College in 1962. It was published in the *Spectator* and in his *Two Cultures? The Significance of C.P. Snow* (London: Chatto and Windus, 1962). See also Roger Kimball, "The Two Cultures' Today," *The New Criterion* 12.6 (February 1994). It appears on the web at http://www.newcriterion.com/archive/12/feb94/cultures.htm. Martin Kettle, "Two Cultures Still," *The Guardian* (Saturday 2 February 2002). For the web version, see http://www.guardian.co.uk/politics/2002/feb/02/books.houseofcommons. Michael Polyani's response to Snow is that a division of labour must occur for the advancement of science and this specialization means that even scientists must have gaps in their knowledge of other scientific fields. See Paul Dean, "The Last Critic: The Importance of F.R. Leavis," *The New Criterion* 14.5 (January 1996), or online at http://www.newcriterion.com/archive/14/jan96/dean.htm.

7 G.H. Hardy, *A Mathematician's Apology* (Cambridge: Cambridge University Press, 1940, rev. ed.. 1967, rpt. 2007), 66.

8 Hardy, 2007: 90.

9 Hardy, 151.

10 Lawrence Martin, Alvin A. Lee, and Manuel Zack, *Harry Thode: Scientist and Builder at McMaster University* (Hamilton: McMaster University Press, 2003), 89

11 Martin *et al.*, 89, see 90.

12 Martin *et al.*, 89.

13 The Oxford English Dictionary, 2nd edn, defines "complementarity" as follows: "A complementary relationship or situation; *spec.* in *Physics*, the capacity of the wave and particle theories of light together to explain all phenomena of a certain type, although each separately accounts for only some of the phenomena."

Part One

The Flying Trapeze:
Three Crises for Physicists

J. Robert Oppenheimer

Foreword

The Whidden Lectures were established in 1954 by E. C. Fox, B.A., LL.D., of Toronto, the senior member of the Board of Governors, to honour the memory of the late Reverend Howard P. Whidden, D.D., LL.D., D.C.L., F.R.S.C., 1871–1952, Chancellor of McMaster University from 1923 to 1941. Their purpose is to help students cross the barriers separating the academic departments of a modern university. The lectures are not restricted as to general theme.

* * *

The seventh series of Whidden Lectures were delivered in January 1962 by the distinguished Director of the Institute for Advanced Study at Princeton, N.J., Dr. J. Robert Oppenheimer.

A graduate of Harvard University who has studied and lectured at Cambridge, Göttingen, Leyden, Zürich, and many other universities abroad as well as in his own country, Dr. Oppenheimer is perhaps best known to the man in the street as the Director of the Los Alamos Scientific Laboratory during the Second World War and subsequently as the Chairman of the General Advisory Committee to the U.S. Atomic Energy Commission. The success of the Los Alamos project in wartime was largely due to his genius and to the inspiration and leadership he gave to his associates. He is, however, more than an atomic physicist. A great humanist who is deeply concerned about man and his survival, he is a versatile scholar of wide interests and deep culture: his early training, indeed, was in the classical languages of ancient Greece and Rome. All who had the privilege of hearing the Whidden Lectures in 1962 will agree that it is difficult to envisage anyone more eminently suitable to deliver them.

E. T. SALMON
Principal of University College
May 1964   *McMaster University*

Preface

The three lectures, *The Flying Trapeze: Three Crises for Physicists*, were given by Professor Oppenheimer from only sketchy outline notes, and were recorded. It was a most stimulating experience to hear these lectures, to witness Professor Oppenheimer's occasional search for the precise word, and to notice the wealth of illustrations that sprang to his mind to illuminate each idea. It was a revelation to me when I looked at the word-for-word transcript of the lectures to see that such sparkling addresses, so clear to the listener, contained so many sentences sufficiently involved to make reading difficult. Moreover, the discussion of each of the three crises, Space and Time, Atom and Field, and War and the Nations, did not fall neatly into the time of one lecture, so that Professor Oppenheimer continued the first topic into the second lecture, and the second topic into the third; this caused him to repeat and summarize certain material. It seemed appropriate in a written account to confine each topic to one chapter. This caused me to coalesce some of the material from the end of one lecture and the start of the next; in the process I have discarded very little that was said, but I have altered the order of a few passages.

I hope that this editing has served to make the verbal transcript more readable, without removing any of the flavour of colloquial verve, and careful phraseology, which combined to make the original lectures such an exciting and satisfying experience. At least the reader may be assured that, although they have been occasionally rearranged, all the significant words are Professor Oppenheimer's.

M. A. PRESTON, M.A., PH.D., F.R.S.C.
Professor of Theoretical Physics
McMaster University

I

Space and Time

This has been a great century in physics, a century of unexpected, profound, and moving discoveries, and of applications that have changed a great deal in the condition of human life. The last years have seen very great progress in the understanding of essential features of life, and I am confident that the years ahead will teach us more than all preceding history of man about how living organisms perform their miraculous functions and about man as a part of nature. We in physics are still engaged in what feels at the moment like a very great intractable struggle to find out the laws of matter, the nature of matter. It is not of that that I want to speak, but of chapters that are to some extent closed, although questions raised by the answers found earlier in the century are still before us, still wide open. I shall, in this and the second lecture, speak of increases in our understanding, changes in our understanding, of the world of nature. In the third lecture I shall speak rather of changes in the human situation brought about by the developments in physics and other sciences.

Our time is marked by the prominence of the sciences. It is marked by very rapid change and very great growth—growth in science, growth in productivity, growth in population, growth in travel, growth in communication. Almost any statistic that you look at shows a sharp curve with a characteristic of doubling in ten or twenty or thirty years. In the case of the sciences, this doubling occurs in about ten years, and there are several quite spectacular figures which mark it. If you think of all those people who devote their lives to studying nature or applying what has been learned in the technical way and call them scientists, then throughout man's history there have been a number of them and of that number about 93 per cent are still living today, so rapidly has the number of people so engaged increased. A friend of mine, in Europe, calculated how fast one of our journals of fundamental physics was growing, and established that if the rate of growth were maintained, then next century the volumes would weigh more than the whole earth. I was called on, not very long ago, by the Scientific Secretary of the Soviet Academy of Sciences, who spent a day with me in Princeton. I believe that his is an important political office, and we talked a little bit about the growth of scientific activity, in which he is engaged as an administrator. I asked him how he saw the future beyond the next five-year plan, say fifty years from now. Without thinking he said, "Then all of us will be scientists"; the horror of it came over him slowly and he added, "No, not quite."

Still, in talking of this as a scientific age and thinking of this as a time remarkably influenced by science, we need, I think, to bear in mind two cautions. One is that we probably have no very good idea today of the range of problems which will be accessible to science. We do not know how much of human behaviour may yield in one way or another to the characteristically objective and often rather unexpected study that is a science, and we may today live in something of an imbalance between what we know of the physical world, what we are beginning to know of the living world, and what we know of the human world. I, however, am deeply convinced that the scientific knowledge which may be available about men—not much today—will always be, as is our knowledge of the physical world, very very incomplete and partial, and that the sense of having to live and act in response to tradition, good judgement, and wisdom, which we have now, will not ever be alleviated by any development of the sciences.

I think we need secondly to remember that a great part of the present scene arises not from what we have learned, but by its application in technology. This, in turn, rests on an organization of the economy and to a more limited, but still real, extent on our political arrangements. Neither of these derives from, nor is in any tight way related to, the sciences, because, although the growth of knowledge is largely responsive to human needs, it is not fully so. The existence of terrible and intractable diseases does cause a very wide and intensive study of problems that may be related to the diseases. Problems of agricultural productivity, problems of gadgetry, perhaps most of all problems of military importance stimulate the vigour and increase the support for research. Still it is a profound and necessary truth that the deep things in science are not found because they are useful; they are found because it was possible to find them.

Think of the long centuries in which attempts were made to change mercury into gold because that seemed like a very useful thing to do. These efforts failed and we found how to change mercury into gold by doing other things that had quite different intentions. And so I believe that the availability of instruments, the availability of ideas or concepts—not always but often mathematical—are more likely to determine where great changes occur in our picture of the world than are the requirements of man. Ripeness in science is really all, and ripeness is the ability to do new things and to think new thoughts. The whole field is pervaded by this freedom of choice. You don't sit in front of an insoluble problem for ever. You may sit an awfully long time, and it may even be the right thing to do; but in the end you will be guided not by what it would be practically helpful to learn, but by what it is possible to learn.

I think that to those who are far removed from the life of the sciences, this sometimes appears to be irresponsible. It seems as though having made something potentially pestiferous, like nuclear bombs, we ought to go ahead and find something potentially helpful in getting rid of them. Indeed we ought; but instead it is much more likely that our thoughts will turn to things that are easier to do than that, that are more at hand than that. It is not irresponsibility; it is characteristic of the special way in which one does advance so rapidly in knowledge, for often one may quickly make an irreversible accession to knowledge by establishing an error. Having proved that something is not right, you do not go back to it again; you have learned your lesson. Progress, which in moral and human things is a very elusive word applicable, certainly, to some aspects of our life, but not to all, is an inevitable thing in the sciences. Progress is coextensive with the existence of the scientific world.

Now the first two of these lectures have to do with just such episodes, where previously held, firmly entrenched errors were with considerable shock and very great grandeur corrected—and in such a way that those errors will not be made again. Moreover, this progress in learning about the world of nature has changed rather profoundly not only what we know of nature, but some of the things that we know about ourselves as knowers. It has changed, to use an old phrase that is beloved of Butterfield, the "thinking caps" of men, as did the revolutions of the late middle ages and the seventeenth century. I may be wrong, but I share with my colleagues, or with many of them, a strong conviction that this experience is one which we would gladly extend beyond the range of limited technical communities. The experience of seeing how our thought and our words and our ideas have been confined by the limitation of our experience is one which is salutary and is in a certain sense good for a man's morals as well as good for his pleasure. It seems to us that this is an opening up of the human spirit, avoiding its provincialism and narrowness. You may think of the example of what it has meant to all of us to learn over the last centuries how different other cultures could be from our own and still in some real sense be cultures.

Progress of this kind is possible only because it blends two almost contradictory traits. The one is a great love of adventure, so that you look for new things and for changed circumstances, look far into the sky, look close into matter, do all sorts of things that take you away from the familiar human experience. That lies on the one hand, and on the other is a great adherence to such order and clarity as has already been attained. One may describe the latter as a sense of conservatism about not giving up any understanding that has been achieved, so that even though you are about to rewrite Newton you are very very reluctant to move very far away from Newton, and even though you may realize that everything that has been said before in physics is only very partially true, you will fight very hard to keep that partial truth. You will be strong through the tradition, and you will use the tradition in describing the new experience until that point comes when you simply cannot go on with it and you have to make a great break.

Many of the men who have contributed to the great changes in science have really been very unhappy over what they have been forced to do. Kepler, who loved spheres, discovered ellipses. Planck, with his famous quantum of action, introduced an element of discontinuity into physics, which seemed to him absolutely intolerably strange and ugly. Einstein, who was able to live with the theories of relativity and regretted only very few aspects of them, also contributed to the development of quantum theory; he proposed the idea of light quanta, but never could reconcile himself to the quantum theory logically built up from this basis. And de Broglie, who discovered that there are waves which are associated with material particles, could never reconcile himself to their interpretation as waves which only represented information and not some disturbance in a corporeal medium.

These changes are forced on physicists somewhat reluctantly because we are both traditional and conservative and at the same time a little too adventurous. In our lifetimes we have seen, in a limited area, our beliefs and our experience radically altered—the popular word is revolutionized, but that is not quite right, for they have been deepened and changed, but not completely overthrown. I have the impression that a general awareness of this and a general experience of it may be of some use in dealing with human problems in a time when the world also is changing so very rapidly.

I have in my enterprise tonight and tomorrow very severe limits; one of them is that especially in physics it is often believed that without the mathematical forms one cannot really say what the discoveries are all about. There is a measure of truth in this; the discoveries could probably not have been made without the mathematical forms which give a quick synoptic and luminous way of representing the order that inheres in nature. It is not surprising that mathematics is involved in nature; it is really a requirement of consistency and the one thing that we are all confident of is that nature may be difficult, but she will not be inconsistent. (It is only we who can be that.) But I think that some understanding of the concepts of physics can be conveyed with very limited use of mathematics, and I propose so to restrict myself. You may think of an analogy. It is certainly better to see Hamlet acted, if it is reasonably well acted, than to read it. It was written to be acted, not to be read in a study. Still, if you read it, you have, with good will and imagination and luck, a good deal of feeling for the meaning of the play. It is certainly a very daring enterprise to try to guess from an English translation what Pasternak's novel is like; but you know a good deal more about it reading it in English than not reading it at all. And I hope that you may, if not at my hands at least in some happier future, feel that mathematics, though a help, is not indispensable for some insight into the essentials of what has been found in modern physics.

In the second lecture, I shall be talking about quite profound changes in our idea of causality, in what we think of determinism in the natural world, and most of all of what we mean and may mean by objectivity. These changes were necessary in order to attain the prize of a reasonable understanding of the ordinary properties of matter, those properties which manifest themselves even when you are not attacking matter with the violence which the great accelerators and the cosmic rays make possible. And in this lecture I want to discuss some changes in the ideas of space and time. Both of these themes are variations on the problem of the consistency of what we know about motion in space and about what is in space, about its field or content.

The quantum theory was the work of many people. I think that we would all agree that Niels Bohr was the heart of this brilliant group. On the other hand, the ideas of space and time, though they go back a long way, were revolutionized in this century by one man, and in some aspects at least it is permissible to think that if he hadn't lived, the revolution would not have occurred. He was Einstein.

The first theory of relativity, at least in the Western world, does not date from the twentieth century. It dates from the thirteenth and early fourteenth, from the Paris school of natural philosophers, of whom Buridan and Oresme are the best known. It was certainly one of the great changes in human thought and it is remarkable because, although it is physics, it did not rest on any elaboration of observational or experimental technique but on analysis and on ordinary common-sense knowledge of how things behave. And it was the opening without which the future development of science is hardly thinkable. This was the discovery: in an analysis of the problem of motion, uniform motion—a body moving with constant velocity—was not something for which you could find or needed to find any explanation or cause; uniform motion was a natural state of matter. Of course, this was not the schoolman's view; it was not Aristotle's view, for whom it was obvious that to keep something moving you had to work on it, and the only natural state was one of rest. The new viewpoint was called the theory of impetus, which we would today say was the theory of momentum, namely that the constant impetus of a body was something that needed no explanation and that all you had to explain was change in its impetus, change in its motion, change in its momentum. This, as you know, was also Galileo's view; and we call the transformation of co-ordinates, which emphasizes this causeless character of uniform motion, the Galilean transformation—although without his permission and without any good historical ground. The idea behind this transformation is that because it involves no cause to have uniform motion there will be a similarity in objects which are in motion with respect to each other. There will be no inherent difference between them. There will be an ability to describe one as analogous to the other. This so-called Galilean transformation tells you how from the co-ordinates x of an object that is at rest at a time t, you can derive the co-ordinates, the time, and the velocity as seen in a system in which that same object moves uniformly with a velocity v.

$$x' = x + vt,$$
$$t' = t.$$

Suppose you have something at rest and it's at the point x and you are looking at it at a time t. Now suppose you move with respect to it with a velocity $-v$. Then the co-ordinate of the object will be given by x', the time won't be changed, and any velocity V that may appear in the original system will appear as a new velocity V' in the new system, $V' = V + v$. This is the Galilean invariance and it's just common sense. It says the particle simply moves along with its co-ordinate increasing because it is in motion, the time isn't changed by this veloc-ity, and the velocities add. This theory of impetus is, of course, Newton's first law; and Newton's laws of motion, which describe how accelerations are produced by forces, are invariant under this simple transformation. You cannot distinguish one uniform motion from another by the application of Newton's laws; they are relativistic in the sense that relative motion is observable, but absolute motion is not as long as it is uniform, that is with no acceleration.

From the time of Newton up to the end of the last century, physi-cists built, on the basis of these laws, a magnificently precise and beautiful science involving the celestial mechanics of the solar sys-tem, involving incredible problems in the Cambridge Tripos, involv-ing the theory of gases, involving the behaviour of fluids, of elastic vibrations, of sound—indeed a comprehensive system so robust and varied and apparently all-powerful that what was in store for it could hardly be imagined. I think the only record I have seen of any explicit doubt on the subject of the Galilean transformation and of Newtonian mechanics was about a century earlier than the theory of relativity in a paper of Euler. Because of the relative transverse motion between a fixed star and the earth, you see the star at a slightly different angle than the true direction. Euler found that he did not get exactly the same result when he calculated this variation from the point of view of the star and the point of view of the earth. The difference was totally insignificant experimentally and he did-n't say anything more about it. He just noted it.

But early in the nineteenth century and increasingly through that century another study in physics was under way, not having to do with the motion of bodies under gravitational forces, but having to do with the domain of light and electromagnetism. It was not neces-sary—although today it is—to decide whether gravity was an action at a distance in which one body affected another very far away or whether gravity spread from one body to another. And there was at that time and is today no really good experimental way of distinguish-ing the two. There are, in principle, very good ways and we feel sure that we know the answer, but we have not yet tried it out. However, with electromagnetic forces the situation is quite different. I think you have all seen what happens when you have a simple bar magnet and some iron filings on a piece of paper. The iron filings assume quite regular patterns, following lines which have something like parabolic shapes around the poles of the magnet. Already in the first half of the nineteenth century Faraday knew about this and his vision was that the space surrounding the magnet, although it had no pieces of matter in it, had something which was physically important present in it, and that was a magnetic field: the power to affect a magnet. Of course, the little iron filings act like magnets and are affected and do respond to this field and make it manifest. In the same way if you have an electrically charged rod or ball and if you come into the near-by area with another charged object with the same charge, you will feel it pushed away a little; if you present an opposite charge, you will feel it pulled in a little. And these are things that happen when the two are not in contact: they arise from a property of the space surrounding the electric charge or the magnet. Faraday talked of these lines and tubes of force, of the electric and magnetic potentials—I don't use this term technically—which exist in space, and for him space became animated with these fields. They were things which anyone could measure: one could measure their directions, one could measure their strengths; they were as palpable as the corporeal bodies themselves, but they existed in a vacuum. Indeed, they exist very well in a vacuum, and have nothing to do with the presence of air; they are modified by any matter if it is there, but they are present without any matter. This picture, of course, is beginning to be the famous aether, the empty space that is capable of having properties.

Faraday showed that if you changed the magnetic field rapidly, you would make an electric field and Maxwell discerned theoretically that if you changed the electric field rapidly enough you produce a magnetic field. This effect was later verified; it is much harder to see than Faraday's result, merely because of practical considerations. In fact, Maxwell predicted that, in the absence of any charges and currents, field pulsations of this kind, in which electric and magnetic fields would generate each other, could propagate freely. He calculated the velocity of the pulsations and found that it was a rather well-known velocity—that with which light propagates.

Thus this field of Faraday's is busy. It not only has fields around charges and magnetic poles—magnetic dipoles really—but it transmits electromagnetic waves. It transmits all the waves which feed the television sets and instruct the rockets and give us our wonderful culture over the radio; it transmits light, it transmits heat; it transmits many forms of very high energy radiation—forms of light which are very penetrating, which play a big part in nuclear physics. (The reality of man-generated long wavelength electromagnetic waves was established late in the last century by Hertz.)

This highly peopled space, full of electric and magnetic phenomena, is related to particles in motion in the following way: if I have a charged object it will, of course, respond to gravity (a universal force), but it will also respond to electric fields and if it is in motion it will respond to magnetic fields. It will feel a supplementary push, the electric field pulling it in the direction of the field, and the magnetic field in general pushing it at right-angles to the field, and to its own velocity. The laws of these effects on charges were reasonably well known at the turn of the century, at least for objects that did not move too fast. But what was very troublesome is that Maxwell's account of the propagation of electromagnetic waves of light and the whole basis of his theory and Faraday's intuitive picture of a space filled with fields was not consistent with the Galilean invariance property.

One can see this from a general viewpoint for, if this space is full of electric and magnetic fields, it need not appear at all the same thing when I move with respect to it. More specifically—and this is really the crux of the difficulty—according to Maxwell's theory the velocity of light is something that is fixed by his equations. His result was very close to the observed measure. But if I move with respect to the medium in which these fields are described by Maxwell's equations then I would expect to apply the formula $V' = V + v$, that the velocity which I see for the light is the sum of the velocity with which I am moving (or its negative) and the velocity of light in the medium; it might be bigger or it might be smaller, depending on whether I am moving towards the source of light or away from it. This is a view which was indeed prevalent at the turn of the century, and which was shown by many indirect methods and one very direct experiment, one of the great crucial experiments in history, to be simply not so.

Before this experiment, the situation presented at least three alternatives. First, one might say that there is a system—the system in which electric and magnetic fields are described and exist and obey Maxwell's equations—which is unique, and absolute rest has meaning by reference to that system, and anything in motion with reference to it may have different physical behaviour because of this motion. To accept this alternative is to give up the invariance law and to give up the whole idea of relativity, that is the relativity of uniform motion. The second possibility was to say that Maxwell's equations, in spite of their describing such an enormous range of phenomena, may somehow not be right, and this was extremely hard to do after a half-century of success. And the third was to say: "There is relativity and Maxwell is right, but the Galilean equations don't describe the transformations of relativity." No one could do that until the situation got really desperate.

And it was made desperate by the Michelson-Morley experiment. In preparing for these lectures I looked up Einstein's lectures in 1921 at Princeton; he said of the Michelson-Morley experiment: "I assume its results are known to you." I thought I should not quite do that because it was done a long time ago. What Michelson did was to measure the time taken by light to move a moderate distance back and forth in the laboratory and to see whether this was the same when parallel to the earth's motion round the sun and perpendicular to it. The expected differences were quite small, and it took a very great technical virtuosity to be able to look for them. But Michelson did the experiment and he did it over and over again. Now, the earth might just possibly be in the preferred rest system of electromagnetic phenomena in January, but then in June it is moving in a very different direction, and with substantial speed; Michelson's sensitivity was enough to have detected very very easily the motion of the earth, by the change in the velocity of light depending on whether the earth was moving with or against or not at all in this luminiferous aether, the seat of electromagnetic phenomena. He got a null result. This was so unexpected that the experiment, with many refinements and variations, was repeated for decades after that as a witness to the traumatic character of this answer.

So we are not allowed to believe that the velocity of light depends on the velocity of the source. We are not really allowed to doubt that Maxwell's equations are true in all co-ordinate systems and we are not really allowed to doubt that the equations of the Galilean transformation are not a good description—they are only an approximate description—of what happens when we observe a system that is in uniform motion with respect to us. At this point three people found the solution, but only one found its full meaning right away, and that was Einstein.

Einstein said: "Let us imagine what the situation would be if we could not communicate with a speed greater than a light signal." That is pretty fast (3×10^{10} centimetres per second) by ordinary standards; we would not normally notice this limitation. We would not find that our bicycles were getting away from us. But it is a finite velocity, and that makes a very big conceptual change. If you do not have instantaneous communication and if you want to compare information at two different places, you must make allowance for the time it takes for the message to get back and forth. For instance, suppose you want to synchronize two clocks that are a long way apart. (They should be clocks of the same type, perhaps natural clocks which are more or less guaranteed the same— "atomic clocks.") A natural way to synchronize them so that they read the same time would be to set the clock at one place half-way between the time at which the signal left the other and the time at which it was received back after reflection. The notion of simultaneity, which intuitively seems to be something that should not depend on any moving around you do, is indeed a valid notion when things are at the same point of space, but is no longer a valid notion over substantial distances and when relative motions at all comparable to the velocity of light come into play.

This means that if it is true that you cannot send signals faster than light, and if it is a physical contradiction to imagine it, then you have this relativity of simultaneity, this velocity dependence of judgements of simultaneity. Also you have other physical effects which are produced for you by the machines that you use for measuring distance and for measuring time. Let me explain that when I say "clock" I mean something that is designed to measure as accurately as possible regular intervals of time, and when I say "distance" I mean something that you measure with a ruler, which has been by remote comparisons calibrated by a standard metre in Paris. The clocks and rulers then are physical objects.

Now, in order to be consistent with the fact that there is a limiting velocity which is not infinite, but is the finite velocity of light (called by everybody c), the Galilean transformation must be abandoned and replaced by a new transformation called the Lorentz transformation, after the first man who wrote it down. This must provide the co-ordinate of a point x and a time t, when I look at it from a system uniformly moving with a velocity $-v$.

$$x' = \gamma(x + vt)$$

$$t' = \gamma\left(t + \frac{xv}{c^2}\right)$$

$$\gamma' = \left(1 - \frac{v^2}{c^2}\right)^{-1/2}$$

$$V' = \frac{V + v}{1 + Vv/c^2}$$

This is a very simple Lorentz transformation; v is the relative velocity of the two systems, and γ is something which is near one when the velocity v is small compared to the velocity of light c and which becomes infinite, marking the limit of the applicability of these transformations, as v approaches c. Moreover, this clearly indicates the limiting character of the velocity of light. You see that it shows that a length interval in one co-ordinate system will appear to be shrunk by the factor $1/\gamma$ when examined in a moving co-ordinate system. You see that the time is not told the same in the two co-ordinate systems and that the difference not only has a difference of scale but depends on the positions of the clocks. This is the point about the judgements of simultaneity. And you see further that if you have a process going on which takes a time t as measured in the system where the object is at rest, then if you move at a velocity v with respect to it, the time will be lengthened, being γt.

To summarize, motion decreases the measurements of length, motion increases the intervals of time, and the two facts together are encompassed in the Lorentz transformation. Further, the formula for the velocity V' indicates that if you add two velocities that are very close to the velocity of light you never get beyond the velocity of light, you just get a little closer to it. This completely consistent system never enables you to talk about or to discuss the properties of relative motion with a velocity greater than that of light, but it does tell you how to talk about real motions in terms of the actual behaviour of actual clocks and rods and atoms and all the rest of physics. These equations give an invariant description of physical phenomena, a description independent of relative uniform motion, one which is as good in one system as in another. This formalism re-expresses the ancient theme of Buridan, that uniform motion requires no cause, but now with this very new wrinkle that couldn't have been anticipated on the basis of ordinary experience, that, because objects cannot be accelerated beyond the velocity of light, the analogue of an infinite velocity is a finite velocity.

From this viewpoint one naturally asks that not only Maxwell's equations of electromagnetism but the equations of motion for charged particles and then also for neutral particles should be invariant, i.e. that they should have the same content, irrespective of the frame of reference in which we describe the phenomena, as long as we are talking only about uniform motion. We do that naturally in talking of ordinary things. If there is a complete symmetry in a problem, so that no direction is singled out, then we certainly would like to talk about it in such a way that that symmetry is preserved in our description; and if there is nothing in space to make one point different from another, we would like to give a description which is as valid in Chicago as it is in Hamilton. And in the same way here we would like a description valid irrespective of the relative velocity of the objects we are talking about and what we ourselves happen to be doing while we are looking at them.

This was done for mechanics and gave at once the rather clear sign that Newton's equations are wrong. This is clear *a priori*, because if the acceleration is proportional to the force and inversely proportional to the mass, there is no reason why you cannot make velocities bigger than that of light. Something must prevent those forces from being so effective, and what it is, to put it a little oversimply, is that the mass of a body is not in fact constant. Indeed, if the theory of mechanics is to be compatible with the requirement of the constancy of the velocity of light and relativity in this restricted sense—the mass of a body must increase with its velocity in just this way:

$$m = \frac{m_0}{\sqrt{(1 - V^2/c^2)}}.$$

Here m_0 is the mass of the body at zero speed and m its mass at speed V. This is the origin of much fertile speculation by Einstein, because if the mass of a body increases with its velocity so does its kinetic energy and it will increase in the same way, viz:

$$\Delta T = c^2 \Delta m.$$

The symbol ΔT means the change in kinetic energy and Δm represents the corresponding change in mass.

Because the total energy is really something that is not lost or gained by a system, but is conserved, what is true of kinetic energy must be true of all energy and, therefore, a change of energy and a change of mass go hand in hand and the change in energy is related to the change in mass by the square of the velocity of light. This is something that it would be nice to have a little mathematics or more time to show; but it is a direct and really quite inescapable consequence of the purely kinematic connexions which I have written down as the Lorentz transformation.

Another important point is that these transformations mix up space and time very much more than the Galilean ones. To a limited extent you cannot interchange space and time. They have inherently different character. A watch is a watch and a ruler is a ruler and you cannot use the ruler to measure the time and the clock to measure the co-ordinates. But they do change with relative motion. Of course, you are not restricted to move in a straight line with respect to something you are studying: you can also turn around or you can take another place in space. This whole set of procedures—rotation, translation (moving to another origin, that is another base point), and moving uniformly in some direction— together are a set of operations that are closed and form the Lorentz group. You cannot, with these operations, convert any space-like interval into a time-like interval or any time-like interval into a space-like one, but you can change the "direction" of a space-like interval and give it some slightly more time-like quality, and you can do the same thing for time-like intervals.

This system, this special theory of relativity, which predicts correctly the behaviour of rods and clocks under motion, became an absolutely all-pervasive feature of physics. We use it literally in almost every branch of nuclear physics and many branches of atomic physics, and in all branches of physics dealing with the fundamental particles. It has been checked and cross-checked and counter-checked in the most numerous ways and it is a very rich part of our heritage. For instance, many of the particles that are produced in the atmosphere by cosmic rays are unstable. They have a natural tendency to come apart into others, to decay. But if they move very fast, their decay rate is slowed down and the rule is simply:

$$\tau' = \tau(1 - V^2/c^2)^{1/2} = \tau/\gamma$$

where τ is the decay rate when the particles are at rest and τ' is the decay rate when they are moving with speed V. This is observed and is a very vivid thing. We have not yet seen people stay young, but we have seen particles stay young by the billions.

There is another point, a little out of chronological order. I have spoken of rotations, translations, and uniform motions as part of the Lorentz group, but there is another part of the Lorentz group that is not so simply connected with these operations. You cannot rotate your right hand into your left. The only way you can get the one to be congruent to the other is with a reflection in a mirror. You may try wiggling your hands about, but it is really not possible to rotate one into the other. One would think that if rotation did not make any physical difference, reflection would not either, that if space were so isotropic that there was no direction singled out in it, then it would not matter if something were right-handed or left-handed. The two arrangements would be equally probable—there is a good deal of this accidental character in human asymmetries. This invariance law was believed for at least thirty years. Many many brilliant examples turned up where you could classify the states of atomic and nuclear systems according to whether they were unaltered by reflection or whether their symbols changed sign under reflection; in both cases you may say that to any allowed motion or phenomenon in physics, the mirror image also is allowed. If you can have something happen with a wheel turning a certain way and an arrow pointing up, then keeping the wheel the same, but reversing the arrow, which is what happens when you hold up a mirror, will also be allowed. Such objects do exist in physics; in fact the neutrino is a very good example of one. It is only a few years ago that some doubt arose as to whether this rule was strictly true—the rule, that is, that to any system found in nature, the mirror image must occur, being compatible with the laws of nature. The doubts were sufficiently anxious and deep that Lee and Yang looked into it and found that no proof of this rule had been really given experimentally in a certain class of very feeble forces and very slow reactions. And so they looked—not they but their friends—and the answer is that nature has, in this special manifestation, a most violent and total prejudice in favour of right-handed and against left-handed arrangements and the other way round in other cases. It is very odd, very unexpected, and possible only because you cannot get from a rotation or a translation to a reflection. What we now more or less believe is that if any configuration is allowed, then if you take its mirror image and replace all the positive charges by negative and vice versa, and let it run backward in time, that will also be allowed. But that is all we are really confident we know.

This theory of relativity has been very much mixed up in all the developments of physics. I would stress that the odd and often seemingly paradoxical things that are embodied in the special theory of relativity are not paradoxes in the sense of being conflicts between different experiments. They do not involve any contradiction on the part of nature; what they do involve is a gross change, a rather sharp change, from what learned people and ordinary people thought throughout the past centuries, thought as long as they had thought about things at all. The simple facts, namely that light travels with a velocity that cannot be added to or subtracted from by moving a source of light, the simple fact that objects do contract when they are in motion, the simple fact that processes are slowed down when they take place in motion, and very much so if they move with velocities comparable to the velocity of light—these are new elements of the natural world and what the theory of relativity has done is to give coherence and meaning to the connexion between them. These contractions of objects and these retardations of events are, of course, reciprocal; and that is a little paradoxical. It is a little hard to think that, if a moving chunk of matter gets flatter and flatter in the direction in which it is moving, and if you happen to be with that chunk of matter, you would get flatter and flatter if you looked at yourself where you originally were. But it is true; and the same kind of thing is true about time; this is the origin of the twin paradox. It is true also that when there are changes in mass, there is in practical terms a corresponding enormously big change of energy, as we know, both to our hope and our caution. We are not sure that in approaching the domain of the very small (and I am here not now talking of ordinary atomic dimensions, but dimensions some million times smaller), we know exactly what it means to say that "nothing" can move faster than light. But we are sure that our doubt is not with moving faster than light; our ambiguity is with "nothing"—we do not quite know what that means in this domain.

I come now to a generalization of the theory of relativity, which starts when you begin to think about motions which are not uniform, and goes on to consider the nature of gravity. General relativity has very very few connexions with any other part of physics and, as I said, is something that we might just now be beginning to discover, if Einstein had not done so more than forty years ago.

This is partly because, compared to electricity, gravity is a very weak force and really manifests itself only when you are dealing with bodies that are pretty substantial, such as the earth, the sun, and smaller things, but not on an atomic scale. Consequently, it is rather inaccessible to experiment, because the objects you deal with are big and not things you can wiggle around very much. You might think that gravitation should resemble electricity in producing fields which exist in the vacuum, which can be measured, and which propagate with the velocity of light. Something like this is true, but there are two enormous differences. One sign of a difference is that like charges repel each other, like masses attract, and this means the two cannot be really quite the same. Another is that gravitation is a quite universal phenomenon; all bodies follow the same pattern when they are acted on only by gravity: this was Galileo's principle of equivalence. However, if you follow out the attempt, and this has only been done in the last year or so, to make a theory for gravity as much like the theory of electricity and magnetism as you can, you find that, quite apart from the rigorously predictable effects of uniform motion on the measurement of space and time, gravitational fields have much deeper and much more tangled effects on the behaviour of rods and clocks.

If you study this further, you have to come to two conclusions, that in important ways gravitation is a very different thing from electricity and magnetism. First, the rods and clocks are so affected that the space that they measure out, which is always flat if you look in a small region of space in a small interval of time, manifests over bigger regions curvature like the surface of a two-dimensional egg. This curvature may vary from point to point and is itself an expression of the gravitational effects which are in this space. And second, because gravitation, like electromagnetism, involves potential energy and because gravitation is produced by all mass, and therefore, by all energy, gravitation produces gravitation and gravitational fields are not linear in the sense that if you have two gravitational waves they do not merely superimpose their effects, but they interact. Also, if you have a gravitational wave and a gravitational field around the sun they interact. All of this can be found out in a sort of pedestrian way by making the analogy with electricity and magnetism.

But for Einstein it was entirely different. He came at it from two points. One was the universality of motion in a gravitational field which enabled him to think that this might be a geometric thing. The second was the fact that the principle of relativity, philosophically, ought not to be limited to uniform motion. If there is nothing else around, how can you tell if something is being accelerated or not? You can only tell that by reference to something that is not being accelerated. But we know that accelerated motion differs from uniform motion in that we do not have to be told when we are undergoing it, because we feel it and phenomena do respond to it. Einstein observed that a uniform acceleration is exactly the same thing as a uniform gravitational field in all its physical effects. This is another principle of equivalence. And he, therefore, was led to the idea that the problem of dealing with non-uniform motions and the problem of explaining gravitation were related and indeed identical.

If you are moving in something resembling free space you really cannot tell how fast you are moving unless you refer your motion to something else, to the earth or the sun or the stars. But if you are moving in a jerky way, if you are being made to move faster, being accelerated or slowed down, you can have all the blinds drawn, you cannot know where anything else in the world is, but you still can tell that something is going on and you can measure it. And, therefore, there can be no elementary possibility of talking about general motions, motion on a circle, motion which speeds up and slows down, motion on a bumpy railroad train being relative, because within the moving thing (this railroad car or elevator or rocket) you can tell by the way you feel, and you can look at gauges to measure that you are being pushed, pulled, hauled around, jerked, whatever it is. One could, therefore, say that relative uniform motion is indeed relative and no law of nature must discriminate in favour of one such motion rather than another, but that the elementary fact about accelerated motions is that, at least in the part of the universe where we live, we can tell whether we are being jerked around or not, and such motion is not relative. Nevertheless, Einstein's theory of accelerated motions is called the general theory of relativity; it is a very unfortunate terminology. One might almost say that this should be called the general theory of un-relativity, except for one clue, a very deep clue, that was known before, but was understood and made very prominent by Einstein.

If you are confined to a box from which you cannot look out and in which you can make only internal measurements, and if you feel a uniform acceleration, you cannot tell whether you are being speeded up by some force acting directly on the box, or whether you are feeling a uniform gravitational field. The simplest way to confirm this is to fall freely and notice that when you fall freely there is no gravity and there is no acceleration; you are, in fact, accelerating, and you are, in fact, in a gravitational field, but the two of them cancel. You should not achieve this state by jumping out of the window, but if you ride in airplanes enough it will be done for you. Therefore, Einstein understood that one could deal with a more general class of motion only if one also encompassed the phenomena of gravitation. I should say that this principle, that gravitational fields and accelerations are in large measure equivalent to each other, is often called the equivalence principle. It is closely related to Galileo's principle that if the only forces involved are gravitational, all bodies move in the same way. If Galileo's principle were not so, you would not be able to replace gravitation by an acceleration which clearly is the same for all bodies. In the way Einstein did this, the theory of gravitation and the theory of general motions were indissolubly linked.

But one could go about it in what appears to be a more straightforward way, and, in recent years, this less beautiful approach has been developed. One could say that gravitational forces, like the electromagnetic forces, are long range, in that they fall off slowly with distance, and that this suggests that one make a theory of gravitation, which is a natural analogue of the intuitive pictures of Faraday and the equations of Maxwell which describe electromagnetism, electromagnetic waves, and the fields around magnets and charges. The principal point of difference for which one must allow from the beginning is this: that two like charges repel each other, whereas all masses attract each other. If you do this you get a description which reproduces Newton's theory of gravity if fields are not phenomenally strong—and there may be no strong gravitational fields in the world—and if in addition they don't change rapidly with time so that the finiteness of the limiting velocity (of light) plays no part. In this theory one has both principles of equivalence, both that of Galileo and that of Einstein. And one has some famous physical consequences which also were predicted by Einstein. For instance, both theories predict that when light falls in a gravitational field it turns bluer; it turns from red to blue, as frequency increases, and the wavelength decreases. The most precise and, I think, by far the most beautiful example of this is a recent experiment conducted at Harvard in which light was simply allowed to fall down from the third floor to the basement of the Physics Building. One could see how much bluer it had become: one part in 10^{14}: not very much. Also, as Einstein predicted, and as had been guessed before, light is deflected when it passes through a gravitational field, near the sun, or, for that matter, near a star. And you also find, as I have already mentioned, that a gravitational field induces more gravitational field, unlike the standard case of light.

Finally, and perhaps most importantly, if you develop this analogy between gravitation and electromagnetism, you find one very major and deep difference. This is the point where really to explain where the difference comes in would take not a little, but a lot of scribbling on the blackboard, but to explain what the difference is, I think, does not. I shall use the word "space" to mean both the three-dimensional space that we usually mean and the extension in time which we have learned to see is not sharply and totally separable from spatial intervals, because they get mixed up when you look at things in uniform motion. You find that if you explore space with ordinary rulers and clocks, this real space is not the space of Euclid, it is not the space of the classical geometers, but it has some structure and some distortion built into it. This is not the space you imagine on paper; it is the space which you measure, typically, with rods. Now it is very hard to think, at least for me, about four-dimensional continua, especially when one of them is not a distance but a time, but it is legitimate to think of an ordinary two-dimensional surface and suppose that the four-dimensional affair is just a mathematically similar abstraction—just as easy to discuss mathematically but much harder for people to visualize. Then what we have been saying is that we are not dealing with the analogue of a plane surface, but with the analogue of something curved in a rather peculiar way. Locally, in a small enough region, any curved surface, if it has no ridge in it, is flat and it looks like a plane; but if you move along it for some distance, the inherent distortion of the space becomes clear; for instance, the sum of the angles of a triangle will not be a straight angle and Pythagoras's theorem will not be true, and all sorts of geometrical complications will be induced. When you have a sufficiently vigorous and wild gravitational field, such distortions will occur in the nature of space and time, and can be detected by actual measurement. From this it then follows that if you accept the gravitational analogy of electromagnetism you are led to things that have no parallel in electromagnetism; and, if you have your eyes open, you reach Einstein's theory, or something very like it and close to it.

But Einstein, forty-five years ago, did not do this. He developed his description of gravity on the basis of a few rather general ideas. One is that gravitational forces are determined by matter and express themselves in the geometry of space and time. Now, what are the determining aspects of matter? Not its colour, for example, but those aspects that are most clearly related to its mass, energy, momentum, or impetus and related things which form a unitary description of matter. I should say, in this context, that electricity and magnetism, because they have energy, also contribute to gravitational fields. The second important point is that the inherent properties of the geometry wholly determine the gravitational forces that act on bodies. We use the word "inherent" to stress that we are not concerned with how you describe the geometry in terms of co-ordinates, but with those properties which constitute the structure of space and time. So that you have on the one hand that the inherent geometry is determined by the distribution of matter and, on the other, that the response of matter to gravity is determined entirely by the geometry. In fact, matter moves as nearly in a straight line as the crinkly character of the geometry permits. These are the two basic points of Einstein, but they would not lead to anything very definite. In a way which is quite characteristic of physics and which will recur later in these lectures, Einstein also had in mind limiting situations where he knew the right answer. One was the gravitational theory of Newton, which is right, as I said, when fields do not vary too much with time and when they are not overwhelmingly strong. The other is that space and time, if you look at a sufficiently small region, must be flat, and in such a region must be described by the Lorentz space of special relativity.

Those are four elements, we may say four of Einstein's postulates; and the fifth one is the one that nobody can ever translate: the theory must be a simple thing. And here it seems to me we really are faced with the fact that only by inventing the right notation and using the right mathematical ideas can you say whether something is simple or not. With a good deal of fumbling, and many years of unsuccessful trying, many years in which the physical ideas which I have just outlined were clear, Einstein finally came upon a branch of mathematics that other people had made and which gave him the perfect vehicle for writing down how it goes with gravitation and what the general theory of relativity is. And no one today, plodding along to remake this theory along more pedestrian lines, can fail to be overwhelmed by the imagination, the daring, and the beauty of what Einstein did. It is a very different thing to say whether this is a correct theory.

It is, of course, correct in all those particulars which I have talked about, but there is very little experimental evidence about the features of the theory which are peculiar to it, and which have nothing in common with electromagnetic theory, with flat space time, or with Newton's theory. We may be a long time wishing that we knew, but I have never known a physicist who did not think that it was probably a very very good guess indeed. And there is not a shred of evidence against it. We have for space and time not finished with the story. What will come is not my business to try to say, but on two fronts there are wide-open questions.

One is on the scale of the very big, encompassing everything that we see with telescopes and that we hear with radio telescopes. That means more than the distance that light can travel in five or ten billion years, which is about where the present limit lies. We see the universe flying apart; we do not see anything very detailed about its spatial structure. And it is a completely open question, not answered now and conceivably never to be answered, whether the volume of space (I am not now talking of time) is a finite or infinite thing. Einstein thought it was finite, but that was because he thought that everything was steady and static. When we look we see that the motion is the characteristic feature; the further away we look, the faster things are receding from us, and in such a world we have no insight into whether this will stop and there is a finite distance to look or whether it will go on for ever and ever.

Another kind of open question I referred to earlier, and that is that when we get to dimensions so small that they are not of the size of atoms, not even of the size of nuclei, but of the size of those objects of which nuclei and atoms are composed, we cannot really be sure to what extent we can discriminate near-by points in space and time and to what extent the designation of such points is still meaningful. But I will say one thing. Here there is no question of curvature of space because gravity is an utterly negligible force, and we assume that here, too, the velocity of light is a finite limiting velocity imposed on all physical disturbances or signals. From this assumption a great deal can be made to follow, and, so far, nothing that follows from it has shown itself to be in conflict with experience. It is one of the powerful tools of modern-day physics.

II

Atom and Field

The subject of my lecture tonight is really the quantum theory. It has two parallel and even complementary historical origins. One is from the properties of electromagnetic radiation, but from other properties than those which were important for relativity. The other is from an attempt to understand the structure of atoms. I mean by the structure of atoms the atoms of the chemist and the spectroscopist, and not the atoms of the physicist who works with a giant accelerator and who smashes everything that he looks at with his violent collisions. This subject is also interesting but it has been opened up really only in the last decades, and is not understood, whereas the quantum theory was very much a complete theory thirty-five years ago.

As to the properties of electromagnetic radiation, I need first of all to come back with a little more than just words to the idea that a changing magnetic field makes an electric one, a changing electric one makes a magnetic one, and that this pumping cycle produces an electromagnetic wave. These waves have certain important, deep, but rather abstract properties, in common with everything else that physicists call waves. A typical electromagnetic wave may have the electric force changing with time periodically, so that it is sometimes positive and sometimes negative, that is, sometimes pointing, let us say, in the positive direction, sometimes in the negative, and going through zero as it changes from one to the other; the magnetic force is doing the same thing at right-angles to the electric force and out of phase with it, so that when the electric force is zero the magnetic force is a maximum, and the whole thing is travelling at right-angles both to the electric force and the magnetic force with the velocity of light. That is one kind of electromagnetic wave and for us it is plenty.

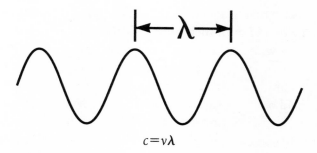

$$c = v\lambda$$

Such a wave is characterized by three numbers: the wavelength λ, the frequency v, and the velocity. The wavelength is the distance from crest to crest of the wave, that is the distance from one point where the electric field is a maximum to the next point at which it is a maximum. The frequency is the rate at which the electric field changes with time at a given point. The product of these two is the velocity of the wave—for an electromagnetic wave, this is the velocity of light, and we write $c = \lambda v$. More generally, we can define in a similar wave the wavelength and frequency for a sound wave, or a water wave, and their product is the velocity of the wave, that is the speed of sound and the speed of progress of the crest of a water wave respectively.

Now the important part of a wave motion, which is true of electromagnetic waves, sound waves, or water waves, and is indeed very easy to observe with water waves, is that if you have two waves more or less in the same part of space and time, they affect each other so that the disturbances add. For example, the electric field that comes from having two electromagnetic waves is the sum of the electric fields of the separate waves; so is the magnetic field. That means that I may have

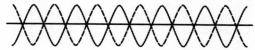

a) Two waves cancelling to give zero disturbances

b) Two waves adding to give a disturbance larger than either

another wave that is added to a given one in such a way that the electric fields add or in such a way that they cancel, depending on how they lie with respect to each other. An important point is that the intensity of light or electromagnetic radiation, the energy it carries, and many of the effects it produces are proportional not to the electric field but to its square. Looking at the diagram, you see that waves can interfere with each other both by adding and producing twice the height of the wave and therefore four times the intensity, or destructively, according to the upper curve (a), so that where one wave is big and positive, the other wave is big and negative, and you get zero for an answer. These are the general phenomena of waves which I need to presume, I hope not wholly irresponsibly, that I have told you about, and which we shall be using all evening in our discussion. We must remember that these properties are true of all waves—water waves, sound waves, and all electromagnetic waves, from those that one uses for the longest wave radio transmission through microwaves, through heat, through light, through ultraviolet light, through X-rays, and up to the highest frequencies there can be.

One consequence of this wave property is that light which comes through different paths may interfere and I will give just two examples of that; one of which we will have to return to.

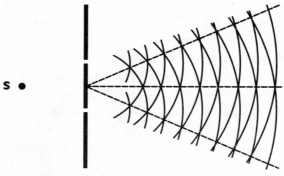

The sketch shows a source S, a diaphragm with very thin slits in it, and out of these slits diverging waves of light. The curved lines represent the crests of these waves: where the crests coincide you will have particularly intense light; where the crest and a trough coincide you will have none at all. You see that the presence of the two slits gives rise to a pattern of brightness and darkness, which either slit alone would not explain and which is characteristic of the wavelength and the separation of the slits. If there were a large number of slits, all spaced the same distance apart, then light would only move in certain directions from this collection of slits, which is called a grating, and these directions are simply related to the ratio of the wavelength and the separation of the slits.

Now, a century of experimentation showed how beautifully the phenomena of the propagation of light—its reflection, its passage through slits, its diffraction from gratings, its dispersion—could be explained in terms of these simple ideas of the interference of waves. There is not to this day the slightest doubt that this is a correct description; it is used every time a radar antenna is designed and any time that one really wants to deal with electromagnetic radiation and its propagation around objects; the light or radio waves from different gaps are brought together and give a resultant intensity depending on the relative phases of the interacting waves. In this case the waves are abstract in the sense that there is no matter moving and, by Chapter I, no aether moving either; but they are concrete in the sense that there are electric and magnetic fields, the ones that Faraday dreamed so much about, which you can measure; every one of these crests corresponds to a measurement of a big electric field at a certain time, and every trough corresponds to a big magnetic field at a certain time. (These measurements would be extremely tedious to do with light, but with long radio waves it is a straightforward experiment that does not teach you very much, but confirms your sanity.) Now, it was exactly at the turn of the century that this harmonious picture of the nature of electromagnetic radiation received a sharp jolt from which it has never recovered. To explain this, it would be easier to skip history entirely, but I will say how Planck discovered it.

When you have a gas of molecules each molecule has, on the average, about the same energy as every other and this energy is a simple measure of the temperature of the gas. If you have electromagnetic waves in an enclosure you can convince yourself that every wavelength should also have about the same energy as every other, and this energy is equal to the temperature of the matter which forms the enclosure and is emitting the waves. This is, on the face of it, absurd, because the theory of relativity says that there can be no limit on how short wavelengths are since all you have to do to make them shorter is get on a fast train, and they will be shorter. Therefore, there will be an infinite energy content to any piece of space that is allowed to come into thermal equilibrium. Energy would simply drain out of matter and everything would be absolutely cold, because all the energy would go into the electromagnetic field. This, it was known, is not true. In struggling to find out why, Planck had a very great advantage. He knew that, for very low frequencies of the light waves, this rule that all the light waves in the enclosure had the same energy was right. He knew that for very high frequencies something quite different happened, and the energy that a wave had was the energy that would be required if one had to create a quantum of energy given by the expression $h\nu$. He introduced the constant h to connect these two régimes which had earlier been studied; it has always since been called Planck's constant. It is, as you see, a constant which, when multiplied by a frequency, gives one an energy, and it will recur; it is the signal, the mark, of atomic physics and is called the quantum of action or Planck's constant. Planck was able to derive a formula which reconciled this behaviour of the equilibrium properties of the enclosed radiation, and also to determine a reasonably accurate value of his constant, but only by employing the technically possible assumption that light was not emitted continuously as a wave should be, but only in energy packets, which correspond to a multiple of the frequency, viz. $h\nu$. He did not believe this, and for many many years struggled to get his formula without making this dreadful assumption which contradicted the whole idea of light as a wave. Because here it was being said, not that light was emitted, like radio waves, simply by charges moving around, but that light was emitted in a whole single operation with a unit of energy, and if that amount of energy could not be emitted, nothing happened; if that could be emitted, it happened; if it could happen more than once, it happened more than once. Well, in this very statistical and complex and dark area it was possible to suppose that Planck had made a mistake, and he lived for years in the confident hope that he had made a mistake.

But he was wrong; and a great blow was struck to his hope when, in the same year that Einstein made the special theory of relativity, he made another paper, which was to prove even more mischievous. The second paper is very closely related to Planck's discovery. If you shine light that is not too red on a metal surface, electrons, which are part of the metal, will come out of it. The very odd thing which had been found in the laboratory was that if you shine the light twice as strongly it does not affect the velocity of the electrons; rather, it affects their number. But, of course, if you are thinking of light as an electromagnetic wave and the wave is more intense, you would expect that the electrons would have more work done on them. But not at all. The energy of the electrons is unrelated to the intensity of the light, but very simply related to the frequency of the light and to Planck's constant.

$$E = h\nu - B$$

The light energy $h\nu$ is the same energy that Planck had introduced five years earlier, E is the energy of the electron as it moves away from the metal and B is not fundamental: it is the work that you have to do to get the electron out of the metal in the first place. This formula has been very accurately and beautifully confirmed. And Einstein said: "This clinches it. Obviously there *are* units of energy in light." When light is absorbed by an electron, it happens in multiples of these units $h\nu$, and then the energy is simply carried off by the electron and that explains the formula.

But, of course, this did not do away with the century of experiences on wave phenomena. Interferometers and prisms, microscopes and radio waves still studied light in terms of the propagation of waves. On the other hand, here was this discontinuous particle aspect, at least to phenomena in which light was absorbed or emitted, which could not be laughed away. Moreover, this was even confirmed by experiments with very hard light, viz. X-rays. In fact, when they collide with electrons, they act as though they had the energy given by $E = h\nu$ and a momentum, or impulse, $p = h/\gamma$, which is just h, the same constant, divided by the wavelength. Thus one could see that light acted in collision with electrons like a particle with a momentum and an energy related to its frequency and wavelength by these very simple rules, consistent with the rules connecting energy and momentum for an electromagnetic wave, but involving both this constant h, and a discrete transfer of energy and of momentum from light to electron in a collision between the two. This experiment, called the Compton effect, had led to a very serious and critical view as to the dual nature of light by about 1923.

Probably the situation could not have been readily understood had it not also been compounded by another and equally puzzling aspect: this time not directly the behaviour of light, but the behaviour of matter on an atomic scale. Let me remind you that, just before this century, Thomson discovered the universal ingredient of ordinary matter, the negatively charged electron which is very light compared to the atom, some 1/2,000th as heavy or less, and which has the unit of charge which we find uniquely throughout the atomic world. Thomson rightly imagined that the number of electrons in an atom was connected with its chemical properties and its place in the periodic table, so that atomic hydrogen would have one electron, helium two, uranium–92. He knew the atoms were neutral, but he did not know where the neutralizing positive charge was; and his best guess was that it was probably extended over a volume of the order of the size of atoms, that is a sphere 1/100th of a millionth of a centimetre in diameter. This was the Thomson model of the atom, and it raised no problems, because it was a rather vague model, and you could not do very much about it. But Thomson was able to show that some regularities, like the occurrence of regular numbers and periods, such as occur in the periodic table, might be expected from such a model. However, this model did not last long, because of the work of Rutherford, which started at McGill, continued at Manchester, and was finally brought to fruition there. Rutherford showed that positive charge of an atom was not spread out over atomic dimensions.

How he did this is itself very beautiful. He had been studying naturally radioactive radiations, coming from uranium, radium, and related heavy elements; he got their family relationships straight and decided which chemical elements were produced by the natural decay of which other elements and which disintegrations followed which; he had distinguished three types of radiation: positively charged and heavy, which were the nuclei of helium and which he called alpha-particles; negatively charged, and light, which were electrons; and neutral, which were very high frequency light. He did not at first know that alpha-particles were helium nuclei, but he thought they were, and he became interested in what happened to them, as they passed through matter. They did not do what they would if atoms had a uniform smooth positive charge, and very light electrons located within it, as suggested by the Thomson model.

In that case there could never be a big force to deflect the alpha-particle, because the smooth charge does not have sufficiently concentrated electricity and the electrons have much too little mass to knock an alpha-particle around, for it is 7,000 times as heavy. But he found that indeed the alpha-particles were, not often but regularly, deflected through very big angles indeed, and from this he concluded that the positive charge was concentrated, and that it was concentrated, along with most of the mass of the atom, in a region with dimensions smaller than 1/10,000th of atomic dimensions. And so he discovered the atomic nucleus which has the positive charge which gives the atom its chemical and most of its physical properties.

This was a marvellous story, but it was only the beginning of really very great puzzles. Think of the simplest of all such atoms, the hydrogen atom. It has a proton, one nuclear particle, at the centre with a unit positive charge, and somehow there is an electron associated with this to make up a system which has a well-defined size. The size is standard; unless the hydrogen atom has been through a wringer or been hit over the head, it always is the same. And it emits a certain characteristic batch of colours when you bash it. Not one of these properties could be intelligible on the basis of Newton's ideas about motion and the idea of how charged particles affect each other, because Rutherford had proved that the field around the proton was the electric field. This field is in its form exactly like the gravitational field around the sun: the forces fall off with the inverse square of the distance and they all point towards the proton, for in this case they are attractive, since the electron and proton are oppositely charged. Consequently, it is just the problem of the planetary motions all over again. Now, one obvious thing that we know about planetary motions is they can be more or less anything: any ellipse, in any plane, with any eccentricity, and any size. Therefore, it is most odd that all hydrogen atoms should have the same size and act in the same way. There is no trace in classical physics of any reason why each hydrogen atom should not be of a different size and shape and behaviour than the next or any other.

Furthermore, although I have not gone into this in detail, we know that if we have a charged particle describing a circular or elliptical orbit, it is accelerated, and an accelerated charged particle will make light waves and lose energy. But hydrogen, unless it is bashed, does not do anything of the kind. It can sit for years and centuries quite content without ever changing. It does not lose its energy and the electron does not spiral in and disappear into the nucleus. And finally the laws relating the colours of light that are emitted from such a classical orbit are a little more complicated, but similar in form to the laws determining the sound frequencies produced by a violin string. There will be a fundamental which is connected to the period of revolution of the electron in the orbit and there will be overtones or harmonics, i.e. multiples of this frequency; whereas the observed frequencies for atomic spectra, hydrogen included, are not harmonics or integral multiples of a fundamental frequency, but rather complicated arrangements of differences between numbers which are not harmonically related. To be specific all the observed frequencies can be written as

$$v = v_i - v_j$$

when v_i and v_j are two of a sequence of numbers $v_1, v_2, v_3....$ In the case of hydrogen, these numbers had been recognized by Balmer, and in general they characterize the atom in question. In other words, the uniqueness of atom systems (which is harder to prove, but just as true, for an atom with 92 electrons) expressed in the law of the light emitted when they are excited, their stability, and the fact that they are all the same size, had no roots in any then existing piece of physics. This was the very great predicament which caused Bohr to make one of those wild guesses which even his own great caution was unable to keep from looking very revolutionary. Bohr said: "For reasons which we don't yet understand, an atom is not characterized by classical orbits, but it is characterized by a set of states which are essentially stationary, which don't change in time." Of these the most familiar and important is the one with the lowest energy, the ground state, and that lasts for ever, unless the atom is disturbed. These states have different energies and those which have more energy than the ground state may not be stable; a transition may occur from such a state to a lower one spontaneously. We remember that each frequency emitted from a given atomic species can be written as $v = v_1 - v_2$, and we may make this into an intelligible equation by multiplying it by h, Planck's constant:

$$hv = hv_1 - hv_2.$$

Then each term in this equation is an energy, and we could assume that the two quantities, hv_1, and hv_2, are the energies of two states in the atom, and the quantity hv is the energy of the quantum of light that is emitted in the transition between them. "I cannot," said Bohr, "describe these transitions. They are not motions in any classical sense. They are something new that I don't understand." Bohr went on to say: "I can give you a rule, in some cases, for I calculated the energies for these states, and this I can do in terms of the properties of the corresponding classical orbits." But Bohr did *not* say, and this turned out not to be true, that these states have anything in common with orbits. For one thing, an orbit is a motion and something changes with time. The stationary state is just what it says: it does not change with time at all.

We have now reached the crisis of quantum theory; but before we get through with this story we will see that we have a vast extension

of our idea of intelligibility in science, that we have a vast generalization of what we mean by objective knowledge, and that we have
a much better analogue to the human predicament than could possibly have been built on Newtonian physics.

Our crisis arose in two studies which, it turns out, are very
closely related. The first was the discovery that, although all electromagnetic waves, including light, are described so perfectly as
wave phenomena showing interference and giving diffraction patterns, nevertheless, in their transactions with matter, they have a
discrete character, behaving like light quanta, with definite energy
and definite momentum, and that they negotiate with matter by
giving up this energy, or by taking it from matter or by colliding
with matter in an elastic collision. Secondly, we had the problem,
created by Rutherford's discovery of the atomic nucleus, of what in
the dickens the electrons were doing in the neighbourhood of the
nucleus. They were not moving on planetary orbits, they were not
radiating, they were not behaving like a small solar system; but they
were, for the most part, in stationary states, essentially stable, the
lowest one completely stable, as Bohr said. When they moved from
one state to another, this was not a motion which could be pictured
in space and time; but the energy difference between the energies
of the stationary states could appear in a form of radiation, the corresponding light quantum. There were rules which were not precise and not generally applicable and which I shall not write down,
that Bohr gave for identifying the energy of these states.

Bohr knew that this was a radical departure and an incompre-
hensible one and he immediately followed it up with a suggestion
very much like that which guided Einstein, namely that this new
scheme, which seemed so wild and unfamiliar, must, in some situations, reproduce the world we knew. Those situations were ones
in which very highly excited states of the atom were involved, in
which many stationary states were involved, and where the dis-
creteness of the stationary state and the finiteness of Planck's constant would not make very much difference. This he called the
"correspondence principle." The new theory must describe the
world of Newton and the world of Maxwell when we are away from

the discrete elements that characterize the quantum theory. This principle turned out to be a most powerful tool; and by 1925 it had been possible to write down laws not involving any image of motion, not involving any clear connexion with Newton's laws or with particles in orbits, but laws which nevertheless were generalizations of Newtonian mechanics and which directly described the connexion between transitions between atomic states and the properties of the atomic state themselves.

I am glad that it did not stay at that, because this is very hard to explain without mathematics. I think my first paper dealt with a simple problem of a molecule with two atoms by this machinery, but it was very hard to interpret what this was about and very hard to solve problems. The solution which most of us find easiest to explain and which is in fact identical with that which the "correspondence principle" led to, came in a very different way. It came in a wild idea that was very soon generalized and verified, and the wild idea was that there should be a wave associated not just with electromagnetism, but also with every kind of particle in nature, specifically with an electron.

These waves are not electric and magnetic disturbances; what they are I will say in a minute. But the relations which characterize the connexion between the wave properties of light and its energy momentum were preserved, viz:

$$E = h\nu$$
$$p = h/\gamma.$$

I have used the same letters, ν and γ for frequency and wavelength, E and p for energy and momentum. This was proposed by de Broglie, who was able to show that one could get a plausible account of the stationary states of the hydrogen atom by the requirement that those states would be realized in which standing waves could be established which were in resonance, that is where the number of wavelengths in the circumference of the Bohr "orbit" would be an integer. This was pretty shaky and it was thoroughly disbelieved—I believe his paper was refused publication. Nevertheless, it was right, and within a year one had found evidence that electrons are indeed in some way wave-like, because they show interference and they diffract just as light does and just as X-rays do.

Also within a year, one found a less sketchy way of describing the relation between the propagation of these waves and the simple forces present in something like a hydrogen atom, where the electron is simply subject to the electric attraction of the proton. This universal wave-particle duality immediately did several things. It explained the existence of stationary states, not as orbits, but as something new with no analogue in classical theory, as things which indeed were steady in time. But they were not static in this sense! If you measured the kinetic energy or the average square momentum of an electron in a stationary state it would not be zero, but it would be the same at any time as it was at any other. It would not change in the course of time. A close connexion between the properties of these waves and Bohr's "correspondence principle" was very quickly set up. But I will not turn to these questions, which are a little mathematical, but rather to the way in which the discovery of the universality of wave-particle duality gave a clue as to the relations between the wave aspects and the particle aspects of light and of all matter. It is also true that a brick is associated with a wave, but it is not a useful thought, because the brick is very much bigger than its wavelength, and we shall never see the interference effects that correspond to macroscopic objects.

The wave-particle duality refers to an individual event and that is a very very striking thing. Let us think again of our two slits. The source may be a light source, or it may be an electron source. The interference acts between the crests of the waves to produce a bright spot in the pattern, or destructively between a crest and a trough to get very little light. This not only describes what happens when you have a lot of light coming from a source, but it describes perfectly well what happens when the light is very faint and you expose a photographic plate for a long time. It describes, in other words, the behaviour of individual quanta of light or individual electrons leaving the source. That fact tells us that the relation of the wave to the finding of the particle is a statistical one: where the wave is strong, we are likely to find the particle, and where the wave, because of destructive interference, is weak, we are unlikely to find it. More than that, the reconciliation

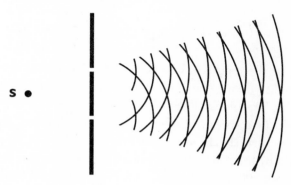

of the wave-particle problem involves the following considerations. If you think of this experiment in terms of a light quantum going through one of the slits and being affected by the other slit through which it does not go, you are led to an impossible description of nature, because then things which are not involved in an experiment may affect the outcome. Thus, our presence here tonight may affect the outcome of an experiment in the reactor building a little away; such an idea has no end. The point then is this: in such a setup you will observe the interference of the light or the electron waves passing through the two slits (or in the more general case, you will get the unidirectional character of light transmitted through a long grating of slits), but you will only do so as long as you leave the experiment as it is with no attempt to find out through which hole the light or the electron passed. Once you arrange to have a little spring in one of the slits, so that when the light is bounced on that slit you notice it, you will have destroyed the interference pattern and you will get only the pattern that you would have if that slit, and that slit alone, were open. How can this be?

It can be because not just the light and the electron, but the slits themselves have the character of being represented by a wave field. Now a wave field, however abstract it may be, has the property that if you want it concentrated in a little region of space you must have different wavelengths present which will reinforce each other in that region of space and cancel outside it. If Δx is a dimension of the region of space, there must be a spread of wavelengths $\Delta \lambda$, such that

$$\Delta(1/\lambda) \gtrsim \frac{1}{\Delta x}; \ \Delta\lambda \gtrsim \frac{\lambda^2}{\Delta x};$$

the smaller the region in which you wish to confine the disturbance, the larger must be the spread of the wavelengths. But if you look at this formula, and remember that $p = h/\gamma$, you will see that there must be a spread of momenta involved. Indeed, the equations show that $\Delta p\, \Delta x \gtrsim h$. In words, the spread in momentum multiplied by the spread in position cannot be less than the quantum of action, Planck's constant. This result is true for the light, for the electron, for the slit, and for anything else that you want to study. This provides a completely consistent restriction on how you may and how you may not use the idea of wave and the idea of particle. The restriction is consistent, because it is universal in that every measuring instrument that you use is as limited in its ability to define at the same time both position and momentum as is the object that you are studying.

In actual fact, these waves represent not electric or magnetic fields, but a state of information. They represent what you have learned by an experiment. Suppose, for instance, that you set out to determine that light passed through the upper slit, or to determine that it was monochromatic light emitted from the source. These two complementary measurements are, in fact, mutually exclusive, because by the time that you had detected the passage of the light through the slit, you would have allowed it to collide with a slit in an effective manner, and thereby to destroy your confidence as to its colour (which is essentially its wavelength). The colour would have been changed by the collision. These waves have a well-defined relation to statistical prediction in that, as in the case of light, their square determines the intensity, which in this case is the probability of finding the particle, either light quantum or electron. They also represent in a general way the kind of information which you can obtain about an atomic system, whether it be its momentum, its position, its energy, or any other possible kind of study you may wish to make of it.

In deciding what measurement is possible, we must take into account the fact that not only the system, but everything we can use to observe it with, is subject to the limitation of complementarity, of which this uncertainty relation between the definition of the momentum of a particle and the definition of its position is the most famous and the most fundamental example. If you have an atom, the stationary states are not orbits. To produce orbits you must take a whole mass of stationary states and build up the waves in a suitable manner by adding the waves of stationary states. So an orbit is complementary to a stationary state; you can realize one or the other, but if you do one, the other is foreclosed. It is also the same with a light quantum; you may have a probability wave for a light quantum, and that is what we have been talking about here; but if you want to build up an electromagnetic wave you must have many light quanta and you must superimpose the waves from many light quanta to make a good old-fashioned electromagnetic wave such as we send and receive. We know that there are indeed many quanta in such waves.

The important point is that it is not merely that we do not always know everything that in classical mechanics we thought we could know, like the position and momentum of an object; if that were so, you could say: "Well, I know its momentum and I will suppose that it is distributed somehow over different possible positions and I will calculate what I'm interested in and take the average." But you must not do that. If you suppose that an object whose momentum you have determined by experiment has a distribution in positions, no matter what the distribution, you will get the wrong answer. It is not that you do not know it; it is that it is not defined. The experiment which gives you the momentum forecloses the possibility of your determining the position. If you welch on it and say, "Well, I want to know the position in the first place," then you can, but then you lose the knowledge which the earlier experiment had given.

One is thus led to a view that a good, well-designed observation gives information. This will determine a wave field, and this wave field develops in time in a quite causal way. That is, if you know it at one time its future will be also known. From this wave field, by taking its square, you can determine the probability for the outcome of another experiment at the future time. These predictions have been checked and checked and checked, and in some wonderful cases are right to one part in ten billion, or something like that. When you make your new observation to check the prediction you generally, but not always, render the old wave function no longer a reasonable description of the system. You also have wild situations in which you may use one particle to study another and in which, depending on what you do with the test particle, you may produce a state for the other which either has a well-defined momentum, or a well-defined position. You cannot do both and you exercise your option by what you do with the observing particle rather than with the observed particle. This gives in a most vivid way a notion of how limited the objectivity of an atomic system is, because apart from a description of what you have done to study its properties, it is not logically possible to assign properties to that atomic system. You cannot say: "I think it is in this part of space and maybe it has such and such a velocity. Let me try it out." You have to take into account, in order to give it any properties at all, what you have done to observe it or what you know of its history. In other words, you have to take into account the relation of this object to the world of nature, not to you as a human being, but to you as one of the many physicists who are in the game.

This theory is, therefore, one which has forced us to a quite different notion of what we mean by objectivity. All over the world, in France, in Japan, in New Zealand, in communist countries, we talk about atomic physics, and we check each other's experiments. In that sense it is a most objective part of our knowledge, and a most well-verified one. These comparisons are possible because we can tell each other how we have gone about an experiment and what we saw and what we found. Mistakes are made, but they are found very quickly. The objectivity which we see in this is not a characteristic that you can look up in a book, it is not an ontological characteristic of the atom at all. It is a characteristic of the way we can talk with each other about it, of the lack of ambiguity and of the reproducibility and the verifiability of our communication with each other.

Quantum theory is, of course, an acausal theory in the sense that events happen for which no precise cause can be determined or given. A given nucleus disintegrates at three o'clock on the afternoon of a certain day. No one in the world could find out when that would happen until it did happen, but he could give a law saying how many in 100,000 nuclei of the same kind would disintegrate in any interval of time. It is a non-determinist theory. There is no possibility, as there was in Laplace's nightmare, of knowing everything about the world right now—not a very plausible assumption—and therefore knowing all about its future—not a very happy outcome. In every experiment, in atomic physics, you look at something, or have other ways of knowing something about the system; it develops according to laws of wave propagation which are simple and well known; then you look again and you get an answer. Everything about this is quite different from the Newtonian picture. You are free in your choice of what you are going to look at to begin with. You are free in what question you ask later; but the event itself is unique. You can try it again and it will not in general give the same answer, because the connexion between the two experiments is a statistical one, not a necessary one.

War and the Nations

I have been discussing the idea of complementarity: that it is impossible to measure precisely two complementary aspects of a physical system. Always when you talk about an atomic system it may be big, it may be a crystal, it may be a nucleus, it may have billions and billions of atoms in it, but always it is a finite part of the world; and in order that you can make an observation of it, you must use the rest of the world for the machinery with which you do it. Especially Bohr has pointed out the analogies between this situation of complementarity and familiar traits in life. He has had, I think, a double purpose: one to illuminate the situation in physics and one to reinforce our interest in complementary aspects of human life.

A favourite one is this. When I write with the chalk it is part of me and I use it without any separation between it and my hand. When I look at it and get interested in what it is and put it under a microscope, it is an object of study. I can do one or the other, but the effective doing of one obviously forecloses the effective doing of the other. I may, as we all have to, make a decision and act or I may think about my motives and my peculiarities and my virtues and my faults and try to decide why I am doing what I am. Each of these has its place in our life, but clearly the one forecloses the other. We may talk, as we increasingly do, about the physical disposition and chemical mechanisms in living objects, but when we talk about living objects we also need to talk about the purpose for which these mechanisms have been developed and have survived. Both methods of description have a valuable part, to give either up is to impoverish our understanding of life; but they are not things that can be done at once without confusion.

There are many other examples. Perhaps one of the deepest, because it is the most familiar, is that we all encounter situations in our life in which we look at the predicament of a man, a friend perhaps, or a son, and see it in the light of what is good for him and of our love for him. We know that others will look at it in the light of what is just and what is proper in society. We know that the good societies, if there are any, the better societies are those in which this conflict and this dichotomy and this element of complementarity is not too terrible. Still, we all know, because of the tragic quality of life, that it will always be there. Those who have lived through the unravelling of the heart of the atomic paradox as it existed twenty-five or thirty years ago believe that one has come to a vision of the physical world with far more room for the human spirit in it than could have been found in the great mechanism of Newton.

Very soon physicists, pleased with what they had found and enormously armed with new theoretical and mathematical methods, turned to other problems—not just atomic physicists, but their colleagues in chemistry, in mathematics, and in other branches of physics. For instance, very soon after the quantum theory was elucidated one began really to make a theory of the electron, the first fundamental particle, other than light, to be studied in detail. And the positron, the counterpart to the electron, which has the same mass, but opposite charge, was discovered, and detailed studies were made of the beautiful processes of materialization and dematerialization, in which a pair of charged particles disappear to give two rays of light (two gamma rays), or in which two gamma rays collide to make a pair. This is as beautiful an example of Einstein's relation between mass and energy as one can ask for. But then we got into another branch of study which in the end involved us as a community in politics in some sense (I mean it in a good sense—the judgement of the good society, not the winning of an election), and in the great questions of national and political power. This, of course, is not unheard of. Archimedes, in Syracuse, had the same troubles, and Hobbes, ten years before Newton's *Principia*, wrote of them with a dry dispassion. This began to happen very slowly and without anyone seeing it, when, armed with quantum theory and eager to understand, physicists turned their attention not to the behaviour of the atomic electrons around the nucleus, but to the nucleus itself.

This field was very much opened up by two developments. One, which occurred in the same year as the discovery of the positron, was the discovery of the neutron, the neutral ingredient of atomic nuclei. The second was the design and construction of accelerators, machines for giving to charged particles sufficient energy to overcome the electric repulsion of atomic nuclei, and to get at them and break them up and to see what they were made of and how they reacted. By 1939 we knew quite a lot of how nuclei behaved, of what their stationary states were like, of how they reacted when bombarded, and of what kind of products would be produced. Although those were the days of small accelerators, a million times less energetic than those now under study, they were good enough to give a very good insight into the behaviour of atomic nuclei. Rutherford was dead then, in 1939. It was he, who, during the First World War, had produced the first artificial transmutation of nuclei, not with an accelerated particle, but with one of his beloved alpha-particles. He went to his death rather doubtful that large-scale energy releases could be practically accomplished on earth, although the energy changes were certainly there to be made. We learned more of this when, on the basis of studies of nuclei and of what the astronomers could tell, it was possible to give a convincing and rather detailed account of some of the principal sources of the energy of the sun and of many other stars in terms of nuclear reactions changing nuclei and releasing energy in the hot central regions of these stars.

Nineteen thirty-nine was the year of fission and was also the year of the outbreak of the Second World War; a good many changes had come to all people, but also to physicists. Early in the 1920s up until the very early 1930s scientists from the Soviet Union were welcome and were frequently found in the great centres of learning in Europe and warm collegial relations were formed then between Russians, Englishmen, Germans, Scandinavians, many of which persist to this day. That was changed, too, in the 1930s. During the 1930s very many men of science, like very many other men, either had to leave or in conscience did leave Germany. Many of them came to Canada, many to the United Kingdom, and perhaps most of all to the United States. Some came from Italy as well.

By 1939 the Western world was no longer a suburb of the scientific community, but a centre in its own right, and when fission was discovered the first analyses of what nuclei were involved and what prospects there were for its practical use for the release of energy were largely conducted in the United States. I remember that Uhlenbeck, who was still in Holland, thought it his duty to tell his government about this development; the Minister of Finance immediately ordered 50 tons of uranium ore from the Belgian mining company, and remarked: "Clever, these physicists."

Actually it was very largely the refugee scientists in England and in the United States who took the first steps to interest their governments in the making of atomic explosives and who took some steps, very primitive ones, in thinking out how this might be done and what might be involved in it. In fact, we all know that it was a letter from Einstein, written at the suggestion of Szilard, Wigner, and Teller, that first brought the matter to President Roosevelt's attention; in the United Kingdom I think it was Simon and Peierls who played this early part. Bohr remained in Denmark as long as it was humanly possible for him to do so. The governments were busy. They had a war on their hands and certainly any reasonable appraisal would have suggested that radar, probably the proximity fuse, and in principle if not in fact rockets would have very much more to do with the outcome of the war than would the atomic energy undertaking. It started slowly under crazy names like Tube Alloys in the United Kingdom, and Department of Substitute Materials in the United States. When I came into it my predecessor had the title Co-ordinator of Rapid Rupture.

There were really very many questions. Would a bomb work and what sort of a thing would it be, how much material would it need, what kind of energies would it release; would it ignite the atmosphere in nuclear reactions and end us all; could it be used to start fusion reactions? There was also the problem of producing, in industrial processes that had no previous analogue in human history, the very considerable number of pounds of the special materials, uranium and plutonium, of which the first bombs had to be made. By late 1941 an authorization for production was really given. There was an uneasy co-operation between the United Kingdom, Canada, and the United States, later substantially to improve, but never, I think, to become completely free of trouble, especially for our friends from the United Kingdom, though we learned much and gained much from all their help. There was also, of course, very much secrecy.

Late in 1942 we decided that we must get to work on how to make bombs themselves. On July 16th, 1945, early in the morning, the first bomb was exploded. It did a little better than we thought it might. One of the guards said: "The long hairs have let it get away from them." That day, the President of the United States, the Prime Minister of England, and Stalin were meeting in Potsdam. I believed, because I was told by Dr. Bush, that the President would take the occasion to discuss this development with Stalin, not in order to tell him how to make a bomb, which the President did not know, but to do something that seemed important at the time, to treat the Russians as allies in this undertaking and to start discussing with them how we were going to live with this rather altered situation in the world. It did not come off that way. The President said something, but it is completely unclear whether Stalin understood it or not. No one was present except Stalin's interpreter of the moment and the President, who does not know Russian. But it was a casual word and that was all.

The bombs were used against Japan. That had been foreseen and in principle approved by Roosevelt and Churchill when they met in Canada and again at Hyde Park. It was largely taken for granted; there were questions raised, but I believe there was very little deliberation and even less record of any deliberation there was. And I would like synoptically, briefly, on the basis of my memory of the time and of talk with many historians who have grappled with it, to tell you what little I think about this. I think first of all that we do not know and at the moment cannot know whether a political effort to end the war in the Far East could have been successful. The Japanese Government was deeply divided and stalemated in favour of war. The dissident part of the Government had made an overture through Moscow to the West. Moscow did nothing about it until Potsdam. Stalin told Truman about it. Stalin did not seem interested, Truman did not seem interested, and nothing happened. This was at the very time when the test bomb was successful and a couple of weeks before the bombing of Japan. The actual military plans at that time for the subjugation of Japan and the end of the war were clearly much more terrible in every way and for everyone concerned than the use of the bombs. There is no question about that; and these plans were discussed with us; they would have involved, it was thought, a half a million or a million casualties on the Allied side and twice that number on the Japanese side. Nevertheless, my own feeling is that if the bombs were to be used there could have been more effective warning and much less wanton killing than took place actually in the heat of battle and the confusion of the campaign. That is about all that I am clear about in hindsight. That, and one other thing: I am very glad that the bomb was not kept secret. I am glad that all of us knew, as a few of us already did, what was up and what readjustments in human life and in political institutions would be called for. Those are the days when we all drank one toast only: "No more wars."

When the war was over, the great men of physics spoke quite simply and eloquently, Einstein in advocacy of world government and Bohr, first to Roosevelt and to Churchill and to General Marshall and then finally quite openly, when nobody else listened but the public, of the need to work for a world which was completely open. He had in mind that we had some very great secrets and that we ought to be willing to relinquish them in exchange for the disappearance of secrecy from all countries and particularly from the secret-ridden communist societies. Stimson, who resigned as Secretary of War in September 1945, wrote: "Mankind will not be able to live with the riven atom, without some government of the whole." Among many reports that we in our innumerable commissions produced, I remember two. One of them, which remains, I think, to this day Top Secret, ended roughly: "If this weapon does not persuade men of the need for international collaboration and the need to put an end to war, nothing that comes out of a laboratory ever will." The other said: "If there is to be any international action for the control of atomic energy there must be an international community of knowledge and of understanding."

All of this was very deep and genuine and I think most of our community, and many other people also, believed it desirable. It was not exactly what Stalin wanted. And it really was not anything to which any government became very clearly or deeply or fully committed. In the absence of a practical way of getting there, the most that could be done was to put forward some tentative and not entirely disingenuous suggestions about the control of atomic energy which, if accepted, would have led in the direction of international collaboration and in the direction of a suitable beginning of world order. That is not how it has worked; and I remind you only of two obvious things. We are in an arms race of quite unparalleled deadliness—I think this is not the place to speak about the amount of devilment that is piled up on both sides, or about the precautions and the difficulties of making sure that it does not go off; on the other hand, we have lived sixteen and a half years without a nuclear war. In the balance, between the very great gravity of the risks we face and the obvious restraints that have seen us through this time, I have no counsel except that of sobriety and of some hope.

It may seem wrong to speak of this as an experience of physicists. It certainly is not an intellectual challenge like that out of which the theory of relativity was born or that which gave rise to the solution of the paradoxes of wave-particle duality and the quantum theory. I doubt if there is a certain specific right idea to be had in the field of how to remake the world to live with these armaments and to live with our other commitments and our other hopes. But it is true that we have been marked by our deep implication in this development, by the obvious fact that without physics it could not have happened, and by the heavy weight which has been laid on so many members of this community in counselling their government, in speaking publicly and in trying above all in the early phases to find a healthy direction. I do not think that even our young colleagues, tearing away at the new unsolved problems of fundamental physics, are as free of preoccupation for their relation to the good life and the good society, as we were, long ago, when we were their age.

There have been, as you know, many deep and painful conflicts among technical people, and I think one can pick up the paper almost any day and find examples of learned men calling their colleagues liars. We are torn by conflicts, and this, I think, was not openly and clearly true in 1945 and 1946. The arms race, the Cold War, the obduracy of the political conflict, and the immense and complex and terrifying scope of the technological enterprise are not a climate in which the simple discussion of physical problems finds very much place. But more than that, of course, these are not physical problems and they cannot be settled by the methods of science. The question of what our purpose is on earth, the question of how we may make a government that will represent these purposes, the question of what our own responsibility is, the question of what business it is of ours to think about these things, are not to be solved in any laboratory or settled by any equation or any mathematics. Part of the conflict among technical people is like the conflict among all people: it comes from conflicting assessments of what our antagonist's course may be, what his behaviour will be—a subject rich in mystery, even for the experts. Part of it comes because we are talking about a world in which there is no relevant previous experience. No world has ever faced a possibility of destruction—in a relevant sense annihilation—comparable to that which we face, nor a process of decision-making even remotely like that which is involved in this. Those of you who have been in battle know how tangled, unpredictable, and unamenable to prior planning the course of a battle often turns out to be, even when it was well planned. No one has any experience with warfare in the nuclear age. These are some of the reasons for acrimonious differences as to what fraction of a population may survive if you do this or do that, or what you may trust our antagonists to do and what you must suspect them of doing. In addition, the community of physicists is certainly no more than any other free of evil, free of vanity, or free of their own glory; we must expect rather ugly things to happen and they do.

But I would really think that on a few rather deep points which do not imply the answers to all the questions in which we could rightly be interested, we are as a community really rather clear as to what our duty is. It is, in the first place, to give an honest account of what we all know together, know in the way in which

I know about the Lorentz contraction and wave-particle duality, know from deep scientific conviction and experience. We think that we should give that information openly whenever that is possible, that we should give it to our governments in secret when the governments ask for it, or, even if the governments do not ask for it, that they should be made aware of it, when we think it essential, as Einstein did in 1939. We all, I think, are aware that it is our duty to distinguish between knowledge in this rather special and proud, but therefore often abstract and irrelevant, sense, and our best guess, our most educated appraisal of proposals which rest on things that in the nature of the case cannot yet be known, like the little cost of some hundred million to build a certain kind of nuclear carrier. We think that it is even more important, and even more essential, to distinguish what we know in the vast regions of science where a great deal is known and more is coming to be known all the time, from all those other things of which we would like to speak and should speak in another context and in another way, those things for which we hope, those things which we value. Finally, I think we believe that whenever we see an opportunity, we have the duty to work for the growth of that international community of knowledge and understanding, of which I spoke earlier, with our colleagues in other lands, with our colleagues in competing, antagonistic, possibly hostile lands, with our colleagues and with others with whom we have any community of interest, any community of professional, of human, or of political concern.

We think of these activities as our contribution, not very different from those of anybody else, but with an emphasis conditioned by the experiences of growing, increasing understanding of the natural physical world, in an increasingly tangled, increasingly wonderful and unexpected situation. We think of this as our contribution to the making of a world which is varied and cherishes variety, which is free and cherishes freedom, and which is freely changing to adapt to the inevitable needs of change in the twentieth century and all centuries to come, but a world which, with all its variety, freedom, and change, is without nation states armed for war and above all, a world without war.

Part Two

The Modern Century

Northrop Frye

Foreword

* * *

The selection of a Canadian scholar to be the Whidden Lecturer in 1967, the year of Canada's centennial, was inevitable. And that the choice should fall on H. Northrop Frye, the first person ever to be named by the University of Toronto as its University Professor, was almost equally inevitable. His reputation as one of the most significant of contemporary literary critics is world-wide and securely established. It is a cause for pride to academic circles in his native country that he should be the subject of a special volume, issued by the Columbia University Press just over a year ago. A graduate of Toronto and Merton College, Oxford, he made his mark some twenty years ago with a penetrating study of William Blake, *Fearful Symmetry*; and since that time a steady stream of books and articles from his pen has made his name one of the most familiar and most respected wherever the study of English letters is seriously pursued. He has lectured in scores of universities throughout the English-speaking world and has received honorary doctorates from many of them.

For the 1967 Whidden Lectures he chose as his theme *The Modern Century*, the century in which, as the saying goes, Canada came of age. He did not restrict his vision, however, to the literary and creative activities that have occurred in this country over the past one hundred years. Rather, he attempted to relate Canadian developments to those of the world as a whole; and it was a stimulating and exciting exercise to accompany him as his purview ranged over other countries, other continents, and other cultures. That the perspective of the many hundreds who had the privilege of hearing him was deepened and broadened, there is not the slightest doubt.

McMaster University is now very pleased to publish the lectures in book form so that an even wider audience may share in the rewarding experience of learning the views of a distinguished Canadian on man's spiritual and intellectual adventures since 1867.

February 1967

E. T. SALMON
*Principal of University College
McMaster University*

Author's Note

The operation of giving the Whidden Lectures for 1967 was made
pleasant and memorable by the hospitality of McMaster University
and my many friends there. To them, as well as to the extraordi-
narily attentive and responsive audience, I feel deeply grateful.

I am indebted to the Canada Council for a grant which enabled
me to work on this and other projects, and to Mrs Jessie Jackson
for her preparation of the manuscript.

The lectures were delivered in the centenary year of Canada's
Confederation, and were originally intended to be Canadian in subject-matter. I felt, however, that I had really said all I had to say about
Canadian culture for some time, with the help of about forty colleagues, in the "Conclusion" to the recently published *Literary History
of Canada: Canadian Literature in English* (1965). Hence the shift of
theme to a wider context. I have tried to make my Canadian references as explicit as possible, for the benefit of non-Canadian readers, but have not invariably succeeded. For example, the titles of the
three lectures are titles of poems by well-known Canadian poets:
respectively, Archibald Lampman, Irving Layton, and Émile Nelligan.

N.F.
*Victoria College in the
University of Toronto
January 1967*

I

City of the End of Things

The Whidden Lectures have been a distinguished series, and anyone attempting to continue them must feel a sense of responsibility. For me, the responsibility is specific: I have been asked to keep in mind the fact that I shall be speaking to a Canadian audience in the Centennial year of Confederation. I have kept it in mind, and the first thing that it produced there was what I hope is a sense of proportion. The centenary of Confederation is a private celebration, a family party, in what is still a relatively small country in a very big world. One most reassuring quality in Canadians, and the one which, I find, chiefly makes them liked and respected abroad, when they are, is a certain unpretentiousness, a cheerful willingness to concede the immense importance of the non-Canadian part of the human race. It is appropriate to a Canadian audience, then, to put our centenary into some kind of perspective. For the majority of people in North America, the most important thing that happened in 1867 was the purchase of Alaska from Russia by the United States. For the majority of people in the orbit of British traditions, the most important thing that happened in 1867 was the passing of the Second Reform Bill, the measure that Disraeli called "a leap in the dark," but which was really the first major effort to make the Mother of Parliaments represent the people instead of an oligarchy. For a great number, very probably the majority, of people in the world today, the most important thing that happened in 1867, anywhere, was the publication of the first volume of *Das Kapital* by Karl Marx, the only part of the book actually published by Marx himself. It was this event, of course, that helped among other things to make the purchase of Alaska so significant: another example of the principle that life imitates literature, in the broad sense, and not the other way round. There is a still bigger majority to be considered, the majority of the dead. In the year 1867

Thomas Hardy wrote a poem called "1967," in which he remarks that the best thing he can say about that year is the fact that he is not going to live to see it.

My own primary interests are in literary and educational culture. What I should like to discuss with you here is not Canadian culture in itself, but the context of that culture in the world of the last century. One reason for my wanting to talk about the world that Canada is in rather than about Canada is that I should like to bypass some common assumptions about Canadian culture which we are bound to hear repeated a good deal in the course of this year. There is, for instance, the assumption that Canada has, in its progress from colony to nation, grown and matured like an individual: that to be colonial means to be immature, and to be national means to be grown up. A colony or a province, we are told, produced a naïve, imitative, and prudish culture; now we have become a nation, we should start producing sophisticated, original, and spontaneous culture. (I dislike using "sophisticated" in an approving sense, but it does seem to be an accepted term for a kind of knowledgeability that responds to culture with the minimum of anxieties.) If we fail to produce a fully mature culture, the argument usually runs, it must be because we are still colonial or provincial in our attitude, and the best thing our critics and creators can do is to keep reminding us of this. If a Canadian painter or poet gets some recognition, he is soon giving interviews asserting that Canadian society is hypocritical, culturally constipated, and sexually inhibited. This might be thought a mere cliché, indicating that originality is a highly specialized gift, but it seems to have advanced in Canada to the place of an obligatory ritual. Some time ago, when a Canadian play opened in Paris, a reviewer, himself a Canadian, remarked sardonically: "Comme c'est canadien! Comme c'est pur!" I should add that this comment was incorporated by the Canadian publisher as a part of his blurb.

Analogies between the actual growth of an individual and the supposed growth of a society may be illuminating, but they must always be, like all analogies, open to fresh examination. The analogy is a particularly tricky form of rhetoric when it becomes the basis of an argument rather than merely a figure of speech. Certainly every society produces a type of culture which is roughly character-istic of itself. A provincial society has a provincial culture; a metro-politan society has a metropolitan culture. A provincial society will produce a phenomenon like the tea party described in F. R. Scott's well-known satire, "The Canadian Authors Meet." A metropolitan society would turn the tea party into a cocktail party, and the con-versation would be louder, faster, more knowing, and cleverer at rationalizing its pretentiousness and egotism. But its poets would not necessarily be of any more lasting value than Mr Scott's Miss Crotchet, though they might be less naïve. It is true that relatively few if any of the world's greatest geniuses have been born in Canada, although a remarkable British painter and writer, Wyndham Lewis, went so far as to get himself born on a ship off Canadian shores, and developed an appropriately sea-sick view of Canada in later life. But we do not know enough about what social conditions produce great or even good writers to connect a lack of celebrated birthplaces with the moral quality of Canadian civilization.

Another aspect of the same assumption is more subtle and per-vasive. It is widely believed, or assumed, that Canada's destiny, cul-turally and historically, finds its fulfilment in being a nation, and that nationality is essential to identity. It seems to me, on the other hand, quite clear that we are moving towards a post-national world, and that Canada has moved further in that direction than most of the smaller nations. What is important about the last cen-tury, in this country, is not that we have been a nation for a hun-dred years, but that we have had a hundred years in which to make the transition from a pre-national to a post-national consciousness. The so-called emergent nations, such countries as Nigeria or Indonesia, have not been so fortunate: for them, the tensions of federalism and separatism, of middle-class and working-class inter-ests, of xenophobia and adjustment to the larger world, have all come in one great rush. Canada has—so far—been able to avoid both this kind of chaos and the violence that goes with the devel-opment of a vast imperial complex like the U.S.A. or the U.S.S.R. The Canadian sense of proportion that I mentioned is especially valuable now, as helping us to adopt an attitude consistent with the world it is actually in. My present task, I think, is neither to eulogize nor to elegize Canadian nationality, neither to celebrate its survival nor to lament its passage, but to consider what kinds of social context are appropriate for a world in which the nation is rapidly ceasing to be the real defining unit of society.

We begin, then, with the conception of a "modern" world, which began to take shape a century ago and now provides the context for Canadian existence, and consequently for our Centennial. A century ago Canada was a nation in the world, but not wholly of it: the major cultural and political developments of Western Europe, still the main centre of the historical stage, were little known or understood in Canada, and the Canadian reaction even to such closer events as the American Civil War was largely negative. Today, Canada is too much a part of the world to be thought of as a nation in it. We have our undefended border with the United States, so celebrated in Canadian oratory, only because it is not a real boundary line at all: the real boundary line, one of the most heavily defended in the world, runs through the north of the country, separating a bourgeois sphere of control from a Marxist one.

Culturally, the primary fact about the modern world, or at least about our "Western" and "democratic" part of it, is that it is probably the first civilization in history that has attempted to study itself objectively, to become aware of the presuppositions underlying its behaviour, to understand its relation to previous history and to see whether its future could in some measure be controlled by its own will. This self-consciousness has created a sharp cultural dialectic in society, an intellectual antagonism between two mental attitudes. On one side are those who struggle for an active and conscious relation to their time, who study what is happening in the world, survey the conditions of life that seem most likely to occur, and try to acquire some sense of what can be done to build up from those conditions a way of life that is at least self-respecting. On the other side are those who adopt a passive and negative attitude, responding to the daily news and similar stimuli, aware of what is going on but making no effort to understand either the underlying causes or the future possibilities. The theatre of this conflict in attitudes is formed by the creative and the communicating arts. The creative arts are almost entirely on the active side: they mean nothing, or infinitely less, to a passive response. The subject-matter of contemporary literature being its own time, the passive and uncritical attitude is seen as its most dangerous enemy. Many aspects of contemporary literature—its ironic tone, its emphasis on anxiety and absurdity, its queasy apocalyptic forebodings—derive from this situation.

The communicating arts, including the so-called mass media, are a mixture of things. Some of them are arts in their own right, like the film. Some are or include different techniques of presenting the arts we already have, like television. Some are not arts, but present analogies to techniques in the arts which the arts may enrich themselves by employing, as the newspaper may influence collage in painting or the field theory of composition in poetry. Some are applied arts, where the appeal is no longer disinterested, as it normally is in the creative arts proper. Thus propaganda is an interested use of the literary techniques of rhetoric. As usual, there are deficiencies in vocabulary: there are no words that really convey the intellectual and moral contrast of the active and passive attitudes to culture. The phrase "mass culture" conveys emotional overtones of passivity: it suggests someone eating peanuts at a baseball game, and thereby contrasting himself to someone eating canapés at the opening of a sculpture exhibition. The trouble with this picture is that the former is probably part of a better educated audience, in the sense that he is likely to know more about baseball than his counterpart knows about sculpture. Hence his attitude to his chosen area of culture may well be the more active of the two. And just as there can be an active response to mass culture, so there can be passive responses to the highbrow arts. These range from "Why can't the artist make his work mean something to the ordinary man?" to the significant syntax of the student's question: "Why is this considered a good poem?" The words advertising and propaganda come closest to suggesting a communication deliberately imposed and passively received. They represent respectively the communicating interests of the two major areas of society, the economic and the political. Recently these two conceptions have begun to merge into the single category of "public relations."

One very obvious feature of our age is the speeding up of process: it is an age of revolution and metamorphosis, where one lives through changes that formerly took centuries in a matter of a few years. In a world where dynasties rise and fall at much the same rate as women's hemlines, the dynasty and the hemline look much alike in importance, and get much the same amount of featuring in the news. Thus the progression of events is two-dimensional, a child's drawing reflecting an eye that observes without seeing depth, and even the effort to see depth has still to deal with the whole surface. Some new groupings result: for example, what used to be called the trivial or ephemeral takes on a function of *symbolizing* the significant. A new art of divination or augury has developed, in which the underlying trends of the contemporary world are interpreted by vogues and fashions in dress, speech or entertainment. Thus if there appears a vogue for white lipstick among certain groups of young women, that may represent a new impersonality in sexual relationship, a parody of white supremacy, the dramatization of a death-wish, or the social projection of the clown archetype. Any number may play, but the game is a somewhat self-defeating one, without much power of sustaining its own interest. For even the effort to identify something in the passing show has the effect of dating it, as whatever is sufficiently formed to be recognized has already receded into the past.

It is not surprising if some people should be frustrated by the effort to keep riding up and down the manic-depressive roller-coaster of fashion, of what's in and what's out, what is U and what non-U, what is hip and what is square, what is corny and what is camp. There are perhaps not as many of these unhappy people as our newspapers and magazines suggest there are: in any case, what is important is not this group, if it exists, but the general sense, in our society, of the panic of change. The variety of things that occur in the world, combined with the relentless continuity of their appearance day after day, impress us with the sense of a process going by a little too fast for our minds to focus on anything in it.

Some time ago, the department of English in a Canadian university decided to offer a course in twentieth-century poetry. It was discovered that there were two attitudes in the department towards that subject: there were those who felt that twentieth-century poetry had begun with Eliot's *The Waste Land* in 1922, and those who felt that most of the best of it had already been written by that time. There also appeared to be some correlation between these two views and the age groups of those who held them. Finally a compromise was reached: two courses were offered, one called Modern Poetry and the other Contemporary Poetry. But even the contemporary course would need now to be supplemented by a third course in the post-contemporary, and perhaps a fourth in current happenings. In the pictorial arts the fashion-parade of isms is much faster: I hear of painters, even in Canada, who have frantically changed their styles completely three or four times in a few years, as collectors demanded first abstract expressionism, then pop art, then pornography, then hard-edge, selling off their previous purchases as soon as the new vogue took hold. There is a medieval legend of the Wild Hunt, in which souls of the dead had to keep marching to nowhere all day and all night at top speed. Anyone who dropped out of line from exhaustion instantly crumbled to dust. This seems a parable of a type of consciousness frequent in the modern world, obsessed by a compulsion to keep up, reduced to despair by the steadily increasing speed of the total movement. It is a type of consciousness which I shall call the alienation of progress.

Alienation and progress are two central elements in the mythology of our day, and both words have been extensively used and misused. The conception of alienation was originally a religious one, and perhaps that is still the context in which it makes most sense. In religion, the person aware of sin feels alienated, not necessarily from society, but from the presence of God, and it is in this feeling of alienation that the religious life begins. The conception is clearest in evangelical thinkers in the Lutheran tradition like Bunyan, who see alienation of this kind as the beginning of a psychological revolution. Once one becomes aware of being in sin and under the wrath of God, one realizes that one's master is the devil, the prince of this world, and that treason and rebellion against this master is the first requirement of the new life.

A secularized use of the idea appears in the early work of Marx, where alienation describes the feeling of the worker who is cheated out of most of the fruit of his labour by exploitation. He is unable to participate in society to the extent that, as a worker, he should, because his status in society has been artificially degraded. In this context the alienated are those who have been dispossessed by their masters, and who therefore recognize their masters as their enemies, as Christian did Apollyon. In our day those who are alienated in Marx's sense are, for example, the Negro, whose status is also arbitrarily degraded, or those who are in actual want and misery. The Negro, looking at the selfishness and panic in white eyes, realizes that while what he has to fight is ultimately a state of mind, still his enemies also include people who have got themselves identified with this state of mind. Thus his enemies, again, are those who believe themselves his masters or natural superiors. Apart from such special situations, not many in the Western democracies today believe that a specific social act, such as expropriating a propertied class, would end alienation in the modern world.

The reason is that in a society like ours, a society of the accepted and adequately fed, the conception of alienation becomes psychological. In other words it becomes the devil again, for the devil normally comes to those who have everything and are bored with it, like Faust. The root of this aspect of alienation is the sense that man has lost control, if he ever had it, over his own destiny. The master or tyrant is still an enemy, but not an enemy that anyone can fight. Theoretically, the world is divided into democracies and peoples' republics: actually, there has never been a time when man felt less sense of participation in the really fateful decisions that affect his life and his death. The central symbol of this is of course the overkill bomb, as presented in such works as *Dr Strangelove*, the fact that the survival of humanity itself may depend on a freak accident. In a world where the tyrant-enemy can be recognized, even defined, and yet cannot be projected on anything or anybody, he remains part of ourselves, or more precisely of our own death-wish, a cancer that gradually disintegrates the sense of community. We may try to persuade ourselves that the complete destruction of Communism (or, on their side, of capitalist imperialism) would also destroy alienation. But an instant of genuine reflection would soon tell us that all such external enemies could disappear from the earth tomorrow and leave us exactly where we were before.

In this situation there is a steady pressure in the direction of making one's habitual responses passive. The first to succumb to this pressure are those whose attitude to the world is deliberately frivolous, who have only an instinct for avoiding any kind of stimulus that might provoke a genuine concern. Such an attitude tries to ignore the issues of the day and responds mainly to the "human interest" stories in the tabloids provided for it, gathering its experience of life much as one might pick up a number of oddly shaped stones on a beach. But even here the effort to shut out anxiety is itself an anxiety, and a very intense one, which keeps the conscious and critical part of the mind very near to the breaking point of hysteria. The mind on the verge of breakdown is infinitely suggestible, as Pavlov demonstrated, and the forces of advertising and propaganda move in without any real opposition from the critical intelligence.

These agencies act in much the same way that, in *Paradise Lost*, Milton depicts Satan acting on Eve. All that poor Eve was consciously aware of was the fact that a hitherto silent snake was talking to her. Her consciousness being fascinated by something outrageous, everything that Satan had to suggest got through its guard and fell into what we should call her subconscious. Later, when faced with a necessity of making a free choice, she found nothing inside her to direct the choice except Satan's arguments, which she perforce had to take as her own, the more readily in that she did not realize how they had got there. Similarly, the technique of advertising and propaganda is to stun and demoralize the critical consciousness with statements too absurd or extreme to be dealt with seriously by it. In the mind that is too frightened or credulous or childish to want to deal with the world at all, they move in past the consciousness and set up their structures unopposed.

What they create in such a mind is not necessarily acceptance, but dependence on their versions of reality. Advertising implies an economy which has some independence from the political structure, and as long as this independence exists, advertising can be taken as a kind of ironic game. Like other forms of irony, it says what it does not wholly mean, but nobody is obliged to believe its statements literally. Hence it creates an illusion of detachment and mental superiority even when one is obeying its exhortations. When doing Christmas shopping, there is hardly one of us who would not, if stopped by an interviewer, say that of course he didn't hold with all this commercializing of Christmas. The same is to some extent true of propaganda as long as the issues are not deeply serious. The curiously divided reaction to the Centennial—a mixture of the sentimental, the apprehensive, and the sardonic—is an example. But in more serious matters, such as the Vietnam war, the effects of passivity are more subtly demoralizing. The tendency is to accept the propaganda bromide rather than the human truths involved, not merely because it is more comfortable, but because it gives the illusion of taking a practical and activist attitude as opposed to mere hand-wringing. When propaganda cuts off all other sources of information, rejecting it, for a concerned and responsible citizen, would not only isolate him from his social world, but isolate him so completely as to destroy his self-respect. Hence even propaganda based on the big lie, as when an American or Chinese politician tries to get rid of a rival by calling him a Communist or a bourgeois counter-revolutionary, can establish itself and command assent if it makes more noise than the denial of the charge. The epigram that it is impossible to fool all the people all the time may be consoling, but is not much more.

What eventually happens I may describe in a figure borrowed from those interminable railway journeys that are so familiar to Canadians, at least of my generation. As one's eyes are passively pulled along a rapidly moving landscape, it turns darker and one begins to realize that many of the objects that appear to be outside are actually reflections of what is in the carriage. As it becomes entirely dark one enters a narcissistic world, where, except for a few lights here and there, we can see only the reflection of where we are. A little study of the working of advertising and propaganda

in the modern world, with their magic-lantern techniques of projected images, will show us how successful they are in creating a
world of pure illusion. The illusion of the world itself is reinforced
by the more explicit illusions of movies and television, and the imitation world of sports. It is significant that a breakdown in illusion,
as when a baseball game or a television program is proved to have
been "fixed," is more emotionally disturbing than proof of crime
or corruption in the actual world. It is true that not all illusion is a
bad thing: elections, for example, would hardly arouse enough
interest to keep a democracy functioning unless they were assimilated to sporting events, and unless the pseudo-issues were taken
as real issues. Similarly the advantages of winning the game of
space ships and moon landings may be illusory, but the illusion is
better than spending the money involved on preparations for war.
Then again, when illusion has been skilfully built up, as it is for
instance by such agencies as the *Reader's Digest*, it includes the illusion of keeping abreast of contemporary thought and events, and
can only be recognized as illusion by its effects, or rather by the
absence of any effects, in social action.

Democracy is a mixture of majority rule and minority right, and
the minority which most clearly has a right is the minority of those
who try to resist a passive response, and thereby risk the resentment
of those who regard them as trying to be undemocratically superior.
I am speaking however not so much of two groups of people as of
two mental attitudes, both of which may exist in the same mind. The
prison of illusion holds all of us: the first important step is to be
aware of it as illusion, and as a prison. The right of free criticism is
immensely important, and the habitually worried and anxious attitude of the more responsible citizen has a significance out of proportion to its frequency. But the alienation of progress operates on him
too, in a different way. He finds, in the first place, his response of
concern becoming a stock response. Many of us have had the experience of beginning to read a journal of critical comment, tuning ourselves in to the appropriate state of anxiety, and then noticing that
we have in error picked up an issue of several months back. In the
split second of adjustment we become aware of a conventionalized

or voluntarily assumed response. I am not deprecating the response: I am trying to describe a cultural condition. But any conventional-ized or habitual response is subject in the course of time to the pres-sure of becoming automatic. As I write this, an official communiqué about education arrives in the mail, and I read: "If we are to keep pace with the swiftly moving developments of our time, we must strive for ever higher standards in every field of endeavour.... No informed person is unaware of the tremendous effort that [it] will take to meet the demands that the years ahead will produce. Yet we are also aware that the general well-being of our nation is depend-ent on our ability to meet the challenge."

One would say that it was impossible to write flatter clichés or more obvious platitudes, and the effect of cliché and platitude ought to be soothing. So it is, and yet every word is soaked in the metaphors of a gasping panic, as though the author had placed a large bet on a contender in a race who was, like Hamlet, fat and scant of breath. The conscious appeal is to the concerned and intelligent citizen, who ought to take an interest in what his public servants are trying to do. A less conscious motive is to prepare him for an increase in taxes. But the combination of urgency in the rhetoric and of dull-ness in the expression of it is, or would be if we were not so famil-iar with it, very strange. Something has happened to atrophy one's responses when the most soporific words one can use are such words as "challenge," "crisis," "demand," and "endeavour." Even the most genuinely concerned and critical mind finds itself becoming drowsy in its darkening carriage. And not only so, but the very ability to rec-ognize the cliché works against one's sense of full participation. Self-awareness thus operates like a drug, stimulating one's sense of responsibility while weakening the will to express it.

The conception of progress grew up in the nineteenth century around a number of images and ideas. The basis of the conception is the fact that science, in contrast to the arts, develops and advances, with the work of each generation adding to that of its predecessor. Science bears the practical fruit of technology, and tech-nology has created, in the modern world, a new consciousness of time. Man has doubtless always experienced time in the same way, dragged backwards from a receding past into an unknown future. But the quickening of the pace of news, with telegraph and submarine cable, helped to dramatize a sense of a world in visible motion, with every day bringing new scenes and episodes of a passing show. It was as though the ticking of a clock had become not merely audible but obsessive, like the tell-tale heart in Poe. The first reactions to the new sensation—for it was more of a sensation than a conception—were exhilarating, as all swift movement is for a time. The prestige of the myth of progress developed a number of value-assumptions: the dynamic is better than the static, process better than product, the organic and vital better than the mechanical and fixed, and so on. We still have these value-assumptions, and no doubt they are useful, though like other assumptions we should be aware that we have them. And yet there was an underlying tendency to alienation in the conception of progress itself. In swift movement we are dependent on a vehicle and not on ourselves, and the proportion of exhilaration to apprehensiveness depends on whether we are driving it or merely riding in it. All progressive machines turn out to be things ridden in, with an unknown driver.

Whatever is progressive develops a certain autonomy, and the reactions to it consequently divide: some feel that it will bring about vast improvements in life by itself, others are more concerned with the loss of human control over it. An example of such a progressive machine was the self-regulating market of laissez faire. The late Karl Polanyi has described, in *The Great Transformation*, how this market dominated the political and economic structure of Western Europe, breaking down the sense of national identity and replacing it with a uniform contractual relationship of management and labour. The autonomous market took out a ninety-nine year lease on the world from 1815 to 1914, and kept "peace" for the whole of that time. By peace I mean the kind of peace that we have had ourselves since 1945: practically continuous warfare somewhere or other, but with no single war becoming large enough to destroy the overall economic structure, or the major political structures dependent on it. And yet what the autonomous market created in modern consciousness was, even when optimistic, the feeling that Polanyi has finely described as "an uncritical reliance on the alleged self-healing virtues of uncon-scious growth." That is, the belief in social progress was transferred from the human will to the autonomous social force. Similar con-ceptions of autonomous mass movement and historical process dom-inate much of our social thinking today. In Communist theology the historical process occupies much the same position that the Holy Spirit does in Christianity: an omnipotent power that co-operates with the human will but is not dependent on it.

Even earlier than the rise of the market, the feeling that man could achieve a better society than the one he was in by a sufficiently res-olute act had done much to inspire the American and more partic-ularly the French revolutions, as well as a number of optimistic progressive visions of history like that of Condorcet. Here the ideal society is associated with a not too remote future. Here too there are underlying paradoxes. If we ask what we are progressing to, the only conceivable goal is greater stability, something more orderly and pre-dictable than what we have now. After all, the only thing we can imagine which is better than what we have now is an ensured and constant supply of the best that we do have: economic security, peace, equal status in the protection of law, the appeal of the will to reason, and the like. Progress thus assumes that the dynamic is bet-ter than the stable and unchanging, yet it moves toward a greater sta-bility. One famous progressive thinker, John Stuart Mill, had a nervous breakdown when he realized that he did not want to see his goals achieved, but merely wished to act as though he did. What was progress yesterday may seem today like heading straight for a prison of arrested development, like the societies of insects. In the year 1888 Edward Bellamy published *Looking Backward*, a vision of a collec-tivized future which profoundly inspired the progressive thinkers of that day, and had a social effect such as few works of literature have ever had. Today it impresses us in exactly the opposite way, as a most sinister blueprint for a totalitarian state.

A more serious consequence is that under a theory of progress present means have constantly to be sacrificed to future ends, and we do not know the future well enough to know whether those ends will be achieved or not. All we actually know is that we are damaging the present. Thus the assumption that progress is necessarily headed in a good or benevolent direction becomes more and more clearly an unjustified assumption. As early as Malthus the conception of sinister progress had made its appearance, the vision of a world moving onward to a goal of too many people without enough to eat. When it is proposed to deface a city by, say, turning park lots into parking lots, the rationalization given is usually the cliché "you can't stop progress." Here it is not even pretended that progress is anything beneficent: it is simply a Juggernaut, or symbol of alienation. And in history the continued sacrificing of a visible present to an invisible future becomes with increasing clarity a kind of Moloch-worship. Some of the most horrible notions that have ever entered the human mind have been "progressive" notions: massacring farmers to get a more efficient agricultural system, exterminating Jews to achieve a "solution" of the "Jewish question," letting a calculated number of people starve to regulate food prices. The element of continuity in progress suggests that the only practicable action is continuous with what we are already doing: if, for instance, we are engaged in a war, it is practicable to go on with the war, and only visionary to stop it.

Hence for most thoughtful people progress has lost most of its original sense of a favourable value-judgement and has become simply progression, towards a goal more likely to be a disaster than an improvement. Taking thought for the morrow, we are told on good authority, is a dangerous practice. In proportion as the confidence in progress has declined, its relation to individual experience has become clearer. That is, progress is a social projection of the individual's sense of the passing of time. But the individual, as such, is not progressing to anything except his own death. Hence the collapse of belief in progress reinforces the sense of anxiety which is rooted in the consciousness of death. Alienation and anxiety become the same thing, caused by a new intensity in the awareness of the movement of time, as it ticks our lives away day after day. This intensifying of the sense of time also, as we have just seen, dislocates it: the centre of attention becomes the future, and the emotional relation to the future becomes one of dread and uncertainty. The future is the point at which "it is later than you think" becomes "too late." Modern fiction has constantly dealt, during the last century, with characters struggling toward some act of consciousness or self-awareness that would be a gateway to real life. But the great majority of treatments of this theme are ironic: the act is not made, or is made too late, or is a paralyzing awareness with no result except self-contempt, or is perverted into illusion. We notice that when the tone is less ironic and more hopeful about the nature and capacities of man, as it is for instance in Camus's *La Peste*, it is usually in a context of physical emergency where there is a definite enemy to fight.

Even in theory progress is as likely to lead to the uniform and the monotonous as to the individual and varied. If we look at the civilization around us, the evidence for uniformity is as obvious and oppressive as the evidence for the rapid change toward it. The basis of this uniformity is technological, but the rooted social institutions of the past—home, school, church—can also only be adapted to a nomadic society by an expanding uniform pattern. Whatever the advantages of this situation, we have also to consider the consequences of the world's becoming increasingly what in geology is called a peneplain, a monotonous surface worn down to a dead level by continued erosion. We are not far into the nineteenth century before we become aware of a different element both in consciousness and in the physical appearance of society. This is a new geometrical perspective, already beginning in the eighteenth century, which is scaled, not to the human body, but increasingly to the mechanical extensions of the body. It is particularly in America, of course, that this perspective is most noticeable: Washington, laid out by L'Enfant in 1800, is already in the age of the automobile. This mechanical perspective is mainly the result of the spreading of the city and its technology over more and more of its natural environment. The railway is the earliest and still one of the most dramatic examples of the creation of a new kind of landscape, one which imposes geometrical shapes on the countryside. The prophet Isaiah sees the coming of the Messiah as symbolized by a highway which exalts valleys and depresses mountains, making the crooked straight and the rough places plain. But, as so often happens, the prophecy appears to have been fulfilled in the wrong context.

The traditional city is centripetal, focused on market squares, a pattern still visible in some Ontario towns. Its primary idea is that of community, and it is this idea that has made so many visions of human fulfilment, from Plato and the Bible onward, take the form of a city. To the modern imagination the city becomes increasingly something hideous and nightmarish, the *four-millante cité* of Baudelaire, the "unreal city" of Eliot's *Waste Land*, the *ville tentaculaire* of Verhaeren. No longer a community, it seems more like a community turned inside out, with its expressways taking its thousands of self-enclosed nomadic units in a headlong flight into greater solitude, ants in the body of a dying dragon, breathing its polluted air and passing its polluted water. The map still shows us self-contained cities like Hamilton and Toronto, but experience presents us with an urban sprawl which ignores national boundaries and buries a vast area of beautiful and fertile land in a tomb of concrete. I have had occasion to read Dickens a good deal lately, and Dickens was, I suppose, the first metropolitan novelist in English literature, the first to see the life of his time as essentially a gigantic pulsation toward and away from the great industrial centres, specifically London. And one notices in his later novels an increasing sense of the metropolis as a kind of cancer, as something that not only destroys the countryside, but the city itself as it had developed up to that time.

The Victorian critics of the new industrialism contemporary with Dickens, such as Ruskin and Morris, concentrated much of their attack on its physical ugliness, which they saw as a symbol of the spiritual ugliness of materialism and exploitation. Critics of our time are more impressed by the physical uniformity which they similarly interpret as a symbol of spiritual conformity. If certain tendencies within our civilization were to proceed unchecked, they would rapidly take us towards a society which, like that of a prison, would be both completely introverted and completely without privacy. The last stand of privacy has always been, traditionally, the inner mind. It is quite possible however for communications media, especially the newer electronic ones, to break down the associative structures of the inner mind and replace them by the prefabricated structures of the media. A society entirely controlled by their slogans and exhortations would be introverted, because nobody would be saying anything: there would only be echo, and Echo was the mistress of Narcissus. It would also be without privacy, because it would frustrate the effort of the healthy mind to develop a view of the world which is private but not introverted, accommodating itself to opposing views. The triumph of communication is the death of communication: where communication forms a total environment, there is nothing to be communicated.

The role of communications media in the modern world is a subject that Professor Marshall McLuhan has made so much his own that it would be almost a discourtesy not to refer to him in a lecture which covers many of his themes. The McLuhan cult, or more accurately the McLuhan rumour, is the latest of the illusions of progress: it tells us that a number of new media are about to bring in a new form of civilization all by themselves, merely by existing. Because of this we should not, in staring at a television set, wonder if we are wasting our time and develop guilt feelings accordingly: we should feel that we are evolving a new mode of apprehension. What is important about the television set is not the quality of what it exudes, which is only content, but the fact that it is there, the end of a tube with a vortical suction which "involves" the viewer. This is not all of what a serious and most original writer is trying to say, yet Professor McLuhan lends himself partly to this interpretation by throwing so many of his insights into a deterministic form. He would connect the alienation of progress with the habit of forcing a hypnotized eye to travel over thousands of miles of type, in what is so accurately called the pursuit of knowledge. But apparently he would see the Gutenberg syndrome as a cause of the alienation of progress, and not simply as one of its effects. Determinism of this kind, like the determinism which derives Confederation from the railway, is a plausible but over-simplified form of rhetoric.

Similarly with the principle of the identity of medium and message, which means one thing when the response is active, and quite another when the response is passive. On the active level it is an ideal formulation which strictly applies only to the arts, and to a fully active response to the arts. It would be true to say that painting, for example, had no "message" except the medium of painting itself. On the passive level it is an ironic formulation in which the differences among the media flatten out. The "coolness" of television is much more obvious in the privacy of a middle-class home than it is when turned on full blast in the next room of a jerry-built hotel. All forms of communication, from transistors to atom bombs, are equally hot when someone else's finger is on the button. Thus the primary determining quality of the medium comes from the social motive for using it and not from the medium itself. Media can only follow the direction of the human will that created them, and a study of the social direction of that will, or what Innis called the bias of communication, is a major, prior, and separate problem.

Technology cannot of itself bring about an increase in human freedom, for technological developments threaten the structure of society, and society develops a proportionate number of restrictions to contain them. The automobile increases the speed and freedom of individual movement, and thereby brings a proportionate increase in police authority, with its complication of laws and penalties. In proportion as the production of retail goods becomes more efficient, the quality of craftsmanship and design decreases. The aeroplane facilitates travel, and therefore regiments travel: a modern traveller, processed through an immigration shed, might think ruefully of the contrast with Sterne, travelling to France in the eighteenth century, suddenly remembering that Britain was at war with France, and that consequently he would need his passport. The same principle affects science itself. The notion that science, left to itself, is bound to evolve more and more of the truth about the world is another illusion, for science can never exist outside a society, and that society, whether deliberately or unconsciously, directs its course. Still, the importance of keeping science "free," i.e., unconsciously rather than deliberately directed, is immense. In the Soviet Union, and increasingly in America as well, science is allowed to develop "freely" so that the political power can hijack its technological by-products. But this means a steady pressure on science to develop in the direction useful to that power: target-knowledge, as the Nazis called it. I am not saying that there are no answers to these questions: I am saying that no improvement in the human situation can take place independently of the human will to improve, and that confidence in automatic or impersonal improvement is always misplaced.

In earlier times the sense of alienation and anxiety was normally projected as the fear of hell, the "too late" existence awaiting those who, as Dante's Virgil says, had never come alive. In our day this fear is attached, not to another world following this one, but to the future of our own world. The first half of the modern century was still full of progressive optimism: an unparalleled number of Utopias, or visions of a stabilized future, were written, and universal prosperity was widely predicted, partly because most of the people being exploited in the main centres of culture were well out of sight in Asia or Africa. After the midway point of 1917 there came an abrupt change. Spengler's *Decline of the West* appeared in Germany the next year. Here it is said that history consists of cultural developments which rise, mature, and decline like organisms. After they have exhausted their creative possibilities, they turn into "civilizations." The arts give place to technology and engineering; vast cities spread over the landscape, inhabited by uprooted masses of people, and dictatorships and annihilation wars become the course of history. A Classical "culture" entered this stage with Alexander, and, later, the rise of Rome. The Western world entered it with Napoleon, and is now in the stage corresponding to that of the Punic Wars, with the great world states fighting it out for supremacy. Spengler is often dismissed as "fatalistic" today, but his paralleling of our historical situation with earlier periods, especially that of the Roman Empire, and his point that our technology could be part of a decline as easily as it could be part of an advance, are conceptions that we all accept now, whether we realize it or not, as something which is inseparably part of our perspective.

The progressive belief suffered a rude set-back in America in the crash of 1929; it was adopted by the Soviet Union as part of its revolutionary world-view, but is gradually fading out even there, much as the expectation of the end of the world faded out of early Christian thought. In our day the Utopia has been succeeded by what is being called, by analogy, the "dystopia," the nightmare of the future. H. G. Wells is a good example of a writer who built all his hopes around the myth of progress, in which the role of saviour was played by a self-evolving science. His last publication, however, *The Mind at the End of its Tether* (1940), carried all the furious bitterness of an outraged idealism. Orwell's *1984* is a better-known dystopia, and perhaps comes as close as any book to being the definitive *Inferno* of our time. It is a particularly searching study because of the way in which it illustrates how so many aspects of culture, including science, technology, history, and language, would operate in their demonic or perverted forms. The conception of progress took off originally from eighteenth-century discussions about the natural society, where the progressive view was urged by Bolingbroke and Rousseau and the opposite one by Swift and Burke. According to Rousseau, the natural and reasonable society of the future was buried underneath the accumulated injustices and absurdities of civilization, and all man had to do was to release it by revolution. Writers of our day have mostly reverted to the view of Swift's *Gulliver's Travels*, that slavery is to man at least as natural a state as freedom: this is the central insight of one of the most penetrating stories of our time, William Golding's *Lord of the Flies*, and is certainly implied, if not expressed, in Aldous Huxley's *Brave New World* and many similar works.

It is natural that many people should turn from the vision of such a world to some illusion or distracting fiction that seems to afford a more intelligible environment. Nationalism is or can be a distracting fiction of this kind. The nation, economically considered, is a form of private enterprise, a competing business in the world's market; hence, for most people, nationality comes to their attention chiefly through inconvenience—customs duties, income taxes, and the like. But it also may provide some sense of a protected place. It can't happen here, we may say, deliberately forgetting that the distinction between here and there has ceased to exist. It is significant that intense nationalism or regionalism today is a product either of resistance to or of disillusionment with progress. Progress, when optimistic, always promises some form of exodus from history as we know it, some emergence on to a new plateau of life. Thus the Marxist revolution promised deliverance from history as history had previously been, a series of class struggles. But just as there are neurotic individuals who cannot get beyond some blocking point in their emotional past, so there are neurotic social groups who feel a compulsion to return to a previous point in history, as Mississippi keeps fighting the Civil War over again, and some separatists in Quebec the British Conquest.

However, one wonders whether, in an emergency, this compulsion to return to the same point, the compulsion of Quixote to fight over again the battles he found in his books, is not universal in our world. In ordinary life, the democratic and Communist societies see each other as dystopias, their inhabitants hysterical and brainwashed by propaganda, identifying their future with what is really their destruction. Perhaps both sides, as Blake would say, become what they behold: in any case seeing tendencies to tyranny only on the other side is mere hypocrisy. The Nuremberg trials laid down the principle that man remains a free agent even in the worst of tyrannies, and is not only morally but legally responsible for resisting orders that outrage the conscience of mankind. The Americans took an active part in prosecuting these trials, but when America itself stumbled into the lemming-march horror of Vietnam the principle was forgotten and the same excuses and defiances reappeared.

All the social nightmares of our day seem to focus on some unending and inescapable form of mob rule. The most permanent kind of mob rule is not anarchy, nor is it the dictatorship that regularizes anarchy, nor even the imposed police state depicted by Orwell. It is rather the self-policing state, the society incapable of formulating an articulate criticism of itself and of developing a will to act in its light. This is a condition that we are closer to, on this continent, than we are to dictatorship. In such a society the conception of progress would reappear as a donkey's carrot, as the new freedom we shall have as soon as some regrettable temporary necessity is out of the way. No one would notice that the necessities never come to an end, because the communications media would have destroyed the memory.

The idea of progress, we said, is not really that of man progressing, but of man releasing forces that will progress by themselves. The root of the idea is the fact that science progressively develops its conception of the world. Science is a vision of nature which perceives the elements in nature that correspond to the reason and the sense of structure in the scientist's mind. If we look at our natural environment with different eyes, with emotion or desire or trying to see in it things that answer other needs than those of the reason, nature seems a vast unthinking indifference, with no evidence of meaning or purpose. In proportion as we have lost confidence in progress, the scientific vision of nature has tended to separate from a more imaginative and emotional one which regards nature or the human environment as absurd or meaningless. The absurd is now one of the central elements in the contemporary myth, along with alienation and anxiety, and has extended from man's feeling about nature to his feeling about his own society. For society, like nature, has the power of life and death over us, yet has no real claim on our deeper loyalties. The absurdity of power is clearer in a democratic society, where we are deprived of the comforting illusions that surround royalty. In a democracy no one pretends to identify the real form of society either with the machinery of business or with the machinery of government. But in that case where is the society to be found to which we do owe loyalty?

There are two contemporary plays which seem to sum up with peculiar vividness and forcefulness the malaise that I have described as the alienation of progress. One is Beckett's *Waiting for Godot*. The main theme of this play is the paralysis of activity that is brought about by the dislocation of life in time, where there is no present, only a faint memory of a past, and an expectation of a future with no power to move towards it. Of the two characters whose dialogue forms most of the play, one calls himself Adam; at another time they identify themselves with Cain and Abel; at other times, vaguely and helplessly, with the thieves crucified with Christ. "Have we no rights?" one asks. "We got rid of them" the other says—distinctly, according to the stage direction. And even more explicitly: "at this place, at this moment of time, all mankind is us." They spend the whole action of the play waiting for a certain Godot to arrive: he never comes; they deny that they are "tied" to him, but they have no will to break away. All that turns up is a Satanic figure called Pozzo, with a clown tied to him in a parody of their own state. On his second appearance Pozzo is blind, a condition which detaches him even further from time, for, he says, "the blind have no notion of time."

The other play is Albee's *Who's Afraid of Virginia Woolf?* The title of this play is echoed from the depression song, "Who's afraid of the big bad wolf?," where the "wolf" was a specific fear of unemployment. I began this talk by saying that the modern century was the first to study itself objectively, and that this has created an opposition between the active mind that struggles for reality and the passive mind that prefers to remain in an illusion. Art, culture, the imagination, are on the side of reality and activity: Virginia Woolf, chosen because of the sound of her last name, represents this side, and the characters are "afraid" of her because they cannot live without illusion. The two men in the play are a historian and a scientist, facing the past and the future, both impotent in the present. "When people can't abide things as they are," says the historian George, "when they can't abide the present, they do one of two things ... either they turn to a contemplation of the past, as I have done, or they set about to alter the future." But nobody in the play does either. George can murder his imaginary child, but the destruction of illusion does not bring him reality, for the only reality in his life was contained in the illusion which he denied.

I have tried to indicate the outlines of the picture that contemporary imagination has drawn of its world, a jigsaw-puzzle picture in which the Canada of 1967 is one of the pieces. It is a picture mainly of disillusionment and fear, and helps to explain why our feelings about our Centennial are more uneasy than they are jubilant. In the twentieth century most anniversaries, including the annual disseminating neurosis of Christmas, are touched with foreboding. I noticed this early in life, for my twenty-first birthday was spent at the Chicago World's Fair of 1933, entitled "A Century of Progress," where the crowds were much more preoccupied with worrying about the depression than with celebrating what had led to it. And yet this picture, as I have tried also to explain, is the picture that the contemporary imagination draws of itself in a mirror. Looking into the mirror is the active mind which struggles for consistency and continuity of outlook, which preserves its memory of its past and clarifies its view of the present. Staring back at it is the frozen reflection of that mind, which has lost its sense of continuity by projecting it on some mechanical social process, and has found that it has also lost its dignity, its freedom, its creative power, and its sense of the present, with nothing left except a fearful apprehension of the future. The mind in the mirror, like the characters in Beckett, cannot move on its own initiative. But the more repugnant we find this reflection, the less likely we are to make the error of Narcissus, and identify ourselves with it. I want now to discuss the active role that the arts, more particularly literature, have taken in forming the contemporary imagination, which has given us this picture. The picture itself reflects anxiety, and as long as man is capable of anxiety he is capable of passing through it to a genuine human destiny.

II

Improved Binoculars

Let us begin by looking at some of the characteristics that we generally associate with the word "modern," especially in the arts. "Modern," in itself, means simply recent: in Shakespeare's day it meant mediocre, and it still sometimes carries that meaning as an emotional overtone. In its ordinary colloquial sense it implies an advanced state of technology and the social attitudes of a highly urbanized life. In some Western Canadian towns, for example, houses with outdoor privies are advertised as "un-modern." But "modern" has also become a historical term like "Romantic," "Baroque," or "Renaissance." It would be convenient if, like "Romantic," the colloquial uses of the word were spelled in lower case and the cultural term with a capital, but this is not established. Like "Romantic" again, "modern" as a cultural term refers partly to a historical period, roughly the last century, but it is also partly a descriptive term, not a purely historical term like "medieval." Just as we feel that Keats or Byron are Romantic and that some of their contemporaries, Jane Austen for example, are either not Romantic at all or are less Romantic, so we feel that "modern" is in part a style or attitude in recent culture, and that some of the artists and writers of the last century have been "more modern" than others.

'Modern," so used, describes certain aspects of an international style in the arts which began, mainly in Paris, about a hundred years ago. Out of compliment to our centenary, I shall date it from 1867, the year of the death of Baudelaire. The larger context of this "modern" is the series of vast changes that began to take place, not around 1867, but a century earlier. These earlier changes included the American and French revolutions, the beginning of the Industrial Revolution, new and more analytical schools of thought, such as the French Encyclopaedists and the British Utilitarians, and the cultural development we call Romantic. By 1867 this movement had entered on a second phase, continuous with but distinguishable from its predecessor, and this begins the modern century properly speaking. The thinkers Darwin and Marx, and later Freud and Frazer, the writers Rimbaud, Flaubert, Dostoevsky, and Nietzsche, the impressionist painters and their successors, belong to it.

During the whole of the last century, there has naturally been the most frantic resistance to "modern" culture, for both the highbrow arts and the popular ones, though for different reasons, have a powerful capacity to stir up guilt feelings, personal insecurities, and class resentments. The Nazis called the modern style a Jewish conspiracy, the Jews being for them the symbols of a racism without a national boundary. The Communist hierarchy calls it an imperialistic conspiracy, and particularly attacks the "formalism" which it asserts symbolizes the ideology of a decadent class. One may suspect from such things as the Sinyavsky-Daniel trial that the periodic "thaws" in the Soviet Union are mainly a device to determine where the really dangerous threats to the bureaucracy are coming from, but even so they show something of the tremendous pressure building up against the barriers of official stupidity and panic, which may eventually break through them. Chinese resistance is still militant, though of course the cultural traditions there are different. Hysterical people in the democracies, in their turn, call the modern style a Communist conspiracy; in Canada it is often called Americanization. It is true that many aspects of modern culture, especially popular culture, are of American origin, like jazz, but America is a province conquered by the international modern much more than it is a source of it.

In literature, the international character of the modern style has been partly disguised by difference in language. Just as we seem to be moving into a world in which we meet the same kind of things everywhere, from hydro installations to Beatle haircuts, so we seem to be moving into a world in which English will become either the first or the second language of practically everybody. But of course it does not follow that English or any other language will become a world *literary* language. The last hundred years have also been a period in which many minority languages have been maintained, revived, or in some cases practically invented, by an intense regional patriotism. Hebrew, Norwegian, Flemish, Irish, and French in Canada are examples. The prestige of such movements is one of several elements that have helped to shape a common view which is the opposite of the one I am advancing here. Culture, it is often said, in contrast to economic and political developments, is local, regional, and decentralized, as dependent on an immediate environment as a fine wine or a delicate and traditional handicraft like peasant costumes. The first step in the creation of an indigenous culture, therefore, is a firm boundary line, and the next step is the cultural equivalent of high tariffs against foreign influences.

This theory of culture probably originated in Romantic theories about a creative "folk," and has been confusing the Canadian scene for even longer than the past hundred years. I held a version of it myself, or thought I did, when I was beginning to write in Canadian periodicals a generation ago. According to Shelley in his preface to *Prometheus Unbound*, the decentralizing of Great Britain into a dozen or more districts, each with its own cultural centre, would help to awaken the country to the kind of cultural vitality enjoyed earlier by such small towns as Periclean Athens or Medicean Florence. It sounds unlikely, but it is a roughly consistent extension of Shelley's association of human freedom with the self-determining of national cultures, particularly Greece and Italy. William Morris, again, thought of culture as essentially "manufacture" in the strict sense, as the work of brain and hand which has a totally different function from that of mechanized industry. Hence his ideal world is one of small and relatively isolated communities, governing themselves by local councils and keeping themselves busy making things. In his view the so-called minor or useful arts are the index of a culture; the major arts are assimilated to them, and both are produced by a domestic economy. In T. S. Eliot, again, we find "culture" associated with an intense decentralization. Eliot's *Notes Toward a Definition of Culture* and similar essays are much preoccupied with Welsh and Scottish nationalisms and with the desirability of having most people not move from the place where they were born.

The attempts to "purify" a language are also part of the resistance to the international modern. It is consistent with William Morris's attitude that he should deplore the mongrel nature of modern English which has helped to make it a world language, its grafting of so many Latin conceptual and Greek technical terms on a Teutonic stock. Morris was one of those who wanted English to throw out its load of loan words and return to more Teutonic methods of making up a vocabulary, such as calling a market a cheaping place or a baby carriage a pushwainling. Such efforts got nowhere in English, but some other languages, such as Persian, or German in the Nazi period, were more successful in driving out foreign influences on vocabulary and syntax, at least for a time. Even in Australia, I understand, there has been a group of poets devoted to putting as many native Australian words into their poems as possible. A late echo of this tendency is the anti-"joual" campaign in French Canada, the effort to set up European French as a standard of correctness against the normal linguistic developments which tend to Anglicize and Americanize French Canadian speech. Outside literature, resistance to the modern style has very little if anything to put in its place. Approved Nazi painting and approved Communist fiction can only fall back on idioms derived from the art before 1867, on worn-out Romantic and Victorian formulas which can no longer be used with their original energy and conviction. If we compare T. S. Eliot's theories about decentralized culture with his own poetry and the quality of his influence, both of which are completely international, it is clear that the theories are merely something dreamed up, and have no relation to any cultural facts.

It is of course true that a coherent environment is a cultural necessity. And many of the world's great cultural developments do seem to have been assisted by some kind of local resistance to imperial expansion. The catalyzer of ancient Greek culture was clearly the successful battle for independence by a province on the fringes of what was essentially, in its civilization, a Persian world. Hebrew culture drew a similar strength from its resistance to Egyptian and Mesopotamian imperialism. Elizabethan England and seventeenth-century Holland were provincial rebels against the centralizing forces of the Papacy and the Hapsburg Empire; Germany in the Napoleonic period and, on a smaller scale, Ireland at the turn of this century joined a cultural efflorescence to a political resistance. In our day similar movements are going on, though more confined to the cultural area. The liberalizing of Communist culture is much more likely to start in Poland or Hungary than in the Soviet Union, and Mexico has maintained a remarkable cultural independence of its northern neighbour. The feeling that Canada in this respect has left undone what it ought to have done amounts to a national neurosis. But what I have described is not a social law: it is merely something that often happens, and just as often fails to happen. And even if it were a social law, there are many elements in Canada's situation that would make the applying of it to Canada a false analogy.

Even apart from this, however, there is still the question: where does the seed come from that grows up in these localities of provincial resistance? Spontaneous generation is no more credible in culture than it is in biology. Seeds of culture can only come from the centres of civilization which are already established, often those centres against which the local culture is revolting. As I have tried to show elsewhere, the forms of art are autonomous: poems and pictures are born out of earlier poems and pictures, not out of new localities, and novelty of content or experience in such localities cannot produce originality of form. We notice that the more popular an aspect of culture is, such as jazz music, films, or the kind of poetry associated with beatnik and similar groups, the more quickly it becomes international in its idiom. To try to found a serious culture in Canada on a middle-class intellectual resistance to popular culture of this kind would be the last word in futility. All this may seem too obvious now to insist on, but many intellectuals, in both English and French parts of the country, have in the past been engaged in an inglorious rearguard action of trying to encourage a regional or tourist's-souvenir literature, and it is perhaps still worth repeating that the practice is useless and the theory mistaken. Complete immersion in the international style is a primary cultural requirement, especially for countries whose cultural traditions have been formed since 1867, like ours. Anything distinctive that develops within the Canadian environment can only grow out of participation in this style.

The distinctively "modern" element in the culture of the last century has played, and continues to play, a revolutionary role in society. It may be easiest to illustrate this from the pictorial arts. In medieval painting the prevailing conventions were religious, and for that and many other reasons the technique of representation was highly stylized. As the centuries went on, we can see a growing realism in the painting which, in its historical context, was an emancipating force. The Byzantine type of stylizing comes to be thought stiff and angular; lighter and springier lines succeed in later Gothic; more human touches appear in the divine faces; landscapes sprout and blossom in the background; an occasional nude appears if the iconography makes it possible, as in pictures of St Sebastian or Mary Magdalene. The growth of realism, in other words, is also a growth in the humanizing of the projected myths, man recovering for himself the forms he had created.

As we pass into the Renaissance, and painting becomes more secularized, it begins to reflect something of the spirit that is also in Renaissance science, the feeling of man as a subject confronting an objective world. With the development of perspective the pictorial vision settled on a fixed point in space. As a result there grew up some curiously pedantic critical theories of painting, which assumed that it was primarily a representational art, and that the function of painting was not to create a vision but to record one. The Elizabethan critic Puttenham, writing in the age of Michelangelo and Titian, even asserted that the painter had no creative power at all, but merely imitated nature in the same way that an ape imitates a man. This dreary doctrine found its way into Shakespeare's *Winter's Tale*, somewhat disguised. I mention it only to emphasize the fact it misunderstands, which is the tremendous projecting force in Renaissance and Baroque painting. In Rubens, the great spiralling and twisting rhythms, usually starting from a diagonal, that, so to speak, pick up the eye and hurl it into the furthest point of the picture, express a kind of will to objectify. The same kind of will is also in Rembrandt, in a quieter and more contemplative form, as the eye is led to the points of light that emerge from the graduated shadows. Rembrandt carried this objectified form of painting about as far as human skill could carry it, and imposed his way of seeing on successors for generations.

When we look at the later work of Turner, contemporary with the great English Romantic poets, there is a different feeling which, in the particular context we are speaking of now, might be called a colossal emancipation of vision. It is not the titles of such pictures as "Rain, Steam and Speed" that make us feel that we are in a new world, but the sense of a new way of seeing. We are not looking *at* nature here, but are identified with the processes and powers of nature, the creative forces symbolized by the swirling colours, the dissolving shapes, and the expanding perspective where we seem to see everything at once, as though the eye were surrounding the picture. This is imitating nature as the Romantic age conceived imitation, where man and nature are thought of as connected, not by the subject-object relation of consciousness, but by an identity of process, man being a product of the organic power of nature. As Coleridge says, it is this latter, the *natura naturans*, that the painter imitates, not the structure of *natura naturata* in front of him. With the great impressionists who followed Turner the realistic tendency achieves a second culmination. Impressionism portrays, not a separated objective world that man contemplates, but a world of power and force and movement which is in man also, and emerges in the consciousness of the painter. Monet, painting Rouen cathedral in every aspect of light and shade, Renoir making the shapes in nature explode into vibrations of colour, Degas recording the poses of a ballet, are working in a world where objects have become events, and where time is a dimension of sense experience. We can, of course, look back on earlier painters and see the same things in Rubens or Tintoretto, but we see them there with the hindsight that impressionism has given us.

In all these centuries the representational aspect of painting is the organically growing aspect, the liberalizing force, the avant-garde movement. It is a realism of form, and as it develops it tends to become something of a conservative social force. Thus Dutch realism often reflects a quiet satisfaction in middle-class Dutch life, and in some modern painters—I think particularly of Vuillard—the visual aspect of our social experience is similarly bathed in a benevolent glow of beauty and charm. There is nothing wrong with this, but it was inevitable that there should also develop, as part of the expanding horizon of pictorial experience, a revolutionary or prophetic realism, of the sort that runs through Brueghel, Hogarth, Goya, and Daumier. This kind of realism is often not realistic in form: it may be presented as fantasy, as in Brueghel's "Mad Margaret" or Goya's "Caprichos." But it tears apart the façade of society and shows us the forces working behind that façade, and is realistic in the sense of sharpening our vision of society as a mode of existence rather than simply as an environment.

By 1867 impressionism was reaching its climax of development, and the "modern" world was taking shape. But there are very different elements in the modern world which are also making pictorial impressions. In advertising, propaganda, and a great deal of mass culture, of the type I referred to in my previous lecture, and which is usually intended to be received passively, the prevailing idiom is one that may be called stupid realism. By stupid realism I mean what is actually a kind of sentimental idealism, an attempt to present a conventionally attractive or impressive appearance as an actual or attainable reality. Thus it is a kind of parody or direct counter-presentation to prophetic realism. We see it in the vacuous pretty-girl faces of advertising, in the clean-limbed athletes of propaganda magazines, in the haughty narcissism of shop-window mannequins, in the heroically transcended woes of soap-opera heroines, in eulogistic accounts of the lives of celebrities, usually those in entertainment, in the creation by Madison Avenue of a wise and kindly father-figure out of some political stooge, and so on. The "social realism" of Communism, though much better in theory than this, has in practice much in common with it. It seems clear that an officially approved realism cannot carry on the revolutionary tradition of Goya and Daumier. It is not anti-Communism that makes us feel that the disapproved writers, Daniel and Babel and

Pasternak, have most to say to us: on the contrary, it is precisely such writers who best convey the sense of Russians as fellow human beings, caught in the same dilemmas that we are. Revolutionary realism is a questioning, exploring, searching, disturbing force: it cannot go over to established authority and defend the fictions which may be essential to authority, but are never real. We may compare in American painting the lively development of the so-called ashcan school with the WPA murals in post offices which glumly rehearsed the progress of transportation from camel to jeep, and which are now mostly covered up.

In this context we can see that realism of form has changed sides: it is no longer a liberalizing and emancipating force, incorporating the hopes and fears of humanity into the icons demanded by churches, public buildings, and well-to-do patrons. The projected image is now the weapon of the enemy, and consequently it is the power to project the image that becomes liberalizing. A new kind of energy is released in the painting that followed the impressionists, an energy which concentrates on the sheer imaginative act of painting in itself, on painting as the revolt of the brain behind the eye against passive sensation. Cézanne is the hinge on which this more specifically "modern" movement turns, but it has of course taken a great variety of forms since. One is the abstraction, or abstract expressionism later, which portrays the combination of form and colour without reference to representation. Another is the action-painting which tries to communicate the sense of process and growth in the act of painting. Still another is the "pop art" which presents the projected images of stupid realism itself, in a context where the critical consciousness is compelled to make an active response to them.

Stupid realism depends for its effect on evoking the ghost of a dead tradition: it is a parody of the realism which was organic a century or two ago. The active and revolutionary element in painting today is the element of formalism. (I know that I am using "formalism" in a looser sense than it is used in Marxist criticism, but I am trying to suggest some of the wider implications of the contrasting views.) I said that to the painters of the age of Giotto the old

Byzantine conventions were beginning to seem unnecessarily constricting. But in the stupid realism of commercial late Roman sculpture, with its stodgy busts and sarcophagi, the sharp angular patterns of Byzantine leap out with a clean and vital flame. The cycle of culture has turned once more, and once again it is the stylized that is the emancipating force. Of course there is always a central place for a realism which is not stupid, which continues to sharpen our vision of the world and the society that are actually there. But the exhilarating sense of energy in great formalism is so strong that modern realism tends to express itself in formalist conventions. In Brueghel's "Slaughter of the Innocents" a conventional religious subject is located in a realistic landscape that recalls the terror and misery of sixteenth-century Flanders; in Picasso's "Guernica" the terror and misery of twentieth-century Spain is expressed with the stylizing intensity of a religious primitivism.

In literature there is a change from Romantic to modern around 1867 that is in some respects even sharper and more dramatic than the shift from impressionism to Cézanne. At the beginning of the Romantic period around 1800, an increased energy of propulsion had begun to make itself felt, an energy that often suggests something mechanical. When the eighteenth-century American composer Billings developed contrapuntal hymn-settings which he called "fuguing-tunes," he remarked that they would be "more than twenty times as powerful as the old slow tunes." The quantitative comparison, the engineering metaphor, the emphasis on speed and power, indicate a new kind of sensibility already present in pre-Revolutionary and pre-industrial America. Much greater music than his is touched by the same feeling: the finale of Mozart's Linz Symphony in c is based on the bodily rhythm of the dance, but the finale of the Beethoven Rasoumovsky Quartet in the same key foreshadows the world of the express train. Bernard Shaw compares the finale of Beethoven's opus 106 to the dance of atoms in the molecule, whatever that sounds like. A similar propulsive movement makes itself felt in those greatly misunderstood poems of Wordsworth, "The Idiot Boy," "Peter Bell," "The Waggoner," where we also have references to "flying boats" and the like, and in many poems of Shelley, where again some of the characters seem to be operating private hydroplanes, like the Witch of Atlas. This sense of the exhilaration of mechanical movement continues into the modern period, especially in the Italian Futurist movement around the time of the First World War. In fact the modern is often popularly supposed to be primarily a matter of "streamlining," of suggesting in furniture and building, as well as in the formal arts themselves, the clean, spare, economical, functional lines of a swiftly moving vehicle.

But in modern literature at least, especially poetry, we have to take account of other tendencies. The decline of admiration for continuity is one of the most striking differences between the Romantic and the modern feeling. It perhaps corresponds to the decline of confidence in progress that we discussed earlier. The Swinburne whose linear energy carries his reader through hundreds of pages of poetic dramas and lyrics is felt, by Eliot, to be a poet "who does not think," as less modern in both feeling and technique than the Hopkins who prefers the techniques of "sprung" to those of "running" rhythm. (Swinburne is more correctly estimated now, but as part of a critical development which has outgrown the anti-Romantic phase of modernism, and has got its sense of tradition in better focus.) In France, one modern poet even maintained that the function of poetry was to wring the neck of rhetoric. Such a poet would be bound to accept the dictum of Poe, a most influential one in the modern period, that a long poem is really a contradiction in terms, for it is rhetoric, in the sense of a conventional form of expression that supplies a continuous verbal texture, which makes a poem long. In French literature this rhetorical continuity is associated particularly with Victor Hugo, who is thought of as a pre-modern Romantic. Modern poetry tends to be discontinuous, to break the hypnotic continuity of a settled metre, an organizing narrative, or a line of thought, all of which, it is felt, are apt to move too far in the direction of passive response. In Eliot's *The Waste Land* the scenes, episodes, and quoted lines are stuck into the reader's mind somewhat as the slogans and illustrations of advertising are—tachistoscopically, as the educators say. But, once there, the reader is compelled to a creative act of putting the fragments together. The continuity of the poem, in short, has been handed over to him.

One may see here a tendency parallel to the formalism of modern painting. What corresponds for the ear to stupid realism in the visual arts is partly rhetoric, in the sense used above, the surrounding of an advertised object with emotional and imaginative intensity, the earnest, persuasive voice of the radio commercial, the torrent of prefabricated phrases and clichés in political oratory. Nineteenth-century social critics who could not always distinguish the paranoid from the prophetic, such as Carlyle and Ruskin, often work themselves up emotionally by means of rhetoric into states of mind where they are possessed by the rhetoric and are no longer controlling it, so that a certain automatism comes into the writing. We see this also in a debased form in propaganda harangues. In general, uncontrolled rhetorical babble is an expression of a sado-masochist cycle, where the thing that is uncontrolled is a desire either to hurt someone else or to humiliate oneself. The definitive presentation of the "anti-hero" in modern literature, Dostoevsky's *Notes from Underground*, emphasizes this feature of uncontrolled mechanical talk, and traces it to an excess of conscious awareness over the power of action. The narrator despises himself, and yet admires himself for being honest enough to despise himself, and hence is continually possessed by rhetorical rages directed either at himself or at some projection of himself. Similar tendencies exist in Shakespeare's Hamlet, which is the chief reason why Hamlet, with his melancholy and his broken power of decision, his self-accusations and his uncontrolled brutality to others, becomes so central a Romantic and modern image of consciousness. The anti-rhetorical tendency in modern literature is part of a general tendency in modern culture to plant a series of anti-tank traps, so to speak, in the way of the rumbling and creaking invaders of our minds.

In the creation of poetry there seems to be an oddly paradoxical element. Something oracular, something that holds and charms and spellbinds, is involved in it, and the oracular permits no distraction or criticism: nothing must dispel its mood. Yet what the oracle expresses is frequently an epigram, a pun, an ambiguous statement, or a conundrum that sounds like a bad joke, like the witches' ellip-tical prophecies to Macbeth. Wit is addressed to the awakened crit-ical intelligence and to a perception of the incongruous. Poetry has often veered between these two aspects of the poetic process: in the age of Pope, wit was the preferred element; with the Romantics a more solemnly oracular tone dominated, or alternated with wit, as in Byron. In the modern period the prevailing tone tended to shift again to wit. The degree of abstraction in painting that we see in Léger or Modigliani, or perhaps even in Cubism, where a represen-tational picture has been assimilated to geometrical outlines, is witty, in somewhat the same way that poetry stepping along in antitheti-cal rhyming couplets is witty. In both it is the *discordia concors* of artistic discipline and natural untidiness that evokes the sense of wit, as when a woman's breast becomes a sphere or an epigram falls neatly into ten iambic syllables. T. E. Hulme, Wyndham Lewis, and others, in the early anti-Romantic phase of modernism, were much struck by this analogy between abstraction and satirical wit, and set it up as a standard against the continuous rhetoric and oracular solemnity that they found in the Romantics, from Wordsworth to Gertrude Stein. Of poets, perhaps Auden in English has given us most clearly the sense of creation as play, an expression of man as *homo ludens*. The contrived and artificial patterns of his verse are consistent with this, just as the light verse they resemble is more contrived than heavy verse, and play-novels like detective stories more contrived than "serious" fiction. Valéry's view of poetry as a game bound by arbitrary rules like chess is similar, and Valéry remarks that "inspiration" is a state of mind in the reader, not in the writer—another example of the modern tendency to turn as much activity as possible over to the reader.

There are many complaints about the obscurity of the arts in the modern world, and about the indifference that the modern artist seems to have for his public. But we can see by now that modern art is directly involved in a militant situation peculiar to our time. It does not simply come into being as an expression of human cre-ative power: it is born on a battlefield, where the enemies are the anti-arts of passive impression. In this context the arts demand an active response with an intensity that hardly existed before. Hence the modern artist is actually in an immediate personal relation with his reader or viewer: he throws the ball to him, so to speak, and his art depends on its being caught at the other end. We have already noticed how in *The Waste Land* (and much other modern poetry) the poet hands the continuity of his poem over to the reader, and one could make out a very good case for saying that the reader of *Finnegans Wake* is the hero of that book, the person who laboriously spells out the message of the dream. *Finnegans Wake* belongs of course to the stream-of-consciousness technique in modern fiction. This technique, which is still going strong in the novels of Samuel Beckett, is continuous, but not rhetorically continuous: that is, the links are associative and not merely ready-made as they are in a propagandist speech, hence they require an active reader to see the sequential logic in them.

One would expect to find in the modern, then, some decline in the prestige of the particular quality in art represented by the term "craftsmanship," or, perhaps more accurately, by the highly significant epithet "finished." The work of art is traditionally something set up to be admired: it is placed in a hierarchy where the "classic" or "masterpiece" of perfect form is at the top. Modern art, especially in such developments as action-painting, is concerned to give the impression of process rather than product, of something emerging out of the heat of struggle and still showing the strain of its passing from conception to birth. Balzac tells a celebrated story about a painter whose masterpiece broke down into a tangle of meaningless lines. But the modern century has to take this parable of the *chef d'oeuvre inconnu* seriously, for the lines are not meaningless if they record the painter's involvement with his subject and also demand ours. Malraux has remarked how much the sketch, the sense of something rapidly blocked out and left incomplete, seems to us the index of an artist's vitality. The same principles hold for poetry, even to the extent that a poet today can get more money out of selling his manuscript excreta to libraries than he can out of royalties on the published volume. Dramatists try to break up the hypnotic illusion of the play by various devices that suggest a dramatic process in formation, such as introducing stagehands or prompters, or breaking down the distinction between actor and role. Such devices are regarded by Brecht as a creative form of alienation, giving the audience a closer view of imaginative reality by chopping holes in the rhetorical façade. Novelists adopt similar devices to break the story-teller's spell on the reader: thus Gide's *The Counterfeiters* is a story about a novelist writing a novel called *The Counterfeiters*. Readers of Canadian literature may see similar tendencies in Reaney's *Listen to the Wind* or Leonard Cohen's *Beautiful Losers*.

The tendency to prefer the imperfect work engaged in history to the perfected masterpiece that pulls away from time is closely related to another tendency which also originates in the opposition to passive anti-art. Advertising and propaganda are interested arts, arts with ulterior motives. Behind them is a course of action which they end by exhorting one to follow. A good deal of literature has followed the same pattern (e.g., *The Pilgrim's Progress*, *Self-Help* by Samuel Smiles) and still does. But as a rule the work of art as such is disinterested: there is nothing beyond itself to which it points as the fulfilment of itself. In modern painting and poetry, especially in the last two decades, there has been a good deal of emphasis not only on this disinterested and self-containing aspect of the arts, but of attack on those tendencies within the arts themselves that seem to lead us passively on from one thing to another. A detective story is a good example of this donkey's-carrot writing: we begin it to find out what we are told on the last page. Writing with this structure is teleological: it contains a hidden purpose, and we read on to discover what that purpose is.

Many modern poets, with William Carlos Williams at their head, regard such concealing of a hidden design as gimmick-writing: for them, the image, the scene, the thing presented, the immediate experience, *is* the reality that the arts are concerned with, and to go beyond this is to risk dishonesty. The theory of the modern style in poetry is set out in the letters of Rimbaud known as the *lettres du voyant*, with their insistence that the genuine poet sees directly, in contrast to the rhetorician who talks about what he sees. The same kind of emphasis has been common in painting for a long time: music has been affected by it more recently, but perhaps more radically than any other art. Classical music, up to quite recent times, has been intensely teleological: in symphonies from Haydn to Brahms we feel strongly how the end of a movement is implied in the beginning, and how we are led towards it step by step. In much contemporary music, both electronic and conventional, the emphasis is on the immediate sense impression of sound: the music is not going anywhere; it may even be proceeding by chance, as in some of the experiments of John Cage. The ear is not thrown forward into the future, to hear a theme being worked out or a discord resolved: it is kept sternly in the present moment. This conception of the unit of experience as a thing in itself is of course an intensely impersonal attitude to art: the writer (and similarly with the other arts) is doing all he can to avoid the sense of impressing himself on his reader by suggesting meaning or form or purpose beyond what is presented. In this conception of *chosisme*, as it is sometimes called, it is not simply continuity, but significance or meaning itself, which has been handed over to the reader.

One may see in most of these modern tendencies a good deal of distrust in the rational consciousness as the main area of communication in the arts. Modern art is irrational in many respects, but it is important to see why and in what ways it is. We spoke of advertising and propaganda as stunning or demoralizing the critical consciousness in order to move past it and set up their structures in the rest of the mind. There is clearly no point in setting the artists to defend a Maginot line that has already been outflanked: the artist has to move directly back into the attacked area, and set up his own structures there instead. Hence the various Freud-inspired movements, like surrealism, which communicate on a normally repressed level; hence too the great variety of modern developments of fantasy and articulated dream, where there is no identity, and where the world is like that of Milton's chaos, with things forming and disappearing by chance and melting into other things. In Kafka, for example, the event, the ordinary unit of a story, is replaced by the psychological event, and the social and other significances of what is happening are allegories of these psychological events. The primary emphasis is on the mental attitude that makes the events possible. Thus *The Castle* is presented as a kind of anxiety-nightmare, yet a theological allegory of God's dealings with man and a political allegory of the police state run in counterpoint with it.

I am not trying to suggest that all these modern tendencies form part of a single consistent pattern: far from it. All that they have in common is an imaginative opposition to the anti-arts of persuasion and exhortation. The obvious question to ask is, of course: granted that the arts in the modern world are full of antagonism to the anti-arts, granted that they parody them in all sorts of clever ways, granted that they encourage an active instead of a passive response, does this really make them socially effective? In a world resounding every day with the triumphs of slanted news and brainwashed politics, what can poetry and painting do, tortoises in a race with hares? This question is one of the most powerful arguments of our enemy the accuser. We are constantly learning from the alienation of progress that merely trying to clarify one's mind is useless and selfish, because the individual counts for so little in society. Marxism, with its carefully planned agenda of revolution, provides the most complete answer to the question: "What then must we do?" The democracies provide more limited and piecemeal forms of social activism, demonstrations, sit-ins, teach-ins, protest marches, petitions and the like, partly (if one may say so with all due sympathy and respect) as gestures of homage to the superior effectiveness to be found in the world of public relations and controversies. Similarly, the artist often feels an impulse to guarantee his vision by his life, and hence we find the pattern of antagonism of art to anti-art repeated in an antagonism of artist to society.

In political thought there is a useful fiction known as the social contract, the sense that man enters into a certain social context by the act of getting born. In earlier contract theories, like that of Hobbes, the contract was thought of as universal, binding everyone without exception. From Rousseau on there is more of a tendency to divide people into those who accept and defend the existing social contract because they benefit from it, and the people who are excluded from most of its benefits, and so feel no obligation, or much less, to it. As everyone knows, Marx defined the excluded body as the proletariat or workers, and saw it as the means to a reconstituted society. Those who accept and are loyal to the social contract are known consistently, throughout the whole period, as the bourgeoisie or middle class, otherwise known, in different contexts, as Philistines or squares. Whenever artists think of themselves as a social group, they seem inclined to define themselves in terms of their opposition to the bourgeois society of the contract, with its materialistic and conformist standards.

Some of them have followed the Marxist form of this opposition, though very few in the English-speaking countries, and very few even of those have been of a type that under a proletarian dictatorship would survive the first purge. Radical sympathies in American fiction have tended rather to take the form of a sentimental populism, of a the-people-keep-marching-on type. During the depression, the contest of labour and management began to assume something of the dimensions of a revolution, and the labour movement still had, like the Negroes today, the dignity of an oppressed group. As a result there was a considerable infiltration of working-class sympathies into the drama, films, and musical comedies of that period. But today few areas of American life are less inspiring to the Muse than the trade unions. The collapse of Communist sympathies in American culture was not the result of McCarthyism and other witch-hunts, which were not a cause but an effect of that collapse. The object of the witch-hunt is the witch, that is, a helpless old woman whose dangerousness is assumed to rationalize quite different interests and pleasures. Similarly the Communist issue in McCarthyism was a red herring for a democratic development of the big lie as a normal political weapon: if internal Communism had been a genuine danger the struggle against it would have taken a genuine form. Sympathy with Communism collapsed under the feeling that, even at its best, and ignoring its atrocities, the bureaucracy of Communism was enforcing much the same kind of social contract as the managerial and authoritarian elements in the democracies. Hence American liberals, even radicals, soon lost all faith in the moral superiority of Communism.

Losing the faith was undoubtedly right: the immense relief with which they lost it may have been less so.

But if the Marxist form of radicalism, of the kind that helps to shape the dramas of Brecht and Gorky, is rare in American literature, there is a type of anarchism in it which is far more common. The figure of the individual who will not play the silly games of society, who seems utterly insignificant but represents an unbreakable human force, runs through its literature from Rip van Winkle and the romances of Cooper to the present day. The patron saint of this tendency is Thoreau, retreating to Walden to build his own cabin and assert that the only genuine America is the society of those who will not throw all their energies into the endless vacuum suction of imperialist hysteria and of consuming consumer goods. Huck Finn, drifting down the great river with Jim and preferring hell with Jim to the white slave-owner's heaven, is a similar figure, one of the bums, hoboes, and social outcasts who reach a deeper level of community than the rest of us. This outcast or hobo figure is the hero of most of the Chaplin films; he also finds a congenial haven in comic strips. The juvenile delinquent or emotionally disturbed adolescent may in some contexts be one of his contemporary equivalents, like the narrator of *The Catcher in the Rye*. Sympathy for the youth who sees no moral difference between delinquency and conformity still inspires such Utopian works as Paul Goodman's *Growing Up Absurd*. An earlier and very remarkable Canadian work of this anarchist kind is Frederick Philip Grove's *A Search for America*, where the America that the narrator searches for is again the submerged community that only the outcast experiences.

This form of proletariat has recently combined with another tradition of very different origin. One distinctively modern element in our culture, introduced in the main by the Romantic movement, is the conception of the serious writer, who is in a prophetic relation to society, and consequently in opposition to it. It is no longer sufficient to say, as Samuel Johnson did, that they who live to please must please to live: the serious writer is committed to saying what may not and probably will not please, even if he hopes to please enough, on a different level of pleasure, to be able to live also. With Baudelaire and his successors this antagonism to society becomes a way of life, usually called Bohemian, the antagonism being expressed partly in the over-simplifying phrase, *épater le bourgeois*. More accurately, the artist explores forbidden or disapproved modes of life in both imagination and experience. The square, the man who lives by the social contract, takes the public appearance of society to be, for him, its reality. Hence his obsessive tendency to appear in public clean, clothed, sober and accompanied by his wife. The artist may symbolize a more intensely imaginative community through dirt or slovenliness, lousifying himself as much as possible, as Rimbaud remarked, or through more openly acknowledged forms of sexual relationship outside marriage. Drugs and narcotics have been associated with the arts for a long time, but took on a new intensity and relevance to the creative process with the Romantic movement. The bourgeois view that the appearance of society is its reality is of course based on illusion, and we have seen how a breakdown in illusion is often more disturbing than genuine dangers. Similarly long hair in young men or pictures portraying a consenting sex act may stir up deeper social anxieties than actual delinquency or rape.

The combination of Bohemian and hobo traditions in the beat, hip, and other disaffected movements of our time seems to be part of an unconscious effort to define a social proletariat in Freudian instead of Marxist terms. Such groups find, or say they find, that a withdrawal from the social establishment is a necessary step in freeing them from repression and in releasing their creative energies. Creation is close to the sexual instinct, and it is in their attitude to sex that the two groups collide most violently, as each regards the other's views of sex as obscene. The Freudian proletarian sees established society as a repressive anxiety-structure, the basis of which is the effort to control the sexual impulse and restrict it to predictable forms of expression. His emphasis on the sexual aspect of life, his intense awareness of the role of the thwarted sexual drive in the cruelties and fears of organized society, make him quite as much a moralist as his opponent, though his moral aim is of course to weaken the anxiety-structure by the shock tactics of "bad" words, pornography, or the publicizing of sexual perversions and deviations.

The collision of youth and age is more openly involved in this kind of movement than elsewhere. In a society dominated by the alienation of progress, the young, whose lives are thrown forward to the future, achieve a curious kind of moral advantage, as though the continued survival of anyone whose life is mainly in the past required some form of justification. Certain other elements in this social movement, such as the growth of confessional and self-analysing groups, show some parallels with Marxist techniques.

The picaresque heroes of Kerouac are "Dharma bums," social outcasts with serious social and even religious ideals. Their environment is the squalid and seedy urban one, the city that is steadily devouring the countryside, yet in their repudiation of everything structured and organized in it they struggle for an innocence that is almost pastoral. They seek a kinship with the nature which, like them, has been repressed, almost obliterated, by organized society. In two writers who have strongly influenced this Freudian proletariat movement, Henry Miller and D. H. Lawrence, pastoralism is a central theme. In the nineteenth century the relation of country to city was often thought of, in writers who had begun to hate and fear the rise of a metropolitan civilization, as a relation of innocence to experience, of the healthy natural virtues of the country corrupted by the feverish excitements of the town. This myth produced a good deal of nineteenth-century literature and social propaganda, ranging in value from Wordsworth's *Michael* to temperance melodramas. The pronouncements on drinking and sexual mores made by those in our society who are most spectacularly not with it, like many members of the lower clergy and the higher judiciary, are still often inspired by such visions of a virtuous rustic daring to be a Daniel in a wicked Babylon.

A number of other writers who continued the tradition of eighteenth-century primitivism also nurtured a tangled garden of metaphors about the need for being "rooted in the soil," as part of a similar opposition to the metropolitan development of society. This form of *nostalgie de la boue* was a strong influence on nineteenth-century fiction (Jean Giono, Knut Hamsun), though the ponderous prose lyrics it tended to specialize in are largely forgotten now. It is an attitude with a naturally strong bias toward racism, and in this form it entered into the *Völkisch* developments in Germany which lay behind much of Nazism. Nineteenth-century French Canada also had its propagandists for the motto *emparons-nous du sol*, idealizing the simple peasant bound to his land and his ancestral faith, a picture with a strong resemblance to Millet's "Angelus," of which the most famous expression is *Maria Chapdelaine*. There were similar movements elsewhere in America, like the Southern agrarian movement of a generation ago. In Miller and Lawrence this pastoral theme is less sentimentalized and more closely connected with the more deeply traditional elements of the pastoral: spontaneity in human relations, especially sexual relations; the stimulus to creative power that is gained from a simpler society, less obsessed by satisfying imaginary wants; and, at least in Lawrence, a sense of identity with nature of great delicacy and precision.

The pastoral withdrawal from bourgeois values merges insensibly into another, the sense of the artist as belonging to an élite or neo-aristocracy. The origin of this attitude is the feeling that in a world full of the panic of change, the artist's role is to make himself a symbol of tradition, a sentinel or witness to the genuine continuity in human life, like the London churches in *The Waste Land*. In religion this attitude expresses itself, as a rule, in adherence or conversion to the Catholic Church. Here it is often the Church as a symbol of authority or tradition that is the attraction: Charles Maurras expressed this most bluntly by saying that he was interested in Catholicism but not in Christianity. Political preferences are rightwing, with emphasis on the traditional functions of aristocracy and royalty, especially among those who actually were of aristocratic origin, like Villiers de l'Isle Adam. Eliot's characterizing of himself as "royalist in politics" is a late and not very resonant British echo of what was mainly a French and nineteenth-century tendency. Economic preferences vary, but are always strongly against the conspiracies of international finance. In the twenties and thirties many of this group were attracted to fascism, which they saw as leading to a new recognition of heroic energy in life, including the creative energy of the arts. Both this group and the pastoralists are haunted by the sense of an invisible serenity which has disappeared from contemporary life but can be re-experienced through tradition. Often this feeling takes the form of a sense of vanished gods, like the "dignified, invisible" presences of Eliot's rose-garden. Yeats tried to identify these presences with his pantheon of Irish gods and heroes; Lawrence with his darker gods and his historical myths like that of the Etruscans; George and other German romantics with the Classical gods; Jung with unconscious archetypes. Christian writers tend to think more conceptually of the organizing ideas of religion, original sin, Incarnation, a personal power of evil, and the like, as giving a new richness and depth of significance to life, whether of joy or terror. "I do wish those people who deny the reality of eternal punishment," said the Catholic poet Lionel Johnson, "would understand their own dreadful vulgarity."

One type who most obviously withdraws from the social contract and sets up a way of life in opposition to it is the criminal. There are two kinds of criminals, professional and amateur: those for whom crime is money and those for whom crime is fun. We are concerned with the latter group. It is obvious that the criminal or conspirator is a ready symbol for the artist who breaks with the social contract; one thinks of Joyce's Stephen Dedalus and his conspiratorial motto of silence, exile, and cunning, or Rimbaud's identification of himself as a child of Satan, linked to criminals, slaves, and outcasts of all kinds. The symbol of the artist as criminal, however, goes much deeper. I spoke of the way in which optimistic theories of progress and revolution had grown out of Rousseau's conception of a society of nature and reason buried under the injustices of civilization and awaiting release. But, around the same time, the Marquis de Sade was expounding a very different view of the natural society. According to this, nature teaches us that pleasure is the highest good in life, and the keenest form of pleasure consists in inflicting or suffering pain. Hence the real natural society would not be the reign of equality and reason prophesied by Rousseau: it would be a society in which those who liked tormenting others were set free to do so. So far as evidence is relevant, there is more evidence for de Sade's theory of natural society than there is for

Rousseau's. In any case there is an unpleasantly large degree of truth in the sadist vision, and a good many literary conceptions have taken off from it, or near it. One is the cult of the holy sinner, the person who achieves an exceptional awareness, whether religious or aesthetic in character, from acts of cruelty, or, at least, brings about such an awareness in us. Dostoevsky's Stavrogin, Gide's Lafcadio, with his *acte gratuit* or unmotivated crime, the hero of Camus's *L'Etranger* and of Chaplin's *Monsieur Verdoux*, are examples. A good deal of contemporary American writing links not merely picaresque law-breaking, smoking marijuana and the like, but outright violence and terror, with serious social attitudes. There is something of this in Mailer, and a good deal more in LeRoi Jones and other "black power" adherents. In D. H. Lawrence, too, a curious hysterical cruelty occasionally gets out of hand, most continuously, perhaps, in *The Plumed Serpent*.

Jean Genet is the most remarkable example of the contemporary artist as criminal: his sentence of life imprisonment was appealed against by Sartre, Claudel, Cocteau, and Gide, and even before his best-known works had appeared, Sartre had written a seven-hundred-page biography of him called *Saint Genet*. Genet's most famous play, in this country, is *Le Balcon*. Here the main setting is a brothel in which the patrons dress up as bishops, generals or judges and engage in sadistic ritual games with the whores, who are flogged and abused in the roles of penitents or thieves. The point is that society as a whole is one vast sadistic ritual of this sort. As the mock-bishop says, very rudely, he does not care about the function of bishop: all he wants is the metaphor, the idea or sexual core of the office. The madam of the brothel remarks: "They all want everything to be as true as possible ... minus something indefinable, so that it won't be true"—a most accurate description of what I have been calling stupid realism. A revolution is going on outside: it is put down by the chief of police, and the patrons of the brothel are pulled out of it to enact the "real" social forms of the games they have been playing. Nobody notices the difference, because generals and judges and bishops are traditional metaphors, and new patrons come to the brothel and continue the games. The chief of police, the only one with any real social power, is worried because he is not a traditional metaphor, and nobody comes to the brothel to imitate him. Finally, however, one such patron does turn up: the leader of the revolution. There is a good deal more in the play, but this account will perhaps indicate how penetrating it is as a sadist vision of society.

All these anti-social attitudes in modern culture are, broadly speaking, reactionary. That is, their sense of antagonism to existing society is what is primary, and it is much clearer and more definite than any alternative social ideal. Hugh MacDiarmid, supporting both Communism and Scottish nationalism, and Dos Passos, moving from a simple radicalism to a simple conservatism, are random examples among writers of what sometimes seems a dissent for its own sake. Wherever we turn, we are made aware of the fact that society is a repressive anxiety-structure, and that creative power comes from a part of the mind that resists repression but is not in itself moral or rational. In Vladimir Nabokov's novel, *Pale Fire*, a gentle, wistful, rather touching pastoral poem falls into the hands of a lunatic who proceeds to "annotate" it with a wild paranoid fantasy about his own adventures as a prince in some European state during a revolution. Poem and commentary have nothing to do with each other, and perhaps that is the only point the book makes. But the title, taken from Shakespeare's *Timon of Athens*, suggests a certain allegory of the relation of art to the wish-fulfilment fantasies that keep bucking and plunging underneath it. Such forces are in all of us, and are strong enough to destroy the world if they are not controlled through release instead of repression. In my last lecture I want to talk about the way in which the creative arts are absorbed into society through education. Meanwhile we may notice that the real basis for the opposition of artist and society is the fact that not merely communications media and public relations, but the whole structure of society itself, is an anti-art, an old and worn-out creation that needs to be created anew.

Clair de lune intellectuel

The modern world began with the Industrial Revolution, and the Industrial Revolution set up an economic structure beside the political one which was really a rival form of society. Industry had often enough taken the form of an organization distinct from the state, but never before in history did man have so strong a feeling of living under two social orders as he did in the period of laissez faire. The separation could not, of course, last indefinitely, because the economic social order had so revolutionary an effect on the political one. Explicitly in Marxism, and more tentatively in the democracies, all society eventually comes to be thought of as consisting functionally only of workers or producers. Marxism moves in the direction of a final or once-for-all revolution in which the productive society becomes the only society; in the democracies the non-productive groups, or leisure classes, gradually become socially unfunctional. In both types of society, however, there are, in addition to the workers and their directors, a large group who exist to explain, manifest, encourage, rationalize, and promote the various forms of production. In Marxist societies those in this second group are known as party workers; in the democracies, especially in North America, they are thought of as advertisers and educators.

It seems clear that even with the heavy handicap of defence budgets, even with the assistance given to those parts of the world which are committed to the West but are otherwise unfortunate, the productive power of American and other advanced democracies has become so over-efficient that it can continue to function only by various feather-bedding devices. One device, of the type satirized in *Parkinson's Law*, is the subsidizing of employment; another, of the type lamented in *The Feminine Mystique*, is the effort to encourage as many as possible of the female half of the population to devote themselves to becoming full-time consumers. But these devices do not conceal the fact that leisure is growing so rapidly, both in the amount of time and the number of people it affects, as to be a social complex equal in importance to employment itself.

Thus the technological revolution is becoming more and more an educational rather than an industrial phenomenon. For education is the positive aspect of leisure. As long as we think of society, in nineteenth-century terms, as essentially productive, leisure is only spare time, usually filled up with various forms of distraction, and a "leisure class," which has nothing but spare time, is only a class of parasites. But as soon as we realize that leisure is as genuine and important an aspect of everyone's life as remunerative work, leisure becomes something that also demands discipline and responsibility. Distraction, of the kind one sees on highways and beaches at holiday weekends, is not leisure but a running away from leisure, a refusal to face the test of one's inner resources that spare time poses. It is to genuine leisure what the feather-bedding devices I have just referred to are to genuine industry and business. Our problem today is not that of a leisure class, but of leisure itself, as an increasingly growing factor in the lives of all classes. In relation to the economy, man is essentially functional, deriving his individuality from his job and his social context. In relation to leisure he is essentially a performer or actor, judged, not by his specific role, but by his skill in performance. That is, any leisure activity which is not sheer idleness or distraction depends on some acquired skill, and the acquiring and practice of that skill is a mode of education.

Education involves, first of all, the network of educational institutions: schools and universities, which occupy most of the time and attention of a large part of the population, and many other types of organization—churches, museums, art galleries, theatres, just to start with. To look at our society realistically today, we have to think of its economic or productive aspect as a part of it: let us say, by a rhetorical statistic, half of it. The other half consists of the educational activities which are growing much faster, proportionately, than industry, and which I shall call the leisure structure of society. The industrial and the leisure structures make up, between them, the program of needs and activities which, in their degenerate form in the ancient Roman world, were described as bread and circuses.

In the democracies, as well as in the Communist states, social development has been mainly a matter of relating the economic structure to the political one. In Canada, as in Britain and America, the left wing tends to favour closer relations, usually stopping short of complete socialization, and the right wing tends to favour economic autonomy, usually stopping considerably short of pure laissez faire. Views on the relation of the political to the leisure structure seem to be the reverse of this. Liberal sympathies are more disposed to keep the leisure structure autonomous, and to feel that the political influence on the leisure structure is normally a bad influence. The right wing are more disposed to mutter about the injustice being done to the anti-intellectual majority of taxpayers, and to call for tighter cultural budgets.

In any event the question of what the government does in relation to the leisure structure is taking on an increasingly revolutionary importance. The word "revolution," which originally suggested conspiracy and barricades in the street, can now, in our society, only be associated with some kind of centralized action, usually by the government, in whatever areas can develop enough freedom of movement to revolutionize anything. At present the so-called mass media are sponsored mainly by advertising, which means that they are related primarily to the economy: these include television, newspapers, and the dwindling body of fiction and picture magazines which function as retail advertising journals. The turning of sponsorship into direct control, as when an editor is dismissed or a program cancelled for offending an advertiser, is felt to be pernicious by those who are not completely cynical in such matters. Every effort of a government, however timid, to set up national film and broadcasting companies, and thus to turn over at least some of the mass media to the leisure structure, is part of a fateful revolutionary process. So is every effort to subsidize creative talent; so, even more obviously, is every effort to plan a city more intelligently than leaving it to speculative blight. We are taking the first cautious steps on this revolutionary road now, and it is highly typical of Canada that it is the *administration* of the leisure structure, questions of dividing responsibility and authority, that should be most eagerly discussed. The complete control of the leisure structure by the political or economic power is a logical development of Marxism, at least in its twentieth-century form, but to us the Marxist attitude to the leisure structure seems a purely reactionary one. If the growth of the leisure structure is as important and central a development as I think it is, some of the major possibilities of further social development remain with the more industrially advanced democracies.

Schools and universities are mainly for young people, and, under the influence of the view of society as consisting primarily of wage-earners, they have traditionally been thought of as places in which the young are prepared for real life. This view is congenial to the normal tendency of the adult to think of the adolescent as a rudimentary and primitive form of himself. In my own student days during the depression, when so many students came to college because of the difficulty of finding jobs, it was felt that the four years spent in study required some justification. What creates a man's self-respect, it was thought, is the holding of a job as the head of a family, and university appeared merely to postpone this function. Young people in working-class homes felt this even more strongly, and, in my experience, did not much care that most of them were unofficially but effectively excluded from the universities. The greatly increased number attending today reflects of course an increase in both population and economic buoyancy; but when it is said that students go to college because industry and business now require more education, I suspect a hangover of the old self-justifying arguments. I think students come to college because they realize, more clearly than many of their elders, that by doing so they are fully participating in their society, and can no longer be thought of as getting ready for something else more important.

It inevitably follows from the same principle, however, that the university, or at least the kind of thing the university does, can hardly remain indefinitely the exclusive preserve of the young. The question of adult education is still too large and shapeless for us to be able to look squarely at it along with all our other problems of expansion, but, apart from the very large amount of education within industry itself, the adult population will also need institutions of teaching and discussion as the organized form of their leisure time: I think particularly of married women with grown-up families. It is difficult for a government not to think of education in terms of training, and to regard the university as a public-service institution concerned with training. Such a conception naturally puts a heavy emphasis on youth, who are allegedly being trained for society, the human resources of the future, as we say. Adult education will no doubt enter the picture first in the context of retraining, as it does now in industry, but before long we shall have to face a growing demand for an education which has no immediate reference to training at all.

We have next to consider the relation of the leisure structure to the arts. Down to the nineteenth century, painters, poets, composers tended to follow the traditions set by their predecessors, imitating them and carrying on their conventions in a more elaborate way. Thus there was a steady increase in self-awareness and complexity, and a process resembling that of aging, with each generation building on what had been done up to that point. With the nineteenth century there came, along with the continuing of this process, a prodigious lateral expansion in influence. It was mainly in the second half of the nineteenth century that the great museums came into being, at least in their present form, and the museums brought together an immense assemblage, not merely of works of art, but of objects that presented analogies to and suggestions for the arts. The result was to provide the artist with an encyclopaedic range of influences; it made the artist an academician instead of an apprentice learning from masters. What the museums did for the visual arts modern recordings have done for music.

The increase of historical knowledge, of which archaeology formed a central part, was so vast as to make it seem as though the cemeteries were on the march, the entire past awakening to an aesthetic apocalypse. Painters and sculptors in particular were presented with a world-wide panorama of creative skills, very largely in the applied or so-called "minor" arts. This was naturally an important influence on the trend to formalism that I spoke of in my last lecture, for what this panorama revealed was primarily a universal language of design. Design in its turn has provided a basis for the unifying of the "major" and "minor" arts. Anyone today comparing an exhibition of modern painting or sculpture with one of textiles or pottery gets the impression that in the modern period there is really only an art of design, which is applied equally to all the visual arts, major and minor. I have referred to the view of William Morris, at the threshold of the modern period, that the minor or useful arts were a key area in social revolution because they represent, more clearly than the major arts, the imagination as a way of life, as providing the visible forms of a free society. Although social developments have not followed Morris's anti-mechanistic anarchism, it is still no doubt true that the principles which link such a painter as Mondriaan to textile or ceramic design are a part of a considerable democratizing of aesthetic experience. If so, Morris was right in seeing a significant social, even a political dimension in modern cultural developments.

Along with archaeology and its "museum without walls," as it has been called, came anthropology and its study of "primitive" cultures, which brought primitive art, with its weird stylizing of form, its openly phallic and sexual themes, its deliberate distortion of perspective, squarely in front of the artist's eye. Of all elements in the modern tradition, perhaps that of primitive art, of whatever age or continent, has had the most pervasive influence. The primitive, with its immediate connexion with magic, expresses a directness of imaginative impact which is naive and yet conventionalized, spontaneous and yet precise. It indicates most clearly the way in which a long and tired tradition of Western art, which has been refining and sophisticating itself for centuries, can be revived, or even reborn. Perhaps the kinship between the primitive and ourselves goes even deeper: it has frequently been remarked that we may be, if we survive, the primitives of an unknown culture, the cave men of a new mental era.

It is not always realized how closely analogous the developments of modern literature are to those in the visual arts. The world-wide panorama of the museums is not attainable in literature with the same immediacy, because of the barriers of language. Linguistics sometimes gives an illusion of having surmounted these barriers, but the illusion of literature in translation is even less convincing. However, the trend to formalism, stylizing, and abstraction is quite as marked in poetry as in painting. The elements of verbal design are myth and metaphor, both of which are modes of identification. That is, they are primitive and naïve associations of things, a sun and a god, a hero and a lion, which turn their backs on realism or accurate descriptive statement. In literature, as in painting, realism was an emancipating force down to the nineteenth century, when it reached its culmination in the great novelists of that period. The modern period begins with Baudelaire and the *symbolisme* that followed him, and literature ever since has been increasingly organized by symbolism, dense and often difficult metaphor, myth, especially in drama, and folktale. This development was anticipated in the great mythopoeic poetry of the Romantics, especially Blake, Shelley, and Keats, who correspond in poetry to the revolution of Turner in painting. Like the parallel developments in visual art, the increase of consciously employed myth and metaphor is also an increase in erudition and the conscious awareness of tradition.

When the Romantic movement began, there was one important primitive influence on it, that of the oral ballads, which began to be collected and classified at that time. The oral ballad makes a functional use of refrains and other strongly marked patterns of repetition, which correspond to the emphasis on design in the primitive pictorial arts. The fact that it depended for survival on an oral tradition meant that whatever personal turns of phrase there may originally have been in it were smoothed out, the poem thus acquiring a kind of stripped poetic surface quite unlike that of written poetry. The literary ballads which imitate these characteristics—the *Lyrical Ballads* of Wordsworth and Coleridge, Blake's *Mental Traveller*, Keats's *La Belle Dame Sans Merci*—come about as close as poetry can come to reproducing directly the voice of the creative powers of the mind below consciousness, a voice which is uninhibited and yet curiously impersonal as well. This was also the "democratic" voice that Whitman attempted to reproduce, and

Whitman is the godfather of all the folk singing and other oral developments of our time which cover so large an area of contemporary popular culture. A different but related Canadian tradition is that of the *chansonniers*, as represented today by Gilles Vigneault.

Fifty years ago it could be said that the university and the creative artist were at opposite ends of the cultural spectrum. The university, on its humanistic side, ran a critical and scholarly establishment concerned with the past, and related itself to the present by translating the values of the past into contemporary middle-class values. Anyone interested in painting or writing was likely to drop out of school as soon as it had wasted the legal amount of his time and devote himself to living precariously by his wits. I spent a dinner talking to such a (Canadian) writer recently: he told me of how he had left school at grade ten and eventually established himself as a writer, of how his life since had been financially difficult, even despairing at times, but redeemed by the excitement of an unexpected sale, or, more genuinely, by occasional gleams of satisfaction over a creative job well done. A century ago this would have been a familiar type of story, but while I listened with interest and respect, because I knew his work and admired it, I felt that I was hearing one of the last legends of a vanishing species, of a way of life that was going and would not return.

For in the last few decades the leisure structure has become much more integrated. The university's interest in contemporary culture is now practically obsessive, nor is its relation to it confined to mere interest. More and more of the established artists are on its teaching staff, and more and more of the younger rebels are their undergraduate students. While serving on a committee for awarding fellowships to Canadian writers, I noticed that practically all the serious English candidates were employed by universities and practically all the French ones by the National Film Board or the Canadian Broadcasting Corporation. What cultural differences this implied I do not know, but for both groups some professional connexion with the leisure structure was so regular as to amount practically to a closed shop. When the beatnik movement began about ten years ago, it seemed as though an anti-academic, even anti-intellectual tendency was consolidating around a new kind of cultural experience. It attracted certain types of expression, such as the improvising swing ensembles and their derivatives, which had traditionally been well outside the orbit of higher education. But the academics got interested in them too, and vice versa.

The nineteenth-century artist was typically a loner: even in the twentieth he was often the last stand of laissez faire, resisting every kind of social mediation between himself and his public. It is still often asserted that he ought to continue to be so, and should avoid the seductions of university posts and foundation grants. The social facts of yesterday are the clichés of today. But he is now in a world where such agencies as the Canada Council represent a growing concern on the part of society with the leisure structure. This has affected all aspects of the arts: we may note particularly the changes in genre. Some arts, like music and drama, are ensemble performances for audience; others, like the novel and the easel-painting, are individualized. In an intensely individualized era like the Victorian age, the novel goes up and the drama goes down. Up until quite recently, the creative person, say in literature, was typically one who "wanted to write," and what he wanted to write was usually poetry or fiction. He might dream of rivalling Shakespeare, but he would be unlikely to want Shakespeare's job of a busy actor-manager in a profit-sharing corporation. It looks as though creative interests were shifting again to the dramatic: it is Pinter and Albee and Beckett on the stage, Bergman and Fellini and others in film, who seem to be making cultural history today, as the novelists were making it a century ago. The creative undergraduate tends less to bring his sheaf of poems to his instructor, and tends more to ask his advice about where he can get financial assistance, private or foundational, as a result of having gone broke with a film-making or dramatic venture. This may be a temporary vogue, but I think not, and of course it is obvious how this kind of creative interest immediately involves the artist in the social aspects of the leisure structure. (Psychotherapy, so profoundly connected with the contemporary imagination, has recently changed its emphasis from narrative and confessional techniques to dramatic ones, which is perhaps another aspect of the same cultural trend.)

In my earlier talks I spoke of the modern imagination as resisting the pressure of advertising and propaganda, which assume and try to bring about a passive response. Advertising and propaganda come respectively from the economic and the political structures, and I touched on the neurosis in modern life which springs from the feeling that these structures are not worth loyalty. For all our dislike of the word totalitarian, we have to recognize that there is a profound and genuine, if ultimately specious, appeal in any form of social activity which promises to expand into a complete way of life, engaging all aspects of one's interests and providing fulfilment for one's cultural, spiritual, and intellectual as well as social needs. A generation ago many people plunged into radical politics in the hope of finding a total program of this kind, but all forms of politics, including the radical form, seem sooner or later to dwindle into a specialized chess game. Many others at various times have sought the same total activity in religion, a more promising place, but often a disappointing one, with rather second-rate cultural rewards. It would simplify my argument considerably at this point if I could say that the leisure structure was the missing piece of society, that it is what we can give an unqualified loyalty to, and that it does fulfil the entire range of non-material human needs. There is however no reason to suppose that the leisure structure, as it grows in social importance, will produce a social institution any better (if no worse) than business or politics do: the most we can hope for is a system of checks and balances which will prevent any one of our new three estates from becoming too powerful. Even Plato hardly went so far as to believe in the perfectibility of intellectuals, and the history of the Christian Church, which started out with a much higher ideal of loyalty, does not encourage us to feel that any social institution can be a genuine embodiment of a social ideal. It is mainly those in the departments concerned with the arts, humanities, and general education who show a clear difference of social attitude, not because their virtue is superior, but because their budgets are low. The rich grants that scientists and administrators can obtain as employees of government and industry will always be attractive, whatever their relation to academic freedom, a relation which in itself will become much hazier as universities become more dependent financially on government.

I should describe the ideal or Utopian features of the leisure structure, along with the political and economic ones, rather differently. The evolution of political democracy, as it fought against entrenched privilege at first, and then against dictatorial tendencies, has to some extent been a genuine evolution of an idea of liberty, however often betrayed and perverted, and however much threatened still. The evolution of industry into a society of producers, as labour continued to fight against a managerial oligarchy, has been to a correspondingly modified extent an evolution of an idea of equality. Matthew Arnold warned the dominant bourgeoisie of Victorian England that a society could pursue liberty to the point of forgetting about equality. Today, with capitalism in a counter-reformation period and with totalitarianism thought of as something foreign, we prefer to be reminded that society—that is, other societies—can pursue equality to the point of forgetting about liberty. But neither political democracy nor trade unions have developed much sense of the third revolutionary ideal of fraternity—the word "comrade" has for most of us a rather sinister and frigid sound. Fraternity is perhaps the ideal that the leisure structure has to contribute to society. A society of students, scholars, and artists is a society of neighbours, in the genuinely religious sense of that word. That is, our neighbour is not, or not necessarily, the person in the same national or ethnical or class group with ourselves, but may be a "good Samaritan" or person to whom we are linked by deeper bonds than nationality or racism or class solidarity can any longer provide. These are bonds of intellect and imagination as well as of love and good will. The neighbour of a scientist is another scientist working on similar lines, perhaps in a different continent; the neighbour of a novelist writing about Mississippi is (as Faulkner indicated in his Nobel Prize speech) anybody anywhere who can respond to his work. The fact that feuds among scholars and artists are about as bitter as feuds ever get will doubtless make for some distinction between theory and practice.

It is a peculiarity of North America today that culture is absorbed into society mainly through the university classroom. Such a dependence of contemporary culture on the educational system, rather than on a self-acquired social education supplementing the academic one, is much less true of Europe. This seems to imply, perhaps correctly, a higher degree of maturity in European society, in this respect at least. When I speak of the North American university's interest in contemporary culture as obsessive I am speaking of a degree of interest that I somewhat regret: it might be better if the university confined itself to supplying the historical dimension of its culture. But the students dictate a great deal of the teaching program of the university, though they seldom realize it, and students of the humanities appear to regard the study of the contemporary or near-contemporary as the most liberalizing element of a liberal education. My notion is that the trend is for the European pattern to fall in with the North American one rather than the other way round, but my observations do not depend on such a prediction.

Whatever the eventual relation of teaching and culture, the academic and the creative aspects of contemporary society have certainly come together within the last generation or so, and their future destinies, so far as one can see into the future, appear to be closely linked. This accounts for a feature of our cultural life which seems more paradoxical than it is. The university classroom is concerned with "liberal" education, and liberal education is liberal in every sense of the word: it emancipates, it is tolerant, it assimilates the learning process to a social idea. Yet so far as it is concerned with contemporary culture, its material includes all the reactionary and anti-social attitudes I glanced at earlier, some of which are, in detail, quite obviously silly, perverse, or wrong-headed. But when contemporary authors are assigned for compulsory reading, and when they are taught in a way that relates them to their cultural heritage, a certain detachment comes into the attitude toward them. Not all the detachment is good, but one thing about it is: the social attitude of the writer is taken over by the social attitude of education itself, and loses its crankiness by being placed in a social context. Study, as distinct from direct response, is a cool medium, and even the most blatant advocacy of violence and terror may be, like Satan in the Bible, transformed into an angel of light by being regarded as a contribution to modern thought. Where shall wisdom be found? Chiefly, for our age, in the imaginative and technical skills of the more or less unwise.

The leisure structure, then, is essentially a structure of education, which means that it is vitally concerned with teaching. One can teach only what is teachable, and what the university must teach is the only thing it can teach: the specific disciplines into which genuine knowledge is divided. What results from this in the mind of the student? Facts, perhaps; ideas; information; the techniques of the present; the traditions of the past. But all these things are quickly acquired by the good student, and, unless used for some definite purpose, quickly forgotten. What emerges from university teaching, as its final result in the student's mind, is something the university cannot, or should not, explicitly teach. As most great theorists of education, from Castiglione to Newman, have recognized, the form of liberal education is social, in the broadest sense, rather than simply intellectual. I should call the social form of liberal education, provisionally, a vision of society, or, more technically, a mythology.

In every age there is a structure of ideas, images, beliefs, assumptions, anxieties, and hopes which express the view of man's situation and destiny generally held at that time. I call this structure a mythology, and its units myths. A myth, in this sense, is an expression of man's concern about himself, about his place in the scheme of things, about his relation to society and God, about the ultimate origin and ultimate fate, either of himself or of the human species generally. A mythology is thus a product of human concern, of our involvement with ourselves, and it always looks at the world from a man-centred point of view. The early and primitive myths were stories, mainly stories about gods, and their units were physical images. In more highly structured societies they develop in two different but related directions. In the first place, they develop into literature as we know it, first into folktales and legends of heroes, thence into the conventional plots of fiction and metaphors of poetry. In the second place, they become conceptualized, and become the informing principles of historical and philosophical thought, as the myth of fall becomes the informing idea of Gibbon's history of Rome, or the myth of the sleeping beauty

Rousseau's buried society of nature and reason. My first lecture dealt primarily with mythology in this sense, particularly with the so-called existential myths.

It seems to me that there have been two primary mythological constructions in Western culture. One was the vast synthesis that institutional Christianity made of its Biblical and Aristotelian sources. This myth is at its clearest in the Middle Ages, but it persisted for centuries later, and much of its structure, though greatly weakened by the advance of science, was still standing in the eighteenth century itself. The other is the modern mythology that began when the modern world did, in the later eighteenth century, but reached its more specifically modern shape a century later, and a century before now.

The older mythology was one that stressed two things in particular: the subject-object relation and the use of reason. Man was a subject confronting a nature set over against him. Both man and nature were creatures of God, and were united by that fact. There were no gods in nature: if man looked into the powers of nature to find such gods they would soon turn into devils. What he should look at nature for is the evidence of purpose and design which it shows as a complementary creation of God, and the reason can grasp this sense of design. The rational approach to nature was thus superior to the empirical and experimental approach to it, and the sciences that were most deductive and closest to mathematics were those that were first developed. Of all sciences, astronomy is the most dependent on the subject-object relationship, and in the Middle Ages particularly, astronomy was the science par excellence, the one science that a learned medieval poet, such as Dante or Chaucer, would be assumed to know.

In the pre-modern myth man's ultimate origin was of God, and his chief end was to draw closer to God. Even more important, the social discipline which raised him above the rest of creation was a divine ordinance. Law was of God; the forms of human civilization, the city and the garden, were imitations of divine models, for God planted the garden of Eden and had established his city before man was created; the ultimate human community was not in this world, but in a heaven closer to the divine presence. Philosophers recog-

nized that the ordinary categories of the mind, such as our perception of time and space, might not be adequate at a purely spiritual
level. It was possible, for example, that a spiritual body, such as an
angel, did not occupy space or travel in space at all. The unfortunate
wretch who attempted to put this question into a lively and memorable form by asking how many angels could stand on the point of
a pin has become a byword for pedantic stupidity, a terrible warning to all instructors who try to make a technical subject interesting.
But as far as popular belief and poetic imagery were concerned, the
spiritual world was thought of as essentially another objective environment, to be described in symbols—city, temple, garden, streets—
derived from human life, though the myth taught that human life
had been derived from them. This mythology, relating as it did both
man and nature to God, was a total one, so complete and far-reaching that an alternative world-picture was practically unthinkable.
This is the real significance of Voltaire's familiar epigram, that if God
did not exist it would be necessary to invent him, which was, in his
day, a much more serious remark than it sounds. One could, theoretically, be an atheist; but even an atheist would find God blocking
his way on all sides: he would meet the hypothesis of God in history,
in philosophy, in psychology, in astronomy. As for morality, its standards were so completely assimilated to religious sanctions that even
a century ago it was impossible for many people to believe that non-
religious man could have any moral integrity at all.

In the eighteenth century there began to grow, slowly but irre-
sistibly, the conviction that man had created his own civilization.
This meant not merely that he was responsible for it—he had always
been that—but that its forms of city and garden and design, of law
and social discipline and education, even, ultimately, of morals and
religion, were of human origin and human creation. This new feeling crystallized around Rousseau in the eighteenth century, and the
assumptions underlying the American and French revolutions were
relatively new assumptions. Liberty was no longer, as it had been
for Milton, something that God gives and that man resists: it was
something that most men want and that those who have a stake in
slavery invoke their gods to prevent them from getting. Law was no

longer, as it had been for Hooker, the reflection of divine order in human life, but in large part the reflection of class privilege in property rights. Art and culture were no longer, as they had been for the age of Shakespeare, the ornaments of social discipline: they took on a prophetic importance as portraying the forms of civilization that man had created. The Romantic movement brought in the conception of the "serious" artist, setting his face against society to follow his art, from which the modern antagonism of the artist to society that I discussed earlier has descended.

A major principle of the older mythology was the correspondence of human reason with the design and purpose in nature which it perceives. This correspondence was still accepted even after God had dwindled into a deistic first cause, a necessary hypothesis and nothing more. The modern movement, properly speaking, began when Darwin finally shattered the old teleological conception of nature as reflecting an intelligent purpose. From then on design in nature has been increasingly interpreted by science as a product of a self-developing nature. The older view of design survives vestigially, as when religion tells us that some acts are "contrary to nature." But contemporary science, which is professionally concerned with nature, does not see in the ancient mother-goddess the Wisdom which was the bride of a superhuman creator. What it sees rather is a confused old beldame who has got where she has through a remarkable obstinacy in adhering to trial and error— mostly error—procedures. The rational design that nature reflects is in the human mind only. An example of the kind of thinking that Darwin has made impossible for the modern mind is: "If the Lord had intended us to fly, he'd have given us wings." The conception of natural functions as related to a personal and creative intention is no longer in our purview.

Modern mythology, at least with us, is naturally not as well unified as the earlier one, but it does possess some unity none the less. It reaches us on two main levels. There is a social mythology, which we learn through conversation and the contacts of family, teachers, and neighbours, which is reinforced by the mass media, newspapers, television, and movies, and which is based fundamentally on

cliché and stock response. In the United States, elementary education, at least before the sputnik revolution of 1957, consisted very
largely of acquiring a stock-response mythology known as the
American way of life. Canadian elementary teaching has been less
obsessed by social mythology, as its children do not require the
indoctrination that citizens of a great world power do, but it has
its own kind, as in fact do all societies in all ages. Social mythology in our day is a faint parody of the Christian mythology which
preceded it. "Things were simpler in the old days; the world has
unaccountably lost its innocence since we were children. I just live
to get out of this rat race for a bit and go somewhere where I can
get away from it all. Yet there is a bracing atmosphere in competition and we may hope to see consumer goods enjoyed by all members of our society after we abolish poverty. The world is threatened
with grave dangers from foreigners, perhaps with total destruction;
yet if we dedicate ourselves anew to the tasks which lie before us
we may preserve our way of life for generations yet unborn." One
recognizes the familiar outlines of paradise myths, fall myths, exo-
dus-from-Egypt myths, pastoral myths, apocalypse myths.

The first great modern novelist is usually taken to be Flaubert,
whose last and unfinished work, *Bouvard et Pécuchet*, included, as
part of its scheme, a "Dictionary of Accepted Ideas." In recent years
there has been a phenomenal growth of books which are written
from within one of the social sciences, but are actually read as social
satires. Anyone can think of a dozen titles: *The Lonely Crowd*, *The
Affluent Society*, *The Organization Man*, *The Academic Market-Place*,
The Status Seekers, *The Insolent Chariots*, *The Hidden Persuaders*,
Games People Play. This last one breaks the rhythm of the conventional titles: a stock phrase preceded by the inside-knowledge suggestion of the definite article. Not all of these are good books, but
they all deal with subjects about which good books ought to be written. The importance of this form of literary fiction, for that is what
it is, is that it studies society from the point of view of its popular or
cliché mythology, its accepted ideas. It is bound to have a revolutionary impact on other fiction by making novelists and dramatists more
aware of the symbolic and ritual basis of social behaviour.

A more complicated mythology emerges in general education and liberal arts courses, where we become aware of the immense importance of the thinkers who have helped to shape our mythology: Rousseau, Marx, Freud, the existentialists, and others whose importance depends on what versions of it we take most seriously. In addition to the art and scholarship which is specialized and works with limited objectives, there is a wide variety of "idea books," books that survey the intellectual world, or a large section of it, from a certain comprehensive point of view. On the book-shelves of my study in front of me as I write I see works of history: Spengler's *Decline of the West*, Toynbee's *A Study of History*, Hannah Arendt's *Origins of Totalitarianism*. Works of philosophy: Whitehead's *Science and the Modern World*, Sartre's *Being and Nothing*. Works of science: Eddington's *Nature of the Physical World*, Sherrington's *Man on his Nature*. Works of criticism: McLuhan's *Understanding Media*, Fiedler's *An End to Innocence*, Harold Rosenberg's *The Tradition of the New*, Irving Howe's *Steady Work*. Works of psychology: Norman Brown's *Life Against Death*, Marcuse's *Eros and Civilization*. Works of religion: Buber's *I and Thou*, Tillich's *The Courage to Be*, Cox's *The Secular City*. This is a purely random list, but it should give an idea of the kind of book that helps to shape our contemporary mythology, and to give coherence and co-ordination to our views of the human situation. All these books deal with ideas, but occasional words in the titles, "Decline," "City," "Eros," "Innocence," indicate their origin in myth. In a sense they are all philosophical, even though most of them are clearly something other than actual philosophy. What I am here calling mythology has in fact often been regarded as the rightful function of philosophy, and we note that philosophers, especially of the existentialist school, have been particularly fertile in naming our central myths, such as the alienation, absurdity, anxiety, and nausea dealt with in my first lecture.

Our mythology, I said, is a structure built by human concern: it is existential in the broad sense, and deals with the human situation in terms of human hopes and fears. Thus, though some of the books I have listed are written from the point of view of a scientific discipline, it does not really include the physical sciences. In our day, ever since Darwin, there have been two world-pictures: the picture of the world we see, which is simply there, and is not man-centred, and the picture of the world we make, which is necessarily man-centred. The arts, the humanities, and in part the social sciences, all contribute to the contemporary myth of concern, but the physical sciences have their own structure, perhaps their own mythology. The earlier mythology was developed out of the idea of God; God has today no status, even as a hypothesis, in physical science, but the myth of concern neither excludes nor necessitates God, who comes into some versions of it and not into others. Of course scientific conceptions are continually being annexed by mythographers: the conception of evolution, for instance, has been applied in dozens of ways. But when the term evolution is used in Bernard Shaw's theory of a divine creative will, in Herbert Spencer's philosophy of ethics, in a Biblical scholar's account of the growth of the idea of God, or in a history of painting, the conception used is not identical with the biological theory: it is only a mythological analogy of that theory. How significant the analogy is has still to be determined, as a separate problem. Naturally science has immense relevance to the myth of concern, especially when it manifests an ability to destroy or to improve human existence—in some areas, such as genetics, it is not always easy to distinguish the two things. But it is a primary function of the myth of concern to judge the effects of science on human life in its own terms. This is what good mythological works written by scientists, such as the books of Eddington and Jeans and Sherrington, help us to do. When a mythologist attempts to show that the conceptions of science support or prove his vision, he weakens his power of resistance to science.

What I am describing is a liberal or "open" mythology, of the sort appropriate to a democracy. I call it a structure, but it is often so fluid that the solid metaphor of structure hardly applies to it at all. Each man has his own version of it, conditioned by what he knows best, and in fact he will probably adopt several differing versions in the course of his life. Myths are seldom if ever actual hypotheses that can be verified or refuted; that is not their function: they are co-ordinating or integrating ideas. Hence, though good mythological books are usually written by competent scholars, the mythology of concern is something different from actual scholarship, and is subordinate to it. Any verified fact or definitely refuted theory may alter the whole mythological structure at any time, and must be allowed to do so. Yet there are certain assumptions which give mythology some social unity and make discussion, argument, and communication possible. It is not addressed directly to belief: it is rather a reservoir of possibilities of belief. It is the area of free discussion which Mill, in his *Essay on Liberty*, felt to be the genuine parliament of man and the safeguard of social freedom as a whole. It is the "culture" that Matthew Arnold opposed to the anarchy of doing as one likes, the check on social and political activism. For activism, however well motivated, is always based on rationalized stock response. Beliefs and convictions and courses of action come out of an open mythology, but when such courses are decided on, the area of discussion is not closed off. No idea is anything more than a half-truth unless it contains its own opposite, and is expanded by its own denial or qualification.

An open mythology of this kind is very different from a closed one, which is a structure of belief. There are two aspects of belief, theoretical and practical. Theoretical belief is a creed, a statement of what a man says he believes, thinks he believes, believes he believes. A creed is essentially an assertion that one belongs to a certain social body: even if one is trying to define an individual belief not exactly like anyone else's, one is still defining one's social and intellectual context. One's profession of faith is a part of one's social contract. Practical belief is what a man's actions and attitudes show that he believes. Pascal's conception of the "wager," the assumptions underlying one's conduct, is a conception of practical belief. Similar conceptions are in Newman's *Grammar of Assent*, and, more generally, in Vaihinger's theory of assumed fictions. A closed mythology, like Christianity in the Middle Ages, requires the statement of theoretical belief from everyone, and imposes a discipline that will make practice consistent with it. Thus the closed mythology is a statement both of what is believed to be true and of what is going to be made true by a certain course of action. This latter more particularly is the sense in which Marxism is a closed mythology, and the sense in which another revolutionary thinker, Sorel, generally conceives of myth.

A closed mythology forms a body of major premises which is superior in authority to scholarship and art. A closed myth already contains all the answers, at least potentially: whatever scholarship or art produce has to be treated deductively, as reconcilable with the mythology, or, if irreconcilable, suppressed. In Marxist countries the physical sciences are allowed to function more or less independently of the myth, because, as remarked earlier, society picks up too many of its golden eggs to want to kill the goose, but as the physical sciences do not form an integral part of the myth of concern, their autonomy, up to a point, would not be fatal to it. A closed myth creates a general élite. In the Middle Ages this élite consisted of clerics; in Marxist countries it consists of those who understand both the principles of Marxism and the way that the existing power structure wants Marxism rationalized.

In the democracies there are many who would like to see a closed myth take over. Some are hysterical, like the John Birch society who want a myth of the American way of life, as they understand it, imposed on everything, or like the maudlin Teutonism which a generation ago welcomed the formulating of the Nazi closed myth in Alfred Rosenberg's *Myth of the Twentieth Century*. It may be significant that the book which actually bears that title should be one of the most foolish and mischievous books of our time. Some are nostalgic intellectuals, usually with a strong religious bias, who are bemused by the "unity" of medieval culture and would like to see some kind of "return" to it. Some are people who can readily imagine themselves as belonging to the kind of élite that a closed myth would produce. Some are sincere believers in democracy who feel that democracy is at a disadvantage in not having a clear and unquestioned program of its beliefs. But democracy can hardly function with a closed myth, and books of the type I have mentioned as contributions to our mythology, however illuminating and helpful, cannot, in a free society, be given any authority beyond what they earn by their own merits. That is, an open mythology has no canon. Similarly, there can be no general élite in a democratic society: in a democracy everybody belongs to some kind of élite, which derives from its social function a particular knowledge or skill that no other group has.

The earlier closed mythology of the Western world was a religion, and the emergence of an open mythology has brought about a cultural crisis which is at bottom a religious crisis. Traditionally, there are two elements in religion, considered as such apart from a definite faith. One is the primitive element of *religio*, the collection of duties, rituals, and observances which are binding on all members of a community. In this sense Marxism and the American way of life are religions. The other is the sense of a transcendence of the ordinary categories of human experience, a transcendence normally expressed by the words infinite and eternal. As a structure of belief, religion is greatly weakened; it has no secular power to back it up, and its mandates affect far fewer people, and those far less completely, than a century ago. What is significant is not so much the losing of faith as the losing of guilt feelings about losing it. Religion tends increasingly to make its primary impact, not as a system of taught and learned belief, but as an imaginative structure which, whether "true" or not, has imaginative consistency and imaginative informing power. In other words, it makes its essential appeal as myth or possible truth, and whatever belief it attracts follows from that.

This means that the arts, which address the imagination, have, ever since the Romantic movement, acquired increasingly the role of the agents through which religion is understood and appreciated. The arts have taken on a prophetic function in society, never more of one than when the artist pretends to deprecate such a role, as, for instance, T. S. Eliot did. It is sometimes said that the arts, especially poetry, have become a "substitute" for religion, but this makes no sense. The arts contain no objects of worship or belief, nor do they constitute (except professionally for a few people) a way of life. If a man is brought up to believe, say, in the immortality of the soul, loses that belief, and then reconciles himself to death by saying that he will continue to live in the memories of his friends, he really does have a substitute for religion—that is, an accommodation of a transcendent religious conception to the categories of ordinary experience. Many "philosophies of life," like that of Sartre in our day, are substitutes for religion in this sense, but the arts are not and never can be. The alliance of religion and art is based on the fact that religion deals with transcendent conceptions and that the arts, being imaginative, are confined, not by the limits of the possible, but by the limits of the conceivable. Thus poetry speaks the mythical language of religion. And perhaps, if we think of the reality of religion as mythical rather than doctrinal, religion would turn out to be what is really open about an open mythology: the sense that there are no limits to what the human imagination may conceive or be concerned with.

I developed my own view of such questions by studying the poetry of William Blake. Most of Blake's lyrical poems are either songs of innocence or songs of experience. One of the songs of innocence is a poem called "The Lamb," where a child asks a lamb the first question of the catechism, "who made you?" The child has a confident answer: Christ made the lamb because he is both a lamb and child himself, and unites the human and subhuman worlds in a divine personality. The contrasting poem is the song of experience called "The Tyger," where the poet asks: "Did he who made the lamb make thee?" Some students of Blake, I regret to say, have tried to answer the question. The vision of the world as created by a benevolent and intelligent power is the innocent vision, the vision of the child who assumes that the world around him must have parents too. Further, it is a world in which only lambs can live: lions and tigers can enter it only on condition that they lie down with the lamb, and thereby cease to be lions and tigers. But the child's vision is far behind us. The world we are in is the world of the tiger, and that world was never created or seen to be good. It is the subhuman world of nature, a world of law and of power but not of intelligence or design. Things "evolve" in it, whatever that means, but there is no creative power in it that we can see except that of man himself. And man is not very good at the creating business: he is much better at destroying, for most of him, like an iceberg, is submerged in a destructive element.

Hence the fragility of all human creations and ideals, including the ideal that we are paying tribute to this year. The world we see and live in, and most of the world we have made, belongs to the alienated and absurd world of the tiger. But in all our efforts to imagine or realize a better society, some shadow falls across it of the child's innocent vision of the impossible created world that makes human sense. If we can no longer feel that this world was once created for us by a divine parent, we still must feel, more intensely than ever, that it is the world we ought to be creating, and that whatever may be divine in our destiny or nature is connected with its creation. The loss of faith in such a world is centrally a religious problem, but it has a political dimension as well, and one which includes the question we have been revolving around all through: what is it, in society, to which we really owe loyalty? The question is not easy to answer in Canada. We are alienated from our economy in Marx's sense, as we own relatively little of it ourselves; our governments are democratic: that is, they are what Nietzsche calls "all too human." We have few ready-made symbols of loyalty: a flag perfunctorily designed by a committee, a national anthem with its patent pending, an imported Queen. But we may be looking in the wrong direction.

I referred earlier to Grove's A Search for America, where the narrator keeps looking for the genuine America buried underneath the America of hustling capitalism which occupies the same place. This buried America is an ideal that emerges in Thoreau, Whitman, and the personality of Lincoln. All nations have such a buried or uncreated ideal, the lost world of the lamb and the child, and no nation has been more preoccupied with it than Canada. The painting of Tom Thomson and Emily Carr, and later of Riopelle and Borduas, is an exploring, probing painting, tearing apart the physical world to see what lies beyond or through it. Canadian literature even at its most articulate, in the poetry of Pratt, with its sense of the corruption at the heart of achievement, or of Nelligan with its sense of unfulfilled clarity, a reach exceeding the grasp, or in the puzzled and indignant novels of Grove, seems constantly to be trying to understand something that eludes it, frustrated by a sense that there is something to be found that has not been found, something to be heard that the world is too noisy to let us hear. One of the derivations proposed for the word Canada is a Portuguese phrase meaning "nobody here." The etymology of the word Utopia is very similar, and perhaps the real Canada is an ideal with nobody in it. The Canada to which we really do owe loyalty is the Canada that we have failed to create. In a year bound to be full of discussions of our identity, I should like to suggest that our identity, like the real identity of all nations, is the one that we have failed to achieve. It is expressed in our culture, but not attained in our life, just as Blake's new Jerusalem to be built in England's green and pleasant land is no less a genuine ideal for not having been built there. What there is left of the Canadian nation may well be destroyed by the kind of sectarian bickering which is so much more interesting to many people than genuine human life. But, as we enter a second century contemplating a world where power and success express themselves so much in stentorian lying, hypnotized leadership, and panic-stricken suppression of freedom and criticism, the uncreated identity of Canada may be after all not so bad a heritage to take with us.

Part Three

The Nemesis of Empire

Edward Togo Salmon

Foreword

* * *

The eighteenth series of lectures was delivered in January 1973 by Edward Togo Salmon, M.A., Ph.D., D.Litt., LL.D., F.R.S.C., F.R.H.S., F.B.A., Messecar Professor of History and University Orator in McMaster University. His topic, *The Nemesis of Empire*, is one of perennial concern to historians and of immediate concern to everyone who has witnessed the decline and dissolution of the British Empire.

Born in England and raised in Australia, Dr. Salmon obtained his classical education in Sydney and in Cambridge, England. After brief service at Acadia University, Dr. Salmon came to McMaster in 1930 to join the Department of Classics and later the Department of History. His energies and capacities soon became manifest not only in his scholarly career, his important publications, and his service to classical organizations at home and abroad, but also in his role as departmental and administrative officer.

His career as Principal of University College during the emotional 'sixties (1961–67) and as First Vice-President of the newly established Division of Arts (1967–68) is memorialized by curricular innovations and by the splendid buildings of the Arts Complex. Few professors have contributed so richly and so decisively to the advancement of the University's distinction and international stature.

Dr. Salmon has been President of the Classical Association of Canada (1952–54), Member of the Executive Committee of the International Federation of Classical Associations (1959–69), Member of the Humanities Research Council of Canada (1965–8), President of the American Philological Association (1971), and Vice-President of the International Council for Philosophy and Humanistic Sciences, a sub-agency of U.N.E.S.C.O., since 1971.

His many administrative roles and public service in no way diminished his productivity as scholar. His *History of the Roman World, 30 BC–AD 138* has entered upon its sixth edition (1968); his *Samnium and the Samnites* (1967) won the coveted Merit Award of the American Philological Association; his *Roman Colonization Under the Republic* (1969) was the product of years of topographical and historical research throughout the length and breadth of Italy.

Elections to Learned Societies have brought distinction to the man and to his University: Fellow, Royal Society of Canada; Fellow, Royal Historical Society; Honorary Member, Australian Classical Society; Honorary Member, Society for the Promotion of Roman Studies; Fellow of the Canadian Institute in Rome; and, most notably, Corresponding Fellow of the British Academy (1971).

Dr. Salmon ranks as McMaster's most distinguished humanist. Visiting Lectureships in Australia, the United Kingdom, Eire, and the United States and his recent Professorship at the Intercollegiate Centre for Classical Studies in Rome (1969–71) have won international respect for his wisdom and scholarship.

The members of the audience who attended his Whidden Lectures were captivated by his distinctive style, by the breadth of his erudition, and by the grace of his oratory. A larger company of his students, many of whom have digressed widely from the Groves of Academe, will recall past lectures, genial words of friendship, and the warmth of his personality when they read this published version. Dr. Salmon is the first member of the McMaster University Faculty to appear as Whidden Lecturer. The Selection Committee thereby honoured the first chairman of the Whidden Lectures Committee and introduced to a capacity audience one of McMaster's most distinguished statesmen and teachers and one of her most zealous servants.

A. G. McKay
McMaster University

I

A Fit of Absence of Mind

Britain's forward step into Europe makes timely a backward glance at her empire. It was often viewed by its advocates as an advanced analogy to the Roman Empire. Both imperial powers had expanded initially without premeditation, programmes, or policies; both had faced acute crises of inadequate government and had renewed their lease of life to become supreme powers.

But besides these superficial coincidences the Roman and the British empires are very unlike in their manner of birth and growth and show significant contrasts which underline their whole history.

Will you let me begin on a very personal note? It is an exceptional honour to be invited to deliver the Whidden Lectures. The many distinguished scholars who have appeared in the series in the past have won for it an enviable reputation, and to be thought worthy of inclusion in their company is a compliment indeed. Nor am I unappreciative of the fact that, although other Canadian scholars have been Whidden Lecturers before me, I belong to McMaster itself. I hope that I shall be easily understood, even though I cannot find the words to tell you how proud this makes me.

But I have yet another and a much better reason for being grateful to the Whidden Lectures committee. Unlike all those who have appeared before me on this platform, I was acquainted, and indeed well acquainted, with Dr. Whidden; and not only with Dr. Whidden, but also with Dr. Fox, that great friend of McMaster whose generosity twenty years ago made this lecture series possible. I had much affection and unbounded admiration for these two great Canadians, and I am deeply thankful that I have been given an opportunity to pay what tribute I can to their memory. To that end I have chosen a theme that would have been dear to the heart of Howard Whidden: he came of British Empire loyalist stock, as did his wife. And I have endeavoured to treat the theme in a manner of which Carey Fox would have approved; his desire always was to have different specialities and disciplines brought more closely together. I have accordingly tried to confront the British with the Romans. The subject is made topical by the New Year's Day entry into Europe's Common Market of the British, who have thereby opened up a new chapter in their long history, turning their backs on their imperial past.

Those of us who were born in Edwardian times have been privileged to witness not only the finest hour, but also the greatest days, of the British Empire. By 1920 the supremacy of the Royal Navy, repelling the challenge of Kaiser Wilhelm's fleet in the wasteful "dreadnought" race, had triumphantly reasserted itself. Great Britain and the Empire had not only fought the war that was to end all wars and make a world fit for heroes to live in, but had also emerged from that bloodiest of all conflicts unbowed, victorious, and enlarged. Those who were schoolchildren in those heady days will remember the excitement of Empire Day festivities. The ritual of the celebrations in the school that I attended did not vary greatly from one year to the next. On the eve of the Empire Day holiday, there would be a general assembly of all the students, featured by a stirring recitation of appropriate verses from Rudyard Kipling, followed by a wheezy gramophone recording of Dame Clara Butt singing Elgar's "Land of Hope and Glory"; all present would then raise their voices in unison to the spirited strains of "Rule, Britannia" and, after some speechifying and flag-waving, would wend their homeward way, proud, exhilarated, and uplifted, to let off fire-crackers around a bonfire in the evening.

In retrospect, half a century later, it all seems completely remote, if not more than a little incredible. It was another world, a world of ebullient chauvinism from which we have since shaken loose to move into the emancipated if somewhat bewildering days of the second half of the twentieth century, when the British Empire has become one with the snows of yesteryear and when uncertainty reigns as to what will replace it as the rock of stability for a wobbling world.

In 1914 Great Britain and her overseas dependencies formed some sort of imperial unity. The declaration of war by Britain on the

4th of August in that year bound the whole of it, and the members of the Empire marched shoulder to shoulder against the Central Powers. In World War II a mere quarter of a century later, they once again marched together, but this time much more in the manner of a fighting alliance than of an organic union. Canada, for instance, made her own declaration of war, and she did not do it merely in tame imitation of Britain, nor even at precisely the same moment. Officially, Canada was at war with Japan before Britain was (or, for that matter, even before the U.S.A. was), and officially she was never at war with Bulgaria at all. Nevertheless there can be no doubt that in World War II the imperial connection still counted for much.

It seems hardly likely that this will ever be the case again. No one believes that there could be similar concerted action in the unthinkable event of the world being subjected to the horror of a third world war. By 1970, another bare twenty-five years later, the various countries of the Empire had decided to go their separate ways, with some of them no longer recognizing even the tenuous link of the British crown. True, most of them have agreed to continue in close consultation, and even to practise a certain amount of co-operation, with one another in the Commonwealth. But this does not disguise the reality that their feet have been swiftly and firmly planted upon different paths, even upon paths that in one or two instances have already led them into war with one another.

The rapidity with which the British Empire has crumbled seems all the more startling in that this has occurred so soon after it had reached its furthest territorial extension. The days immediately after World War I saw it at its zenith. It was in the halcyon days of the early twenties that Cecil Rhodes's imperial dream of an all-red route from the Cape to Cairo was translated, if only briefly, into reality; and as its inhabitants of the time were so fond of repeating, the Empire had become the mighty organism spread over one-quarter of the world's surface on which the sun never set.

But by definition every zenith is the start of a decline. Already, during World War I, the Empire had sometimes been unofficially referred to as the British Commonwealth of Nations, and in 1922 this expression was actually used in an official document of the very highest importance.[1] At the imperial conference in 1926, the Balfour Declaration attempted to define the concept, and the definition was published and even spelled out in some detail in the Statute of Westminster in 1931. The British Empire thus became the British Commonwealth; and not many years were to elapse before the adjective British had disappeared from the title, and nothing remained of the British Empire other than a handful of islands scattered here and there over the world's oceans.

So remarkable a reversal has inevitably opened the floodgates to a veritable spate of interpretations, explanations, and conjectures. In recent years particularly, much has been written about the end of the British Empire.[2] My hardihood in taking up the theme yet again is due not only to the interest which a "decline and fall" is bound to arouse in a Roman historian, but also to the hope that a look at the British Empire in the light of the Roman experience may well prove illuminating.

I hasten to add that this implies no suggestion that I find history to be self-repeating. The theory that it is remains unconvincing despite an erudite and novel restatement of it by A. J. Toynbee. H. A. L. Fisher himself could not discover in history "a plot, a rhythm, a predestined pattern."[3] Most of us recognize, with Fisher, the part played by pure chance and blind coincidence in the affairs of men, and agree with Walpole that history does not repeat itself no matter how much historians may repeat one another. Mommsen, the greatest modern student of ancient Rome, insisted that men's actions are only too often governed by passion rather than by reason; and passion is too unpredictable to conform to any pattern.

Analogies, however, do obviously exist between the Roman and the British imperial histories. In fact, of all the earlier empires, the Roman is the only one that is even remotely similar to the British in extension, variety, and duration, although one should add that it was also markedly different in many ways. The Romans, too, encompassed much of the world of their time; and their regime, like that of the British, was featured by a long period of peace on the world-wide scale, actually the longest in history. Indeed, Rome served as an inspiration and even to some extent as a model for the

British, especially at the time when the latter became imbued with the concept of imperial purpose.

If it is a matter of interest to us to understand what happened to the Empire of which we so recently formed a part, its evolution will be seen more clearly perhaps when compared and contrasted with that of its Roman forerunner.

The starting point for the two imperial expansions is one of difference: in time, in historical background, and in circumstance. Rome had to fight for survival against strong rivals, even inside Italy. Defeat in her early struggles would have meant subjection, and for her the only alternative was supremacy. The Samnite and the Punic Wars had steeled Roman tenacity and self-discipline to the utmost. After the fall of Carthage there were no equal rivals for dominion, although even yet there were many reversals in both internal and external matters still to come. The Roman senate, effectively the government of the Roman Republic, was fully involved from the outset.

Contrast England. England's, and later Great Britain's, expansion originated from private enterprise, with trading posts and with settlements that were barely official. The competition with Spain, with Portugal, with Holland and, above all, with France put much wind into the sails of the companies of Merchant Adventurers, as well as into those of the Royal Navy. But, apart from the crown patents and charters accorded the companies, there was at first not much real commitment by the government.

Besides contrasts, however, there are broad coincidences. Both Rome and the British imperial power grew without premeditation, programme, or policy, and merely as events dictated, the Romans mostly for strategic reasons, the British mostly out of the necessity to trade. This haphazard opportunism was followed for a long time in both cases by inadequate administration of the annexed territories. Ultimately the problems and crises of the first phase of development in each of the two empires were solved, in the Roman world by the reforms of the emperor Augustus shortly before the birth of Christ, and in the British by the effects of the great changes in the social and political spheres and by the rise in moral and humanitarian standards that bred a sense of imperial mission in the nineteenth century.

In the case of any empire there will probably be some difficulty in pinpointing the precise date of its earliest beginnings. It has sometimes been implied that the Roman Empire began when Rome, the city republic on the River Tiber, brought the whole of Italy under her control between the fifth and the third centuries BC. This, however, seems very doubtful. It is something like saying that the start of the British Empire is to be sought in the achievement of the kingdom of Wessex in suppressing the independent existence of the other Anglo-Saxon realms that disputed the soil of England with it. It is, of course, true that the supremacy established by Rome in Italy before 100 BC was very different, both in legal theory and in actual fact, from the unification imposed by Wessex on the England of the heptarchy before AD 1000. Nevertheless, neither the one nor the other accomplishment can really be considered imperial expansion. It is conceding but little to the salt water fallacy to subscribe to the usual opinion that, in the case of both Rome and England, empire began with the annexation of territories overseas, provinces in the case of the Romans, colonies in the case of the English.

When, shortly after 300 BC, Rome had established her hegemony in Italy, she put an end to the cherished and immemorial habit of the Italic peoples of going to war with one another, and she obliged them to expend their martial energies in another way, namely in helping her to defend Italy, and what she considered to be the interests of Italy, against external attack. But she did not demand taxes or tribute from the Italians, she did not impose her laws or her language upon them, and she did not annex, much less annihilate them: technically they were her allies. It was not until 90 BC, by which time many of the Italians had adopted Latin and Rome's ways, that they were incorporated into the Roman state. And when that finally happened they were brought in, not as subjects but as Roman citizens. In Italy Rome had unified a nation, not created an empire.

But, even before 90 BC, the Roman Empire had already begun, in the third century BC in fact, when Rome annexed Sicily after the victory which she and her Italian allies had won over Carthage in the

First Punic War. Out of the Sicilian acorn grew the mighty oak-tree, which we call the Roman Empire and which was to sink its roots so deep that countries like France, Spain, Portugal, Switzerland, and Romania still speak the language of the Romans in one or other of its Neo-Latin forms. It spread its branches all over the Mediterranean world and the present-day Middle East and North Africa, over central and western Europe, and even over Britain. And it cast its shadow still further afield, as far as India and Central Asia.

For the Romans the annexation of Sicily in the third century BC was an act of prudential self-defence. The Carthaginians had penetrated into the island in force and thus posed a threat to mainland Italy; and there was even the very real risk that they would allow none but their own ships to sail through the narrow straits that on the one side separate Sicily from mainland Italy and on the other divide Sicily from North Africa. To put an end to this menace, the Romans forcibly ejected the Carthaginians from the island and, to make sure that they never came back, annexed it themselves. Sicily thus became the first segment of the Roman Empire, Rome's first province.

It was once again for reasons of defence that Rome decided on possession of parts of Spain, about the year 200 BC. Her object was to deny the Iberian peninsula as a base to any would-be aggressor against Italy. The Romans were hardly likely to forget that Hannibal the Carthaginian had mounted his assault on Italy from there.

Still later in the second century BC, it was once more the need for security, real or fancied, that caused the Romans to consolidate their power on the other side of the Adriatic, in the lands now occupied by Yugoslavia, Albania, and Greece.

At no time in their history were the Romans prepared to tolerate a strong large power as their nearest neighbour, if they could possibly prevent it. Accordingly they sought to establish across the Adriatic a system of small states, no single one of which would be strong enough to bring the others under its control and thus become a potential threat to Italy. The British preoccupation that no power in Europe should become a threat to Britain and her cross-channel policy of preventing such a threat come to mind. The Romans actually set up a balanced system of trans-Adriatic states in 196 BC, and for the next half century they went to considerable effort and trouble to maintain it. Ultimately, however, they had to concede that the preponderance of the state of Macedon was such that it was bound to upset any balance of power immediately east of the Adriatic; and it was then, in 146 BC, that the Romans first resorted to annexation in that area and got their first possessions in the Greek-speaking eastern end of the Mediterranean. It hardly looks like premeditated aggression.

Indeed it is not difficult to demonstrate that the Roman senate (and it was the senate that decided policy under the Roman Republic) was anything but eager to embark on wars of conquest.[4] The priestly law of Rome forbade wars of aggression in any case and, besides, it was undesirable for her to become responsible for the direct administration of territories beyond the seas. Therefore, in the senate's view, additional commitments were generally to be avoided: they should be accepted only if they contributed to the defence of Italy. Even when Hellenistic monarchs bequeathed their kingdoms to Rome, as they occasionally did in the second and first centuries BC, vaguely in the same way that Edward the Confessor is reported to have left England by testamentary disposition to William the Conqueror, the Roman senate did not invariably take up the legacy, even though it would have meant acquiring empire without effort. In 96 BC the senate avoided taking Cyrene at the first time of asking; and in 88 BC again it refused to accept Egypt, potentially a most valuable acquisition, when one of the Ptolemies offered that kingdom to Rome in his will. (Both countries did become Roman later.)

On the other hand, the Romans were prepared to accept such bequests of kingdoms whenever they thought it in their interest to do so: they obtained Pergamum in this way in 134 BC and Bithynia in 74 BC. They, of course, also showed little hesitation in seizing territories by conquest, whenever they felt that this was necessary in defence of their own security.

A defensive war is admittedly a highly subjective and very elastic concept, and it would be naïve to think that there were not often other and unavowed motives mixed up with the Romans' concern, genuine or feigned, for their own security. To serve their personal ambition, powerful individuals sometimes transgressed official policy. Roman commanders were capable of gratuitously attacking some backward tribe, in the certain knowledge that no government will determinedly discipline or readily repudiate a striking military success, even one achieved against orders; and Roman generals hungered for military success, even if cheaply won over primitive peoples, since it paved the way to the celebration of a triumph, that gorgeous processional spectacle which ensured a man's political future and, in the poet Horace's words, for a giddy moment made him the veritable equal of the gods.

Once Rome had become mighty, the temptation to use her power was overwhelming, always of course in the ostensible interests of her own security. Even the gentle Virgil, in the last century before Christ, proclaimed it Rome's duty to humble the proud in defensive wars;[5] and, a hundred years later, the Elder Pliny seems to have taken it casually for granted that Rome's mission should be to continue expanding her world empire and enforce a Roman peace.[6] Inevitably, therefore, the real reasons for annexations were only too liable to become mixed and murky. The Roman conquest of Britain in AD 43 is an instructive example. Officially it was another case of self-defence, an attempt to protect Roman possessions in Gaul against threats from across the Channel. But, in fact, it looks much more like a case of sheer aggression, possibly with the object of bolstering a precarious regime with a resounding military success abroad. Or it may even be that on this occasion there was an economic motive and that the Romans were attracted by the precious stones and the minerals with which the island was reputedly stuffed.

Economic motives, it must be admitted, do not seem to have normally affected Roman policy very much, even if they may have done so in the case of Britain. Usually it was not with some idea of acquiring markets or control of raw materials that Rome made additions to her Empire. Roman history cannot show anything really to parallel the kind of initiative allowed to the East India Company in Asia, the Company of Adventurers of London Trading into Africa, or the Hudson's Bay Company in Canada; and it follows that it also cannot show the sort of development that such initiative led to.

Nevertheless, economic considerations were by no means invariably ignored. The Romans were certainly not indifferent to the spoils of war or to the tribute that could be extracted from a subjugated people; and there might be other material gains, as well. Augustus' abortive attempt in 25 BC on the fabled land once ruled by the Queen of Sheba may have been due to a desire to obtain control of the desert caravan trade. Again, the Roman general, who informed a group of Gauls in AD 70, after a short-lived rebellion, that Rome had not gone into their country in the first place out of any desire for gain, sounds more disingenuous than convincing.[7] Furthermore, examples can be adduced of the Roman armed services being obliged to intervene when traders got into trouble in foreign parts. As early as the third century BC an army was sent across the Adriatic to protect Italian merchants who had ventured into today's Yugoslavia.

Nevertheless, despite many cases of unofficial and even of official abuses of power and of other forms of irresponsible behaviour, it is still the case that Rome did not pursue a policy of aggrandisement aiming at providing opportunities for enrichment in the first place. Her usual motive in annexing provinces was to strengthen her imperial defences. She was engaged on the search for secure, natural, and if possible impregnable frontiers and to that end carried her conquests forward to rivers, to mountain ranges, to deserts, and to sea-coasts.

The genesis of the British Empire, too, is to be sought in the annexation of transmarine territories. Traditionally it dates from 1583, the year when Sir Humphrey Gilbert laid claim to Newfoundland for the English crown; his expedition, however, ended up ineffectually, he himself being shipwrecked and losing his life. The real beginnings came a score or so of years later, with the establishment of the settlements in Virginia, and in particular the one at Jamestown in 1607.

But whereas it was a desire to feel secure that chiefly induced the Romans to annex areas and convert them into provinces, it was an eagerness to expand trade that acquired colonies for the English. In the first instance it was a competitive and enterprising search for trade routes to the Far East that took them into all parts of the Atlantic; and it led them into the venture that has come to be known as the first British Empire. In fact, in the case of the English, so predominant was the economic motive that with them trade, instead of following the flag as it is proverbially supposed to do, often preceded it.

The story of the earliest English colonies is a chronicle of private companies being authorized by royal charter to trade and, if need be, to found settlements and maintain armed forces in specified regions overseas, entirely at their own risk and at their own expense. The American colonies got their start in this way; and the beginnings of the Empire in India were not essentially different. The flag often did not arrive until somewhat later, when London decided to make the settlements thus brought into being the direct responsibility of the crown. Two of the thirteen north American colonies that fought Britain in the 1770s, Pennsylvania and Maryland, remained proprietary colonies almost down to the very outbreak of the War of Independence. Indeed, the flag sometimes took its time in arriving, the British government, like the Roman senate, being very reluctant to assume the additional commitments that enlargement of the Empire entailed. The Gambia and British Honduras had been British trading-posts for something like two hundred years before the British government showed much official interest in them. In their case relative obscurity and unhealthy climate might account for the neglect. But it is to be noted that considerable prodding of the London authorities was needed, before even so magnificent a country as New Zealand was officially pronounced British.

It can, of course, be readily admitted that in the case of the British, as of the Romans, other subsidiary reasons besides the principal one often played a part in the decision to make a colony. North Americans need no reminder that the flight from religious and other forms of persecution or that the compulsion the British felt themselves to be under to keep other powers out, such as the Spanish, the Portuguese, the Dutch, and the French, contributed to the birth of some colonies.

Especially in the growth of the so-called Second British Empire was the economic motive frequently combined with, and sometimes obscured by, other causes, a fact that enabled Sir John Seeley, late in the nineteenth century, to make his oft-quoted quip about the Empire seeming to have been acquired in a fit of absence of mind.[8]

Captain Cook went to the Pacific at the behest of the Royal Society as well as of the British admiralty: besides investigating and mapping the antipodean lands his task was to observe the transit of the planet Venus. And his successful accomplishment of both these missions did not so much open up a new area for trade, immediately anyway, as provide England with a dumping ground for her felons and gaolbirds.

Humanitarian zeal and religious fervour were also incentives. After 1807 Wilberforce's campaign against slavery and, later in the century, Dr. Livingstone's missionary explorations led to the enlargement of the Empire of Africa. Elsewhere, in places like Sarawak and Burma, a determination to free native peoples from tyrannical rulers or to terminate chaotic threats to international peace was the motive.

Strategic considerations also were often very much to the fore, needless to say: even Adam Smith, after all, allowed that "defence is of much more importance than opulence."[9] It was the need for military bases, provision points, and coaling stations to enable the Royal Navy, the Empire's instrument of power, to protect the route to India that brought places like Malta, Perim, and Aden under the Union Jack; and Britain's action in taking Cape Colony from the Dutch and Mauritius from the French after the Napoleonic wars was scarcely any different: it had the safeguarding of the Indian Ocean as its object.

Nevertheless, the thought of trade was always uppermost. Even where the British professed other reasons for their action, they were never entirely oblivious of the commercial prospects. In the Indian Ocean area for example, Stamford Raffles was eager to have Java as well as Mauritius annexed after the Napoleonic Wars, undoubtedly because of its economic possibilities, although his publicly announced reason was the desirability of liberating the Indonesians from what he described as the brutal and degrading rule of the Dutch. Fortunately no doubt for the reputation of perfidious Albion, Raffles's proposal was not carried out. He made up for it, however, by establishing Singapore as an entrepôt of trade; and, like Hong Kong, another island off the coast of Asia that became a

British colony in the nineteenth century, Singapore has been amazingly successful in the role.

Even in the late Victorian age, when liberal humanitarianism was very much in vogue, and nowhere more so than in the British Empire, the urge to annex colonies for purposes of trade was still very strong. The notorious "scramble for Africa" was largely a race for materials, markets, and money, and men like Cecil Rhodes ensured that Britain was a leading contender. In a single ten-year period she added well over a million square miles to her African possessions, an area equivalent in size to one-third of all Europe.

It will be seen, then, that even though empire began for both the Romans and the British when they expanded out of home territory into areas overseas, the start, growth, and ultimate wide extension of the two dominions were due to markedly differing causes. In one respect at least, however, there was similarity: both the Romans and the British, in the early stages of their empire-building, behaved as if empire existed largely, if not wholly, for the benefit of the imperial power.

For many years the main concern of the Romans was to get what they could out of their empire without bothering to consider whether they owed it anything in return. They may not have acquired their provinces in the first place for the sake of trade or commerce, but once firmly in possession of them, they proceeded to exploit and plunder them. They clearly did not go so far as to kill the geese that were laying the golden eggs, but they did despoil their nests with ruthless regularity.

The quality of the officials that the Roman Republic sent to its provinces was often objectionable, or worse. Some of its governors were avariciousness personified; and the natives they governed had no real safeguards against their cruelty or their methods of extortion, whether through local leading men in the provinces or through any other means. Gaius Gracchus in the second century BC made the revealing remark that wine-jars usually came back from the provinces filled with gold and silver;[10] and, a little later, a native of Dalmatia observed that the Romans did not send watchdogs or shepherds to guard their flocks, but ravening wolves.[11] Nor was the Dalmatian exaggerating. Cicero has left us a monumental picture of rapacity and viciousness in the person of Verres, the governor of Sicily, who plundered that province unconscionably in the first century BC. Admittedly Cicero was speaking as legal counsel for some of Verres's victims and may have exaggerated his account to some extent. But it is significant that elsewhere, in a work that has nothing to do with the obnoxious Verres and his nefarious activities, Cicero again condemns the excesses of provincial administration under the Roman Republic. His actual words are: "It is difficult to find words to express how fiercely we Romans are hated by the peoples of our Empire because of the wicked and wanton behaviour of the governors we have sent to them of recent years."[12]

One instrument that could minister to a governor's greed was the armed force under his command. The Roman Republic of the days before Christ, remarkably enough, did not have a standing army. This is all the more surprising in view of the fact that the Romans, in marked contrast with the British, always made the army their instrument of power. The practice of the Roman Republic was to raise field forces if, as and when they were needed, conscripting Roman citizens for the purpose. As it happens, field forces were needed with sufficient frequency for there always to be some of them in being somewhere. Even so, a standing army was officially lacking and this made any methodical or continuous planning for garrisoning and defence purposes impossible. Instead, the Roman senate decided each year where to send troops and in what numbers. The system was far from ideal, for the senate might misjudge the need or, even worse, it might play politics and vote troops only for those provinces where it suited the personal interest of its most influential members to have them sent. But the system was made to order for any unscrupulous person who happened to be governor of a province in a year when troops were posted to it. For, in the absence of permanent army quarters, he billeted the troops in the towns of the province. There the behaviour of the conscripts was regularly so unbridled and outrageous that most communities were prepared to pay virtually unlimited sums to be exempted from the evil of having troops billeted on them; and many governors allowed themselves to be bribed by wealthy cities, the wealthier the better, into quartering the soldiers elsewhere.[13]

And the governors not only gouged their provinces. They also often failed in their elementary duty of defending them. In the last century BC provinces were liable to be overrun by invading enemies; and it was not entirely inadequate provision by the Roman senate that was responsible for this state of affairs. It was the governors who were chiefly to blame, since they were prone to devote more of their attention to plundering their charges than to protecting them.

Exploitation, moreover, was not confined to the ranks of the Roman officials. It was also practised, and on a massive scale, by private individuals, operating from positions of favour and advantage and working under the protection of officialdom.

There was a seemingly ineradicable and abiding tradition among the aristocrats who constituted the governing class in the Roman Republic that it was their prerogative and privilege to manipulate the public state machinery for their own ends. As a consequence, the Roman senate was frequently under pressure from private individuals or groups, who were seeking to influence public policy for their personal profit. Sometimes such groups actually succeeded in promoting their economic fortunes with the backing of Roman expeditionary forces. In the late second century BC, for instance, a Roman tax-farming company was enabled to extend the range of its profit-making activities in Asia Minor.[14] And in the first century BC the future leader of the conspirators who assassinated Julius Caesar, the celebrated Brutus, Shakespeare's "noblest Roman of them all," did not hesitate to use public means, that is Roman troops, in order to collect, brutally and callously, debts that were owed to him privately.

It is true that the Roman senate did not always tamely yield to such attempts at undue influence and sinister persuasion. Sometimes it sought to curb the greedy designs of Roman capitalists. In 167 BC, for instance, it would not allow Roman corporations to lease the gold and silver mines of Macedon, giving two reasons for its refusal: first, the said contractors might oppress the natives, and secondly, they might build up private interests in Macedon too dangerous to contemplate.[15] But the slowness of communications and the long distances involved ran counter to any good intentions the senate may have had. It was a physical impossibility for it to supervise the provinces closely and continuously. The plain truth is that the administration of the provinces of the Roman Republic in the days before Christ was often deplorable and scandalous.

Moreover, the provinces suffered, like Rome herself, from the recurring crises of the last century of the Republic. These were the times of Sulla, of Pompey, and of Julius Caesar, when the whole Roman world was torn asunder by driving ambition and ruthless self-interest. The strongest and most sacred principles of government were threatened and Rome seemed about to fall apart. It was then that Augustus came, just in time to resolve a most dangerous crisis in the life of the Roman state; and he made it his task to restore the forces which had been the foundation of Roman life and government: he proceeded to revive respect for tradition and to extend Roman authority. Liberty was not revived. Ultimately, however, the application of Augustus' policies brought stability, peace, and the Roman civilization to the world.

This remarkable lease of life which Augustus succeeded in fashioning for the Roman Empire could, I suspect, have enheartened those British imperialists who, after the loss of the American colonies and the perils resulting therefrom, sought inspiration in Roman history. For down to 1776 the English colonies had been regarded largely as business arrangements, outlets for emigration, and sources of revenue. Most of them, as already noted, had been brought into being by private enterprise or religious dissent, not by acts of state; and this had given the colonists an independence of outlook that objected to the restrictive trading practices established by eighteenth-century England. They themselves did not seek to share in the life and government of the mother country, nor did England seek to attract them. In the eighteenth century, England pursued a mercantilist policy specifically designed to extract the maximum profit from her colonies. In Africa the British built up a virtual monopoly of the slave trade. In India there was rampant profiteering. Robert Clive's personal gains were admitted to amount to well over two million of today's dollars, and his calm announcement to an investigating committee of the House of Commons, "I stand amazed at my own moderation," suggests that other nabobs were getting more. All this obscured whatever merits there may have been in the British administration of those days. The court of law that finally, after many years of litigation, acquitted Warren Hastings of lining his own pockets could hardly have denied that his activities in Bengal had been intended to further, first and foremost, the interests of Britain. The corruption and the abuses of the East India Company, through which the British wielded their power in India at that time, were so notorious that they were just as violently denounced as those of Verres had been by Cicero: the mildest description that the playwright Sheridan could find for the company's rapacious officials was that they were "highwaymen in kid gloves." One source of the company's wealth was the fabulous profits made by smuggling opium from India to China; and the British government shared in these profits by taxing them.

It was the sobering loss of the American colonies that first obliged British statesmen to take stock. Undoubtedly there was a consciousness of neglect in past British colonial administration, and to some it appeared inevitable that all the colonies were soon to be emancipated. Meanwhile, however, the rallying of the Empire loyalists to Canada and the increasing adherence to British administration in India proved that the life of the Empire was not at an end after all. Simultaneously in Britain itself extraordinary transformations were taking place: these were the effects of the Industrial Revolution, which changed the life and orientation of the middle class, and the just as remarkable moral revolution, which aroused a religious, evangelical, and humanitarian enthusiasm, that had actually begun some generations earlier but only now became a mounting force of enormous importance leading, amongst other things, to the abolition of the slave trade. Moreover, influences coming from egalitarian France and the more urgent tendencies to liberalism in Britain itself caused profound changes in government and in its sense of responsibility to the governed. Adopting these new ethical and political attitudes, the British nation sought to rationalize its behaviour and to ask itself whether what it was doing was either morally right or materially worthwhile.[16] And it was in that age of missionary zeal that there emerged a view of the purpose of empire that was often compared at the time to that of Rome. The British Empire, it was thought, would bring a new era of peace in which unity and good government would spread over the world as in the best years of the Pax Romana.

Not that Britain was geographically well situated for such a role. Whereas Rome, centrally placed in her Mediterranean and Continental empire, was able to maintain relatively easy intercommunication and exchange with her provinces and become a nucleus from which romanization could spontaneously radiate, Great Britain could not form a similar link with her colonies, separated as she was before the steamship era by several weeks of travel from the nearest of them. Only later, when the Royal Navy developed swifter connections and made Britain less remote, could her accumulated store of civilization be effectively transmitted. Interchange with countries of high culture, such as India, then grew much more active, although for Britain imperial communications never ceased to be a very awkward strategic problem.

According to Thucydides,[17] fear, self-interest, and glory are the three mainsprings that move mankind, and all three are manifest and larger than life in the history of the two empires. Glory and honour, overlooked and rather forgotten today, were tremendous driving-forces. Cicero says that a thirst for glory steeled the Romans to fight their wars to victory;[18] and to many Victorians and Edwardians the road to Mandalay seemed something more than a mere traffic artery with commercial possibilities, while forbidden Lhasa became the goal of a British expeditionary force largely because it was there. Even today glory still retains its lustre in literature. *La Gloire de l'Empire* has been chosen, in irony or in earnest, by the brilliant French author, Jean d'Ormesson, for the title of his recent *tour de force* on an imaginary state and its rise to greatness.[19] And even the barest accounts of the daring enterprise and exploits of Elizabethan mariners, with their practical genius and their panache, have not lost their power to enthral.

If selfish exploitation with its limited scope had continued to characterize the Roman and the British Empires, they would have been little more than episodes in the human story: they would certainly not have made the impact that they unquestionably did on history. It was when the swashbuckling attitudes and the buccaneering habits of their earlier periods gave way to broader and more responsible approaches that they attained their true greatness. As a result, instead of remaining episodes, they became epochs.

II

Land of Hope and Glory

Both Rome and the British Empire, once they reached their culminating maturity, achieved that rarest phenomenon, a long interval of peace. The advantages of peace were immense in both empires, the more impressive when set against the previous circumstances of the subjected lands and peoples. It achieved security and prosperous order, and spread and preserved the highest forms of civilization of the time. Roman engineering and British technology changed and improved conditions in the world. But while the assimilating principles of Roman government led to a unity hitherto unknown in the ancient world, the British ideal of imperial trusteeship promoted nationalism and independence in the dependent countries.

The Roman Empire enjoyed its heyday in the first two centuries AD, during which period it reconciled its inhabitants to the idea of Roman rule and achieved a considerable degree of unity. It owed this success chiefly to its remarkable absorptive powers.

The Empire consisted of all sorts and conditions of men speaking a wide variety of tongues, professing all kinds of religious beliefs, different from one another in their ways of life and the cultural levels that they had attained, the Romans themselves being the ruling people. But the Romans were not an exclusive sect, intent on keeping all the lesser breeds beyond the pale. It was possible for the inferior, subject peoples of the Roman Empire to obtain Roman citizenship and thus themselves become Romans.

From their earliest beginnings the Romans had been quite willing to admit others to their citizenship, and for a very practical reason. As Philip the Fifth, king of Macedon in the third century BC, noted, the policy enabled them to outnumber their rivals.[20] But it was a generous as well as a practical policy and the Romans adhered to it, almost uninterruptedly, throughout their history.

Admittedly, to acquire Roman citizenship was a privilege, not an obligation, and in the first two centuries AD it was usually reserved for those who were prepared to talk, think, and act like Romans. Not that this meant forced, compulsory assimilation. Non-Romans were not obliged to learn Latin, become converts to Rome's religion, or adopt Roman customs. The Roman authorities were gratified if the native provincials did so, but they did not use compulsion. They preferred the carrot to the stick, relying chiefly on the force of attraction and privilege.

After 27 BC the maladministration of earlier years decreased markedly. Rome then ceased to be a Republic. She came under the rule of emperors, the first of whom, Augustus, reformed and revitalized her Empire. The evidence of improvement is clear and insistent. For one thing, the Roman provinces now obtained much greater security, and came to enjoy the boundless majesty of the Roman peace, to use the famous expression of the Elder Pliny; and the Elder Pliny ought to have known, for he was himself an official of the Empire, and in more than one province.

Now a province of the Roman Empire was not like a province of Canada. It did not have a legislature or anything resembling our provincial departments. It was, in fact, a geographical expression, not a political entity, but rather a collection of political entities. It was an aggregate of separate states, roughly comparable to our counties in size. Some of them were tribal, others urban. The Romans preferred and favoured the latter sort, the city-states as they have been called; but their Empire always contained many of the former, tribal communities whose degree of development did not warrant their organization as civic commonwealths of the municipal kind.

Thus a Roman province had no centralized administration except in the person of its frequently changed governor. Apart from him the only province-wide institution was a committee of dignitaries who could serve as a sounding-board for provincial complaints, but whose principal function amounted to little more than encouraging the natives to practise the Roman equivalent of standing to attention for the playing of "God Save the Queen." For prudential reasons Rome took care to have no provincial organs of administration: a province might be large enough to be dangerous. Instead, she granted self-government at local level, the level of the small states collectively making up the province. It was in them that the everyday tasks of administration were carried out by local councils and local officials chosen from the local inhabitants. These, manifestly, were not sovereign states, since they were not permitted to have a foreign policy of their own. But they were self-governing states; and even though in the last analysis they were controlled by Rome and paid taxes to her, their autonomy was surprisingly extensive. So was their security.

It was the merit of the emperor Augustus to make careful provision for the peace of the provinces. The Roman armed services in the days of the Republic had been curiously makeshift. Field forces had been raised as needed by conscripting Roman citizens, the inducted soldiers remaining on active service for the duration of the need. For this haphazard arrangement the emperor Augustus substituted a permanent standing army in which the men serving were not short-term draftees but career soldiers, who had signed on for a long period, usually for twenty-five years. The Roman imperial army Augustus thus created amounted in all to between 300,000 and 350,000 men in the first two centuries AD, and, although this is a very large figure by ancient standards, it would be wrong to think that it made the Roman Empire bristle with armaments. On the contrary, except in frontier districts, the army was usually very unobtrusive; and, even in the frontier districts, it was barely large enough to do its job. Partly for political prudence and partly for reasons of economy Augustus had made the imperial army as small as possible: it did not have any central reserve and, for certain stretches of the boundaries, it had to rely on the peace being enforced by neighbouring external tribes, paid to perform this task by the Roman authorities, in somewhat the same way that in the Indian Army the British supplemented the forces of their Empire with hired regiments of Gurkhas from Nepal.

On the whole, the Roman imperial army discharged its task with great efficiency during the first two centuries AD. Although fighting occurred not infrequently along the frontiers, the peace of the

inner provinces was largely undisturbed. Even the rigours of billeting decreased, since permanent camps were built for the troops
in many areas.

The Pax Romana thus enforced made the Roman Empire very
attractive for those who lived within its borders. It came to be
regarded as the region of ordered and civilized living, the *oikumene*
to use the Greek word commonly adopted to describe it, a word
that has now passed into our own language even if normally with
a rather different connotation. The world beyond was the barbarous region where lawlessness and anarchy were rife. Inside the
oikumene the rule of law prevailed.

It would be absurd, of course, to suggest that the millennium had
now arrived and that Augustus' reforms had transformed the mis-
ruled world of the Roman Republic into a Utopia of unalloyed hap-
piness. Things had undoubtedly improved, but they had not become
perfect. Opportunities for illicit money-making still existed, ranging
all the way from simple acceptance of bribes for favours to prostitu-
tion of the courts of justice, and worse. The Elder Pliny records having seen Lollia Paullina, who had been briefly married to the emperor
Gaius, gleaming with pearls and emeralds. The observant Pliny notes
their worth which, translated, would be about four million of today's
dollars, and these gorgeous jewels had not been lavished upon her
by her prodigal emperor husband, but, as she readily declared, had
been inherited from her grandfather, purchased (so Pliny indignantly
stressed) with loot from the provinces.[21]

One area offering scope for unscrupulousness was provincial
taxation. Rome's action in taxing her provinces at all seems shock-
ing to people nurtured on the doctrine of no taxation without representation. Yet it is difficult to see how there can be administration
without taxes.

One aspect of Roman tax-raising, however, seems very unfair. The
provinces in effect subsidized Italy, since its inhabitants paid much
less. And it was not just the varying levels of the taxes, but also their
very existence that was the source of evil. It opened the door to corruption and illegal exactions. Bribery to avoid discrimination or to
obtain privilege at the hands of Roman officials was common, and

the emperors could not stop it, no matter how conscientious they were, since really close control from Rome was impossible in an age of oar-propelled ships and animal-drawn wagons.

The historian Tacitus describes some of the ingenious but rascally tricks to which the officials resorted; and it was largely the activities of a money-grubbing procurator that provoked the bloody revolt of British tribes under Boudicca in AD 60/61.[22] That revolt was mercilessly suppressed, but in fairness one should add that the peccant procurator was immediately removed.

The Romans could claim, of course, that if they were taking taxes out of the provinces, they were also giving something in return: they were providing law, order, and peace. Cicero actually made this claim under the Roman Republic. But it could be put forward with far greater justice from the time of Augustus on and indeed Tacitus does so. The Roman imperial army did then provide security.

The peace was favourable to economic initiative, and enterprising men who knew how to exploit it naturally prospered. Fortunes were not made only by the ruthless exploiters of provincials. For men of enterprise, ability, and industry opportunities to prosper were not lacking; and, even though there were degrees of privilege, there is abundant evidence to show that all classes in the Empire might do well, if luck was on their side. Even for slaves the outlook was not altogether bleak. Inscriptions and literature alike reveal that many of them won their freedom and put it to good use.

Augustus insisted that the most privileged group in the Empire should be the Roman citizens.[23] In the first instance, this meant the inhabitants of Italy. But, by Augustus' day Roman citizens were also to be found in increasing numbers outside of Italy, in other words, in the provinces; and there they were better off than their non-Roman fellows. Their social status was higher; they enjoyed better protection at law; and their opportunities for preferment into positions of prestige and influence were infinitely greater. Nor did the Empire make particularly heavy demands upon them. In the first two centuries AD Roman citizens were seldom, if ever, conscripted for service in the armed forces. On the contrary, those of them who wished to do so could pursue the even tenor of their way, and might even pass their entire lives, without their peace and quiet ever being unduly disturbed. This, incidentally, was in marked contrast with the boisterous state of affairs that had prevailed in the Roman Republic during the last century BC, when the inhabitants of both Italy and the provinces had found civil wars, confiscations, and violence ruinously rampant.

But the well-ordered existence enjoyed by the Roman citizens was within the reach of all, since, as we have noted, all inhabitants of the Empire were eligible for the citizenship. In any province, once one of its small states became thoroughly Roman in language, habits, and outlook, it was likely to be designated as legally "Roman": that is, it ceased to be "peregrine" (foreign), its burgesses becoming Roman citizens. Provincial communities were continually acquiring Roman citizenship in this way.

For non-Roman individuals, as distinct from entire communities, there was another and a quicker route to the citizenship, by way of service in the Roman imperial army. Roman citizens could, of course, enlist if they had a mind to, but in fact they seldom did; and as the Empire got older, their reluctance to do so became ever more marked. It almost looks as if exemption from military service came to be regarded as one of the chief privileges of the citizen-born. They were the favoured group: and they complacently assumed that the invincible Empire needed no exertions from them. So the Roman imperial army came to be recruited from those who did not possess the Roman citizenship, that is from the provincials. But, if these men did not possess it when they joined the army, they certainly did when they left it. Some of them, the legionaries, got the Roman citizenship on enlistment; others, the auxiliaries, on their discharge. But one way or another, all who served obtained it. The army was thus a most potent factor in spreading the Roman citizenship. And not merely the citizenship. The army was also instrumental in spreading Roman ways and the Latin language. It was the provincial communities, the small states of the Empire, the local towns and municipalities that provided the backbone of the Roman army, supplying it not only with its other ranks, but also—and increasingly—with its centurions or junior officers. After their years of service these men, now become Roman citizens, settled down, not as a rule in Italy (which few of them knew at all well, since units of the Roman imperial army were not normally stationed in Italy during the first two centuries AD), but in the provinces, either in those provinces from which they had originally come or in those where they had done their service. Many of them, especially the ex-centurions, played an active part in the affairs of the provincial communities where they settled;[24] and once ex-soldiers had romanized a community, Roman citizenship would soon be forthcoming for it, even for its stay-at-homes who had never joined the army.

But although Roman citizenship improved men's status, it did not automatically elevate them to influence. The Romans were no believers in equality, and they reserved positions of eminence for the talented and the energetic, preferably among the well-to-do.[25] To that end, the Roman population was carefully stratified.

Below the all-powerful emperor at the summit stood the senatorial aristocrats, wealthy, haughty, and few: in the whole Roman Empire at any one time there were hardly more than seven hundred of them; and, no matter where they originally came from, once they became Roman senators, they tended to congregate in Italy. Below these senators there was a second aristocracy, it too quite wealthy but considerably more numerous. This was the equestrian order, with their numbers running into the thousands, although, being spread over the whole Empire, they could not have seemed particularly common. Together, the two aristocracies provided the Empire with its highest officials, administrators, and senior army officers, certain posts being exclusively reserved for senators, and others no less exclusively for equestrians.

The overwhelming mass of Roman citizens, however, were simply plebeians and had little or no say in the formulation and direction of policy, or in the appointment of officials, except possibly at the purely local level: and even there, in the municipal towns and other small states that made up the Empire, the voice of the ordinary man in the street did not sound very loudly. At the municipal, as at the higher, level an oligarchy was in control.

Thus the Roman Empire, quite obviously, was hierarchical, with Roman citizens, the preferred group, themselves divided into categories.

But this was no closed caste system. There was social mobility as well as social stratification. We have already seen that "peregrines," that is non-Romans, could, and did, become Roman citizens, and in ever-increasing numbers; and, within the Roman citizen body, plebeians who prospered could become members of the equestrian aristocracy. Equestrians, in their turn, might become senators. Finally, it was from the ranks of the latter that emperors were obtained. Nor was a man's ultimate origin seriously held against him. Even if race prejudice does occasionally manifest itself in the literature of the Roman Empire, as for instance in the writings of the satirist Juvenal, racism was certainly ignored in practice.

The entire process is illustrated by the evolution of the senatorial aristocracy. Just before the birth of Christ the Roman senate consisted almost exclusively of Italians, a very high proportion of them coming from the city of Rome itself. Yet by AD 68, when the first dynasty of Roman emperors came to its end with the death of the notorious Nero, many of the senators were no longer Italians but Roman citizens from the provinces, prevailingly the western provinces, such as Gaul and Spain. Such provincial senators seem to have come at first from Italian families that had emigrated into the overseas provinces, years and in some instances centuries earlier. But soon unadulterated provincials, from families without any Italian background whatsoever, began to find their way into the senate at Rome, and, once started, this trend gathered speed. By AD 100 it was not merely the western provinces that were supplying senators, but the eastern ones as well, the ones that normally, and with full Roman encouragement, spoke Greek. By AD 200 senators from Italy were no longer in the majority.

The equestrian aristocracy was equally diversified. Its members came from every nook and cranny of the Roman world, some of them being even of servile extraction.

Thus the aristocracies from which the high imperial officials were obtained might be anything in origin. The emperor's body of advisers, for instance, the *consilium principis* as it was called, contained notables from many different regions of the provinces; and these were the men right next to the seat of power.

Governors of provinces, commanders of legions, and various other lofty dignitaries were all likely to be men of provincial extraction. Moreover, the policy of not sending a man to a post in his province of origin, in case he might build up a home power base there, had the effect of thoroughly scrambling the aristocracy. The co-opting of provincial notables undoubtedly deprived the provincial communities of many men of talent, but it also meant that with the passage of time the governing class in the Roman Empire became cosmopolitan to an extent not even remotely attained in the British.

The Roman emperors themselves, being regularly drawn during the first two centuries AD from the ranks of the Roman senate, conform to the pattern. By AD 100 a man from the western provinces had become emperor: he was from a family, originally Italian, that had emigrated many years earlier to Spain. By AD 200 there was an emperor of provincial birth from Africa who seems to have had no Italian blood whatever in his veins. Until then all the emperors of provincial extraction had come from the Latin-speaking west. But soon after AD 200 the purple of the Caesars was being worn by someone from the Greek-speaking east, in the person of a Syrian.

And these emperors were cosmopolitan as well as provincial. Antoninus Pius (AD 138–61), who had a Gallic background, was married to a woman with a Spanish one. Antoninus' successor, Marcus Aurelius (AD 161–80), also had a Spanish background, while his wife's was very mixed: Spanish, Gallic, and Italian. Septimius Severus (AD 180–211), the emperor from Africa, had a woman of Carthaginian or Libyan origin for his first wife and of Syrian for his second. But despite their heterogeneous backgrounds these emperors were not generally regarded, and certainly did not regard themselves, as non-Roman. On the contrary, they were much more likely to be positively ultra-Roman in sentiment. Septimius Severus, for instance, who is said to have been more at home in Punic than Latin, gives the impression of being intent on conforming completely to Roman mentality and conduct. It was with his active encouragement that the famed jurists Papinian and Ulpian developed Roman law, Rome's most precious bequest to later ages, into its most mature and classical form. Septimius' outlook was certainly anything but narrowly north African. His aim was to promote the good government and welfare of the Roman Empire as a whole.[26] Nor was Septimius alone in such devotion to Rome. Some little time after him, an Arab became emperor, and the most notable event of his reign was the celebration, with éclat and splendour, of the one thousandth anniversary of Rome's foundation.

Nothing, of course, could illustrate the success of the Roman policy of assimilation so spectacularly as the rise of provincials to the absolute pinnacle of power. It meant more than mere acculturation of indigenous natives. It implies genuine integration; and as Sir Ronald Syme stressed in a former and very notable series of Whidden Lectures, this was a fact of cardinal importance.[27] In the past Romans had gone out from Italy into the provinces; now in due course and in the fullness of time, provincials in their turn were coming to Rome, there to reinforce and renew the governing classes.[28]

It is this remarkable and widespread assimilation of the upper strata that so sharply differentiates the Roman Empire from the British, where unification of this kind did not occur. Like the Romans, Englishmen did go out into the empire. But there was little traffic in the opposite direction, no reverse flow, so to speak. The Roman world, like modern America, was an extraordinary melting pot, and in it the pervasive Roman ingredient was a unifying factor. The common ground for its men and women, the one thing that characterized them, was their adoption of Rome's language, manners, and outlook: they could all become Roman citizens and consider themselves Roman.

It might be argued that successful assimilation of this kind prevailed only in the upper levels of the population and that the situation must have been very different among the common people. As it happens, little is known about the latter, apart perhaps from those living in Rome itself, and they actually are proved by inscriptions on tombstones to have been quite cosmopolitan. The lower classes in the Empire at large are seldom mentioned in Roman literature, and they did not record anything in their own native tongues. Not that the absence of documents in languages other than Latin and Greek means that the native vernaculars had died out in the first two centuries AD. They certainly continued to be spoken, for they came to the surface again in the fourth century AD, when the Roman Empire was breaking up and revitalization movements, as the anthropologists call them, got under way. Probably the lower orders were not as cosmopolitan and commingled as the aristocracies. The poor could not afford to move far from their places of origin and were not likely to meet, and intermarry with, their opposite numbers from other parts of the Empire.

In this connection, however, the effect of the army should not be overlooked. For a considerable part of the first two centuries AD, the emperors thought it dangerous to have soldiers serve in their countries of origin; and by serving away from their native heaths, the soldiers became much more romanized than they would otherwise have been. Inevitably, too, they formed unions with women from the districts where they served and they must have helped to romanize them to some extent. If the policy of having soldiers serve far from their original homes had been persisted in, romanization would probably have made still more extensive and penetrating headway throughout the Roman world. It might have been as thoroughgoing everywhere as it came to be in the Iberian peninsula and in Gaul, where, despite the survival of Basque in Spain and the continuance of spoken Celtic near Paris and elsewhere until the fourth and even the fifth century AD,[29] the triumph of Latin was so overwhelming that it has remained as the official language, in the form of Spanish, Portuguese, and French, right down to the present day.

In any case, one should not attach undue importance to the slowness, or even the failure, of romanization among the lower orders. In any community the group that set the fashion and decided what attitude should be adopted towards the Empire, was the well-to-do minority. They were the leaders of their communities, and on the whole they were pro-Roman.

One might well ask why. The glib reply that in those days the force of nationalism was much less strong than it is today is not the full explanation.[30] It undoubtedly played a much smaller part in the ancient world than in the modern; but its absence does not sufficiently account for the Roman absorptive success.

It is more useful to consider the positive aspects of the Roman Empire. As we have seen, it was regarded as synonymous with the inhabited, civilized world. Those who entered it, whether forcibly or voluntarily, from the outer and more barbarous reaches had come in from the cold, so to speak. What they found was a broad expanse of peace and a fair semblance of order, where rights of property were safeguarded and the well-to-do were bound to be persons of consequence in their own communities and might even enjoy the prospect of still wider horizons. Even those who did not rise high in the Empire's service could not help but be conscious of their membership in a great political organization, where Roman practicality had improved upon Greek instruction to achieve remarkable progress in the art of civilized living. The Roman policy that favoured material betterment, and the Roman peace that made it possible, caused all provincial communities, urban and tribal alike, to remain contented with their lot.

The cities, which it was the conscious aim of Roman policy to develop, were especial showplaces of the Roman achievement, with their chequer-board layouts, their substantial public buildings, their monumental squares, their luxurious bathing establishments, and their amenities of every kind. The striking spectacle they presented was cause for justified civic pride. Life in them was no doubt to a certain extent standardized, but it was a standard at a higher level than the comparatively low level of technology on which it was based might have led one to expect. To this day one cannot gaze without feelings of surprise and wonder at such monuments as the temple of Jupiter at Baalbek in Lebanon, the triumphal arch at Timgad in Algeria, the amphitheatre at Nîmes in France, the theatre at Merida in Spain, the thermal establishment at Bath in England, the palace at Spalato in Yugoslavia, or the remains of the Danube bridge at Turnu Severin in Romania. The engineering achievement is the more impressive when one considers the network of Roman roads that connected the cities and the magnificent aqueducts that converged on them, bringing in their water supply "as on triumphal arches," as has been finely said.

Over this whole vast area of ordered living, people and goods could, and did, move with great facility and in confident security. True, there were taxes to pay and even some duties on goods in transit; but they seem very mild compared with modern governmental levies. Even though the ordinary man was debarred from political activity and obliged to show respect to his superiors, any man of energy and talent might become one of the superiors. Think of the amazing career of a certain Marcius Agrippa about the year AD 200. This person had started life as a slave, but after winning his freedom he made his way into the equestrian aristocracy and later, more surprisingly, into the senatorial: he even became consul at Rome and governor of more than one important province.[31] Marcius Agrippa was clearly quite exceptional. The average man certainly did not have so heady, enterprising, and exhilarating an experience, and probably felt himself confined to the pursuit of the normal, the unexciting, and the routine. But even if life was humdrum and stereotyped, it could also be comfortable. Edward Gibbon summed it all up two hundred years ago in a famous exaggeration: "If a man were called to fix the period in the history of the world during which the condition of the human race was most happy and prosperous, he would, without hesitation, name that which elapsed from the death of Domitian to the accession of Commodus"[32] (in other words, AD 96 to 180).

It was their contemplation of the panorama of empire that attracted and caught men's imaginations and accounts for their ready acceptance of the notion of a Roman Empire. Even its Greek-speaking inhabitants were won over, despite the determined resistance to romanization which conviction of their own cultural superiority prompted them to offer. When Aelius Aristides, a prominent literary figure of the second-century Greek-speaking world, produced a celebrated oration praising Rome in the most fulsome terms, he was not simply an obsequious time-server. For all the extravagance and flattery of his language, he was undoubtedly saying what many of his compatriots felt.[33]

This was the general attitude of the propertied classes throughout the Empire; and the masses were content to follow their lead, or if they did not actively subscribe to the sentiment they were at least content to tolerate the system.

Land of Hope and Glory

Even the barbarians living beyond the frontiers were aware of the advantages the Empire conferred. Many of them acquiesced readily, and even eagerly, in their own incorporation, and cases are known of some who actually petitioned for it.[34] Once within the Empire's borders they settled down without more ado, even at a time when the borders were unusually disturbed, as in Marcus Aurelius' reign (AD 161–80). Even in the third century AD, when a time of troubles came upon the Empire and insurrectionary, separatist movements broke out, the numerous uprisings were not so much revolts against Roman authority as protest movements reasserting the Roman character of the Empire, which the rebels thought was being undermined. Later, in the fourth and fifth centuries, when the barbarian invaders (Germans mostly), who had ravaged the Empire in the third century AD, returned to dismember it completely, they regularly disclaimed any intention or desire of destroying it. On the contrary, whenever they managed to seize and occupy parts of the Empire, they promptly recognized the "Roman" emperor as the legitimate sovereign authority of the very lands they had annexed. Such was their respect for the Roman Empire and for what they believed it to represent.

The magnetic attraction of the British Empire was not as potent, or at any rate not as durable, as that of its Roman paradigm. The Roman Empire, like the dawn goddess's lover Tithonus, went on for centuries. Over seven hundred years elapsed between the annexation of Sicily and the overthrow of the last "Roman" emperor in the west, named Romulus Augustulus ironically enough, in AD 476. The Greek-speaking eastern half, proudly proclaiming itself Roman and offhandedly referring to the Romans proper as Italians, lasted even longer, until that fatal 29th of May in 1453 when the Osmanli Turks burst into Byzantium. And in the minds and memories of men the empire lived longer still. For centuries, medieval and renaissance Europe nursed the notion, and paraded the formality, of a Holy Roman Empire whose demise, it was believed, would bring the coming of the Antichrist. Perhaps not everyone will agree that, when the Holy Roman Empire was officially pronounced dead on the 6th of August in 1806 and found Napoleon at the height of his glory, medieval fears were justified. But no one will deny that the impact made by the Roman Empire can fairly be measured by the hundreds of years that it remained a forlorn ideal and a nostalgic aspiration.

The British Empire was very short-lived and almost transitory by comparison. The American colonies formed part of it for less than 200 years. India remained in it rather longer: yet Clive's victory at Plassey occurred less than two centuries before 1948. Many of the African colonies needed much less than even a hundred years for their emancipation. Even so, it is probably remarkable that the British Empire should have lasted as long as it did. After the loss of the American colonies in 1776 its prospects must have seemed dim indeed, despite the continuing allegiance of Canada to the British crown. But by one of those curious coincidences of which history can show so many, developments at once conspired to give birth to a second British Empire. These were the consolidation of British power in India, the opening-up of the antipodean lands, and the birth of the Industrial Revolution.

When James Watt, observing a boiling kettle in his grandmother's kitchen in the 1760s, was inspired to see how Newcomen's crude experiments could be improved into a workable steam engine, modern technology was born. It is true that, for something like 10,000 years before that, man had possessed a technology of sorts. It had been in the year 8000 BC or thereabouts that palaeolithic man had stopped being an animal who simply seized and grabbed whatever he needed from nature and became a food producer himself, providing for his own needs. Even so, the primitive technology that he began to develop in those far-off stone age days did not advance very fast or very far. For centuries progress was very slow. From 8000 BC to the 1760s AD man's output of goods and services *per capita* did not increase to any startling or spectacular extent. Even the Roman Empire, with all its amazing engineering triumphs, had been technologically stagnant. Why it should have been so has been much debated. There is general agreement that it was not because of a too great reliance on slave labour and its lack of incentives. Perhaps, as one of our most distinguished Whidden lecturers suggested, it was due to an ignorance of algebra.[35] Whatever the reason, it was not until the 1760s that technology took the great leap forward that made the Industrial Revolution possible, and thereafter the pace was rapid. Its effect was to transform the face of the world, and Great Britain was the pioneer and for a long time virtually monopolized the process. She was the workshop of the world, as a popular saying of the last century expressed it.

That this had much to do with the success of the British Empire is obvious. It was industrial strength that enabled Britain with her relatively small population to overcome Napoleon, to become mistress of so far-flung an empire, to maintain control over long and complex sea routes, and to hold her empire with few forces. The peacetime British Army seemed contemptibly small to the German Kaiser; the part of it stationed in India, easily its largest component, numbered considerably fewer than 100,000 men. And to the argument that it was the Royal Navy rather than the Army that was the instrument of power, it can be replied that personnel serving in the fleet were not overwhelmingly numerous either. It was the quality and range of the technology developed by Great Britain that made the Pax Britannica possible.

Some historians go further and argue that her advanced technology kept Britain's empire together and made the overseas territories content to remain a part of it.[36] It provided them with irrigation works, factories, steel plants, and all the myriad products spawned by the Industrial Revolution; with hospitals, schools, and universities; and above all with the communications (the ports, roads, bridges, railways, telegraphs, and telephones) without which primitive communities had little chance of entering the modern world. For long Britain alone could supply the sinews for the defence of the Empire, and she did so, virtually unaided almost down to the very end of the nineteenth century. The Empire was, quite literally, dependent upon the land of hope and glory.

Things changed, of course, during the nineteenth century. Long before the outbreak of World War I the industrial supremacy of Britain had begun to falter in face of the growing industrial strength of Germany, the United States, and more recently Japan; and by the time of the first world war her technological superiority was clearly a thing of the past. This was to be only too fatally demonstrated in World War II, when the Japanese sank two of the mightiest war-ships in the Royal Navy with comparative ease and then, immedi-ately afterwards, went on to capture Singapore with forces markedly inferior in numbers to the colony's defenders.

But to recognize the fall of Singapore on that dire 15th of February in 1942 as betokening unmistakably the end of the British Empire, even though Britain and the Commonwealth were ultimately to emerge victorious from the cataclysmic contest of which it was but one incident, does not mean that the Empire began and ended with technology. It was not a structure bolted and rivetted together merely by Sheffield steel.

The smallness of the forces with which it was held and the will-ingness of its peoples and nations, once they obtained independ-ence from Britain, to remain closely associated with her in the Commonwealth indicate that the imperial tie depended on some-thing more than a certain skill in mechanical, electrical, and civil engineering. Britain's subjects, like Rome's centuries earlier, found the empire, of which they formed a part, by no means totally unac-ceptable. Indeed some native peoples, the islanders of Fiji, Tonga, and the Gilbert and Ellice group for instance, actually joined the Empire of their own accord, in the same way that alien tribes had sometimes sought admission into the Roman Empire. But the attrac-tiveness did not lie exclusively in the material sphere. Countries like Australia, New Zealand, much of Canada, and parts of Southern Africa felt an attachment to Britain because she had supplied them with the immigrants who settled in them. Clearly, for the Indian sub-continent, for large parts of Africa, and for the islands of the south seas, this could not be the explanation; and it may be doubted whether it was the entire explanation even for the white dominions.

Language had something to do with the matter. English was the mother-tongue for most of the inhabitants of the white dominions. This, once again, was not the case with India and the native colonies. But it is probably true that all of them appreciated the gift of her lan-guage from Britain. English as a world tongue enabled them to participate more fully and more easily in international society and to play some role on the world stage; it introduced them to the world of English literature and a much better understanding of English ideals and institutions; and it supplied them with a lingua franca.

But it was not only by bestowing her language any more than by bestowing her technology that Britain reconciled the countries overseas to her imperial role. She won them far more by the methods and, above all, by the spirit and purpose of her rule.

The methods, as it happens, bore some resemblance to those of the Romans. The imperial worthies of England, and especially the men who fashioned the second British Empire, almost without exception had had a classical education, and their study of Latin and Greek had made them very familiar with the Roman Empire as depicted by Tacitus and others. Their interpretation of it, whether fanciful or not, provided inspiration and some instruction, even though theirs was a very different world and a very different age—an age familiar with the lessons of 1776, exposed to French egalitarian doctrines, and imbued with the spirit of Victorian humanitarianism.

The Romans could teach them something about the responsibility of governors to the governed and also something about methods of indirect rule. In fact, like the Romans, the British availed themselves of the ruling and administrative elements already existing in the overseas territories. British Residents, Political and District Officers and Commissioners and other officials regularly sought to work through sultans, emirs, tribal chiefs, and similar native authorities. But the British faced a situation of infinitely greater complexity than the Romans ever did. Extreme differences of climate and environment presented them with races and cultures that were starkly unlike one another. No uniform system of dealing with them was possible, and no precedents existed, not even in the Roman Empire which was the only previous one to be even remotely similar to their own. To cope with the bewildering diversity with which they were faced the British were forced to improvise. The system that they devised varied all the way from rudimentary paternalism in the most primitive areas to responsible government, with features that Britain herself thought worthy of imitation in the white dominions. In India some states had representative government granted by Britain, while the princely ones resembled the so-called client kingdoms of the Roman Empire: their rulers, maharajahs, rajahs, and princes, recognized Britain as the paramount power. But in many particulars British administrative methods were quite dissimilar from Roman, and the results they produced were naturally also very different. Integration of the Roman kind was conspicuous by its absence.

Of course, the hereditary nature of the British monarchy made it impossible for a Canadian, an Australian, a New Zealander, or even a princely Indian, to ascend the throne at Westminster in the way that Spaniards, Africans, and others had become emperors at Rome. But there was theoretically no reason why truly eminent sons of the overseas empire should not have occupied other lofty posts. Yet they did not do so. The British Prime Minister, and his Cabinet ministers too, regularly came from Great Britain. Admittedly to become prime minister or cabinet members at Westminster men from the overseas empire would have had to stand for election to parliament in the old country, and individuals have occasionally and successfully done so, including a native or two of India. But it is hardly likely that they would ever have got to the highest positions in the land. As long ago as the fourteenth century the English people showed by their rejection of Piers Gaveston how they resent authority being wielded over them by the overseas subjects of their own monarch. The British Prime Minister in the earlier part of this century who was born in Canada of an Ulster background is the exception to prove the rule, and Bonar Law, be it remembered, had not been long out of his cradle when he left Canada for good to settle in Britain.

It should not have been beyond the wit of man to devise a political system that would have harnessed and exploited to advantage the best and most capable talents from all over the Empire. Yet the only overseas members who went to Westminster in their own right were Irishmen, remarkably enough.

Only during the supreme crisis of war was there some change. An imperial war cabinet composed of the dominion prime ministers was improvised in World War I; and in the cabinets that directed the British effort in both the world wars of this century, the overseas countries had some representation, Smuts of South Africa participating in that of World War I and Casey of Australia in that of World War II. But even this small degree of integration ended with the fighting; and the white dominions had their own delegations at the peace conferences and entered the League of Nations after the first, and the United Nations after the second, world war as separate members.

Moreover, dominion abilities were not much used at lower levels of administration than the cabinet. In the main, officials for imperial posts came from schools like Eton and Harrow, or the universities of Oxford and Cambridge.

One result of the exclusion of the dominions was to throw them back upon themselves. Able men channelled their political ambitions into the service of their own communities rather than into the service of the Empire as a whole; and the countries overseas thus retained virtually exclusive use of the abilities and talents of their own distinguished sons. This brought them incalculable benefit, but it also contributed powerfully to the growth of local nationalisms.

This aspect of British imperial affairs is in striking contrast with the situation in the Roman Empire. It is explained by the entirely different purposes the two empires were seeking to serve. The aim of the Romans was assimilation, that of the British almost exactly the opposite. They came to conceive their task as being the protection and the advancement of the native races. Where the Romans tolerated local languages, cultures, and ways of life, the British promoted them, insisting that the development of the indigenous peoples came first. Undoubtedly there was some hope of economic advantage mixed in with their policy of assisting the less developed countries to political maturity. But, on the whole, their impulse to promote native well-being prevailed; and the spokesman of the British government in 1923, a Conservative government as it happened, was quite sincere in saying: "His Majesty's Government think it necessary to record their considered opinion that the interests of the African nation must be paramount.... His Majesty's Government regard themselves as exercising a trust on behalf of the African population."[37]

Thus the British were deliberately preparing the native races, first for representative government, and then after that for responsible government. The British officials in the overseas dependencies themselves tried to set an example of the kind of administration that they hoped the native peoples would ultimately establish. The British Residents, District Officers, and magistrates conscientiously strove to be objective, fair, and incorruptible. As one of them recorded: "We see ourselves as Trustees who are to hand over their trust at the earliest practical moment."[38]

There was perhaps some cant in their moral arrogance, and many of them could undoubtedly be described as smug, stand-offish, and insufferably superior. They could, however, rarely be described as dishonest or callously indifferent.

The pace of progress towards full responsible government varied from one country to another in the British Empire. A series of reforms had brought India very close to the status of the white dominions, when World War II broke out and probably caused some postponement of the final step. In Africa where conditions seemed less mature, the transition was slower.

In the case of both India and Africa, and of the colonies generally, impatient critics, many of them in Britain itself, levelled charges of dilatoriness on the part of officials and of bad faith on the part of the government in Westminster.[39] Others, however, remembering the laboured birth of responsible government in Canada and Australia and noting what has been happening recently in certain regions, wonder whether the approach towards self-government may not in some cases have been too swift. In any case, no one will deny that the Empire did represent an amazing experiment in human organization.

But the British attempt to convert native peoples into modern nations ended as the Roman attempt to transform native peoples into Romans had ended, in the loss of empire.

III

Westward the Course of Empire

Both the Roman and the British imperial powers disintegrated under the changing conditions within them. In Rome, the constant adoption of new elements from the provinces, which had been an invigorating factor in Roman life, got out of hand and became excessive. The character and the structure of Roman government were gradually flooded with foreign practices and remained Roman only in name before it collapsed. The British imperial government was caught in the ferment of nationalisms which it had encouraged and which precipitated its dissolution.

The disintegration of the Roman Empire has been a theme for discussion and speculation for the past fifteen hundred years, in fact ever since the days of Saint Augustine.

The usual explanation, that it perished because it was laid in ruins by repeated attacks of invading "barbarians," Germans for the most part, while no doubt true, appears much too superficial and limited. It does not reveal why primitive and disunited barbarians, and not particularly numerous barbarians either, were able to wreak their will and make a mockery of the boundless majesty of the Roman peace. No single cause can give a complete answer. An overriding explanation must go deeper. I suggest that it is to be found in the way that the Empire was gradually transmuted into something new and strange, so that as a *Roman* empire it simply ceased to be. An increasing and ultimately an overwhelming flood of men, attracted by the prestige of Rome but of outlook different from hers, infiltrated into the centre of power. The quality, system, and principle of Roman government were diluted in this foreign stream, and the governing class, no longer based on Roman traditions and purposes, became in fact un-Roman.[40]

Originally, Romans were to be found only in Rome and its

immediate environs, in the part of Italy known as Latium. They were a group of farmer-soldiers, devoted to their own community and dedicated to its survival. That survival, they were convinced, depended upon a right relation with its gods and upon their own willingness to submit to the authority deriving from high birth, valour, and service to Rome; and out of this conviction they were ready to defer to the policies of their leaders and to follow them with obedience, discipline, and tenacity. Within their own community they were guided by a legalistic instinct for what was customary; outside it, they were prompt to defend it, and to assert it. And the name Rome summed up their community: their aspirations, laws, hopes, and ambitions all centred on Rome.

By the last century BC they had expanded from Latium all over the Italian peninsula, and where they had not installed themselves as settlers they had annexed and incorporated. But they accomplished this spread over Italy without becoming themselves radically changed. No matter how different in language, outlook and general culture the other peoples of Italy originally were from the Romans (and some of them were very different), close and enduring contact had made it possible for all of them over the centuries to coalesce without basically altering the character of the Romans themselves. No doubt developments, the passage of the years, and the admixture of Italian elements made the Romans of the first century BC somewhat different in character from those of the sixth and fifth. Even so, a real fusion of Romans and Italians had taken place. It had largely meant the conversion of the Italians to Roman viewpoints, habits of thought, and patterns of life. The two could not be easily distinguished from one another, and in fact the Greek-speaking inhabitants of the eastern end of the Mediterranean did not make any distinction between them. By the beginning of the Christian era the unification was complete, and henceforth all Italians could fairly be reckoned Romans.

Unification of provincials with Romans, however, did not prove similarly possible. The Romans did have a remarkable talent for assimilating others; but the tribes and peoples of their Empire were too multifarious, the distances, both physical and spiritual, separating them from Italy were too great, and the number of Italians settled in their midst too small to make their total romanization possible. Accordingly the fusion of old Romans and new, of Italians and provincials, of westerners and easterners, and of all the assorted types within the Empire was never fully accomplished. The ripples caused by a stone thrown into a pond get smaller and feebler the further they are from the point of impact. So it was in the Roman Empire, despite repeated and frequent extensions of the Roman citizenship, which reached their climax c. AD 212 when the emperor Caracalla decreed that all freeborn inhabitants of the Empire, with very few exceptions, were henceforth to be Roman citizens, in other words officially Romans.

At the time of Caracalla's decree much of the Roman Empire must have been still unassimilated. The diverse peoples and races that composed it had not been completely made over; and variations in the duration of their submission meant differing degrees in the extent of their acculturation. Even in the most thoroughly romanized provinces, those of the Iberian peninsula and Gaul, many of the lower classes could have been only superficially affected, if that, to judge from the survival of the local vernaculars into the Late Empire.

A high degree of romanization had indeed taken place among the upper classes all over the Empire. But even in their case it was never absolute, no matter how self-consciously Roman a provincial notable might try to become. Provincials might, and indeed they often did, become fervent Roman patriots: one thinks of Julius Classicianus from Gaul, the servant of the Empire in Britain; of Licinius Sura from Spain, the intimate of the emperor Trajan; of Plutarch, the engaging writer of biographies, and of Herodes Atticus, the noted philanthropist, both of them from Greece. Yet they must always have been Romans with a difference. Their way of looking at things, even if they were not always aware of it, would not be exactly the same as the Romans' way; and the vestigial remains of their alien background assumed importance as, in the course of time, age-old Roman institutions and customs changed. The Roman senate itself was greatly altered as the result of the steady infiltration of provincials into its ranks.

Transmutations of national character and culture are by no means easy to trace. Change of language, even when it can be clearly documented and measured, is not in itself conclusive, as English-speaking Irishmen abundantly prove. What really matters is intellectual, emotional and spiritual re-orientation, and this is not easily quantifiable. It can be revealed, however, by men's customs and practices.

One age-old Roman habit, to which Cicero under the Republic and Tacitus under the Early Empire call attention,[41] was that of having high state officials serve indifferently in either civilian or military posts. One year a man might be an important administrator; in the next he might serve as a general. Normally the Roman emperors continued this republican practice, since they were not eager to create specialists who might too easily be mistaken for symbols of state authority.[42] Nevertheless, in the first two centuries AD a tendency to depart from the venerable practice gradually developed. Functionaries began to be reassigned to the same areas or to similar tasks, once they had acquired experience and demonstrated competence in them. An army officer who did well in a certain province was likely to find himself posted to it time and again: Agricola, for instance, was ordered to Britain repeatedly during the first century AD. A civilian, who possessed a certain type of expertise, was likely to be called upon to exercise it on more than one occasion: the Younger Pliny, for instance, served on several financial boards about the beginning of the second century AD. As time went on, specialization of this kind led, logically and inexorably, to the separation of civilian and military functions; and, from the middle of the second century AD on, it proved possible for a man to have an all-military career, without serving much, if at all, in civilian posts.

The consequences of this may have been unforeseen, but they were certainly far-reaching. Whereas previously a serving soldier could hardly rise above the rank of centurion, from the late second century AD on he could advance into the highest officer class; and from there it was but a short step to the imperial purple.

This was soon revealed. In AD 235 a Thracian peasant, who had passed his entire adult life in military camps, was acclaimed by his troops as emperor of the Romans. Thus, a man practically without any experience of civilian life had come to occupy the most powerful position in the Roman, and indeed in the then known world.[43] Ominous as this development was, it became even more so a quarter of a century later when senatorials were completely debarred from serving as officers. For the quality of the troops was by then becoming increasingly dubious.

By the third century AD military disorder had made a vastly increased army necessary. According to Lactantius, a contemporary, the army had grown by AD 300 to a size four times as large as it had been under the emperor Augustus at the time of Christ. This would mean a standing army of a million men or more, a staggering and impossible figure. Lactantius must be exaggerating. Nevertheless, it is quite certain that by his day the army had been greatly enlarged. The emperor Septimius Severus had found it necessary to increase it with a central reserve about AD 200; and just over half a century later the emperor Gallienus strengthened the army still further by adding a large cavalry striking force to it.

The enlargement of the army did more than just revive the horrors of billeting. It created a most awkward problem, since it came at the precise moment when recruits of average good quality were proving difficult to find. From AD 212 on, when all inhabitants of the Empire had been declared Roman citizens, the law of diminishing returns applied. Those born with the Roman citizenship had rarely volunteered for the standing army of the Roman Empire. Provincials, however, had been willing to do so since by serving in the army they obtained the citizenship. But now in AD 212 this principal inducement for them to join up was abolished at a single stroke. Consequently the army had to get its soldiers, more and more, from the wildest and most primitive districts, if not from outside the Empire altogether. It even found itself obliged to accept recruits who, in an earlier age, would have been rejected for failing to meet its physical standards. Under these circumstances, it would not be long before the army would no longer deserve to be called Roman: it would be largely barbarized. Yet this was the force to which was entrusted the defence of the Roman Empire against external attack and the defence of Roman values and traditions. One may well suspect that the military disorder that made the larger army necessary was due, at least in part, to the quality of its recruits.

The vicious circle was thus complete; and the gravity of the situation was all the greater owing to the tendency for officers to come up through the ranks, often without any other qualification than rude fighting ability. The centurions, the real professionals of the Roman imperial army, instead of being reasonably good types from developed and romanized provincial communities, were now likely to be of the same stamp as the men they led: rough, uncouth, and brutal. It is quite literally true that, from the third century AD on, such men were only too likely to make their way into the highest positions in the Empire, even, as we have seen, into the office of emperor itself.

Developments in the civilian sphere were also disturbing. The provincials, who won their way to the loftiest administrative positions and helped thereby to give the Roman Empire its cosmopolitan flavour, were naturally the most thoroughly romanized of their kind. But, as Plutarch protests,[44] their appointment to important imperial posts meant serious loss for their own communities, whose romanization slackened and whose administration deteriorated. The quality of local administration would presumably have declined in any event in the euphoric atmosphere of the Roman peace and the carelessness that it engendered. But the brain drain to Rome inevitably aggravated the decline.

Already by the beginning of the second century AD the affairs of some communities were so chaotic that they were on the brink of bankruptcy. The reaction of the emperors, at that time men of enlightened responsibility, was to send out high-ranking commissioners of their own careful choosing to the affected areas to put matters to rights. These *correctores*, as they were called, assumed charge over entire regions and the communities within them. True, they were only temporary appointments, but as usual the temporary became the normal and the *correctores* soon developed into a permanent institution. And, of course, they deprived the local officials of their functions. The inevitable effect was substantially to expand the embryonic bureaucracy of Augustus' day. It now began to grow with accelerating speed. By the late third and the fourth centuries AD it had burgeoned into the corrupt and greedy monster graphically depicted in the contemporary lament that there were more tax-collectors than taxpayers.

This brought genuine local self-government to an end, and local self-government had been one of the most vitalizing forces in the Roman Empire. Deprived of local outlets for their energies and ambitions, the leading men still remaining in the provincial communities lapsed into indifference and apathy. This in itself was serious enough. But there was also another effect, which does not seem to have been generally appreciated.

As we have seen, the Roman Empire promoted urbanization, since the Romans accepted wholeheartedly the Greek idea that only in the context of the city-state could true civilization flourish. In many parts of her Empire, therefore, Rome had converted tribal communities into urban commonwealths. For un-urbanized rustics such a transformation is always uncommonly difficult. We ourselves have witnessed of recent years the sometimes violent dislocations that result when country dwellers are converted too rapidly into city dwellers. In the Roman Empire their readjustment was reasonably smooth so long as they were being shepherded into their new condition by their own traditional and familiar leaders. But after the second century AD they were liable to find the local men, whom they had always been wont to follow, replaced by newcomer *correctores* appointed by the distant emperor; and, if this disruptive distortion of the traditional patterns of their tribal society did not make them resentful, it certainly left them rudderless and bewildered. The effect of the separation of the natives from their habitual local leaders was truly disastrous. It meant a withering away at the grass roots and must have been in large part responsible for the Empire's obvious loss of dynamism.

Religious vitality suffered no less than civic. In an earlier age their religious beliefs and practices had promoted the discipline, the cohesion, and the greatness of the Roman people. Their native religion guaranteed the traditional ordering of their society, and it did much else besides. Polybius, that very acute observer from Greece, writing in the second century BC, attributed the Romans' rise to supremacy precisely to their religion which was instrumental in keeping them strong and united; and Cicero and Horace, writing a hundred years or so after Polybius, subscribe to his opinion.

Now the native religion of the Romans was by definition a bond with the gods, to whom dutiful respect was paid through acts of public ritual to ensure their favour for the Roman state.[45] To discover the will and intentions of the supernatural powers it had been the habit of the Romans, from time immemorial, to resort to a cult practice described as "taking the auspices": in other words, they looked for omens. If they found unfavourable omens, it meant that the divinities were angry; whereupon they sought to regain divine goodwill by carrying out prescribed acts of ritual with the most painstaking and scrupulous care.

Meticulous observance of the necessary rites went on unchanged, at the official level, for centuries. In private and at unofficial level, it is true, any kind of weird or outlandish belief and practice was tolerated, provided that it did not promote crime, foster immorality, or provoke public disorder. But the due and proper performance of the rituals demanded by the native Roman religion always remained part of the duties of the servants of the Roman state.

At a place called Dura on the River Euphrates, in eastern Syria, excavation has revealed the quarters of a unit of the Roman imperial army of the third century AD, by which time, as we have just seen, the soldiers were being obtained from the most remote and backward districts of the Empire. Yet inscriptions found on the site prove that these rough types of the third century AD regularly and officially carried out in the Syrian desert the acts of ritual that had been prescribed, centuries earlier, for cultivating the good graces of the deities of agricultural Italy;[46] and they were doing this in a period and in a place where the mystic religions, and even sophisticated faiths such as Christianity and Judaism, had made considerable headway. Dura actually displays the earliest surviving Christian chapel and one of the earliest surviving synagogues.

It is difficult to believe, however, that when Roman soldiers of non-Roman birth and rude upbringing carried out acts of Roman ritual in this way, they really appreciated the significance of what they were doing or could themselves have attached deep importance to it. They were content to assimilate their own indigenous native divinities to appropriate Roman ones and thereby reconcile their own cults with those of Rome. But that is far from saying that they really understood the rites they were celebrating. And what is not understood will end up, sooner or later, by being simply discarded.

Of even greater import was the change that had come over the religious attitude of the upper classes. Now that the governing personnel were recruited from anywhere in the Empire, they inevitably included devotees of the occult and of the grosser forms of magic. This made them very different from the Roman leaders of earlier days who, despite all the trust that (like all the ancients) they reposed in omens and portents, had scorned the cruder forms of superstition. No matter how much the lower class plebeians in Rome believed in voodoo, magical incantations, werewolves, human-headed snakes and the like, the governing élite of the early days had disdained such absurdities. Now, centuries later, the leaders were hardly any more enlightened than the mob. They still meticulously observed the old rituals, but in a very different spirit. Dio, writing in the early third century AD, conveys the impression that by then the leaders of society and culture were just as superstition-riddled as the masses; and a state whose spiritual pilots and best educated people have rejected rationality has already lost its values and forgotten what it really stands for.[47]

The history of the auspices which enabled the Romans to keep in well with heaven is instructive in this regard. The ancient belief of the Romans, a belief going back to the earliest beginnings of their city, was that the true and only proper custodians of the auspices were a small group of exclusive and hereditary aristocrats known as the patricians.[48] In the absence of a regular priestly caste, which was something that the Romans lacked, it was this handful of aristocrats who were regarded as the ones possessing the right to deal with the gods on behalf of the Roman people. The patricians, of course, normally delegated this right to the head of the state by conferring the auspices upon him. But whenever the headship of the state fell vacant, the auspices "returned to the patricians" (as the Roman saying expressed it). These, however, began to die out, and to prevent their total disappearance the emperor Augustus created new ones. Thereby he completely changed the character of the patriciate, since it had hitherto been a strictly hereditary aristocracy. The auspices nevertheless seem to have remained under its control, and this, I suggest, explains why in the days of the Roman Empire a new emperor always felt it necessary to seek official recognition in person from the senate in Rome. For it was only there, in the senate, that he would find the patricians who alone could confer the auspices upon him.

By the third century AD, however, Roman emperors, like the Roman governor Gallio in the New Testament, knew none of these things. As often as not, they were men of non-Roman extraction, men like Maximin the Thracian, Philip the Arab, Decius the Pannonian, and Diocletian the Illyrian, who had made their way up from the ranks. Ultimately the practice whose *raison d'être* was not really understood was simply allowed to lapse into desuetude. By the middle of the third century AD the emperors ceased creating new patricians and by its end they ceased to seek official recognition, and the auspices, from the patricians in the Roman senate.[49]

By AD 300 the Roman people no longer enjoyed its old relationship with the gods, while gross forms of superstition and preposterous magic remained.

The emperors themselves did not entirely escape the prevailing patterns of thought. Constantine the Great (AD 312–37), for instance, allowed certain beneficial types of the magical arts to be legally practised. During his struggle for empire he had witnessed the halo phenomenon, as it is called, in the heavens: it had taken the form of a cross on the face of the sun. At that time not yet a Christian, he regarded what he had seen, not so much as a mystical revelation, but rather as a victory omen; and, to ensure the protection of the powerful and to him unfamiliar god of the Christians, he sent his soldiers into the crucial battle of the Mulvian Bridge with an emblem painted on their shields that could be interpreted as Christian. The battle resulted in shattering defeat for his rival for the purple, Maxentius, a devotee of magic, be it noted; and Constantine proceeded at once to recognize Christianity as an official religion of the Roman Empire.[50]

As might have been expected, it is in art that the change from earlier Roman standards is clearly apparent. The most important among the pervading influences were those from the Greek-speaking Near East. These currents spread over the cities of the Mediterranean and into Rome itself. A certain naturalism that had always been present in Roman sculpture and recurrent in Roman painting, the sense of space in the reliefs and frescoes, the descriptive composition, all these Roman features became largely superseded by new concepts and styles, in which the rigidity of the static compositions and the schematic patterns were already anticipating the unreal surfaces and the rhythms of Byzantine art. A most striking change is seen in the imperial portraits. In those of the first two centuries AD, whether lifelike or idealized, the human and individual quality is stressed. But by the close of the third century the group portrait of the tetrarchs in Venice is a geometric scheme, devoid of any individual humanism. Under Constantine and later the oriental conception of imperial majesty has full sway, in the colossal statues at Rome and Barletta with their rigid formality of style and inscrutable gazes.

Caracalla's enfranchising act exactly one hundred years before Constantine's victory had thus had the most far-reaching repercussions on all aspects of Roman imperial life—the army, administration, religion, art, everything. Above all, the lower classes everywhere had been made Romans overnight. But these lower classes were quite unlike the plebeians of the pre-Christian Roman Republic, even though for reasons of historical continuity the emperors had professed to regard the heterogeneous mob in the city of Rome itself as genuinely descended from the settlers of Romulus, pampering and indulging it.

In AD 212 itself Caracalla's action passed without much comment, either because by then the Roman citizenship was no longer much esteemed, or because by then so large a proportion of the provincials already had it that for the remainder to get it was hardly thought worthy of much notice. Even so, the all-embracing act was of the utmost

consequence. Its effect was to make the Roman citizen body anaer-
obic, to use a word that the ecologists have recently brought into
vogue. That is, the amount of extraneous material injected into it
overtaxed its powers of absorption and, like parts of Lake Erie and
the Baltic Sea, it lost its innate capacity for self-regeneration. The original Roman element was simply swamped.

The great mass of Roman citizens were now Roman only in
name. The Roman citizenship no longer inspired vigour and responsibility in those who possessed it. Already at the beginning of the
second century AD Tacitus was hinting that the citizenship had
come to mean very little, and this may help to explain why those of
citizen birth in the Roman Empire, unlike the sturdy Romans who
repelled Hannibal in the third century BC, were so reluctant to
become soldiers. Officially they formed part of the nation that ruled
the world, and they evidently felt that this entitled them to sit back
and enjoy the benefits of Rome's supremacy. Surely there was not
much point in their becoming members of the ruling race, if it
meant that they had to be also a nation of soldiers. The soldier's dangerous trade should be left to the subject peoples.

In earlier days Rome's fortunes, according to Ennius the father of
Roman poetry, stood firm on her ancient customs and on the stal-
wart qualities of her men. But by the third century AD the visions
of glory, which earlier Romans had had, were no longer a stirring
sight. Pride and *élan* belonged to the past and a nation, that had
once cherished the Roman citizenship, now in the days of its depre-
ciation sank into listlessness. Dynamic drive had disappeared from
the Empire, and with it much else besides.

Crisis was not long in coming. After AD 235 and the assumption
of the imperial purple by a rude product of the barracks, there was
a half century of incredible chaos and confusion. Civil war raged all
over the Empire, as commander after commander strove to make
himself supreme. Some succeeded, some failed, and some set up separatist regimes. They were all alike in being short-lived. In the fifty
years between AD 235 and 285 the number of emperors to receive
official recognition from the Roman senate was at least fifteen, and
the number of pretenders that arose to dispute the title with them

infinitely more: it quite literally defies counting. Naturally, as the assorted rivals for the power of the Caesars were fighting one another, the barbarians seized their chance and attacked across the frontiers, looting and spoiling and spreading alarm and despondency on the grand scale. Superimposed upon this military nightmare came social and economic ruin of truly monumental proportions: disease, famine, shortages, inflation, brigandage, piracy, crime, and downright savagery. Trade by barter became common, and ordinary organized living had, to all intents and purposes, broken down.

It is really extraordinary that the Roman Empire did not perish utterly amid the stress, disorder, and violence of this appalling half century. But somehow some sort of restoration was effected, at least in name. But the price was high: nothing less than massive transformation. The Roman Empire emerged from its ordeal entirely changed.[51]

Yet it must be emphasized that it had not been brought to this sorry pass because men had been deliberately disloyal to it or had simply rejected it. On the contrary, not even the most contumacious elements in the Empire would have claimed that they were bent on destroying it or on promoting revolution. By the third century AD all parts of the Empire were, in their own somewhat self-conscious estimation, Roman. This was true even of the Greek-speaking areas. Dexippus, a Greek historian and soldier, is an example: he was the patriotic supporter of the Empire who stoutly defended Athens against the Goths in AD 268.

By then men may not have fully understood the cult of Vesta, the goddess on whom depended the safety of Rome, but they worshipped her with an outward devotion to match that of the earliest Romans.[52] In fact, as the Empire faded, the more desperate became the efforts to revive the old religion. It was precisely in the third century AD that the note of revival was most insistently sounded.

The ephemeral "barrack emperors," as they have been called, of that tristful third century regarded themselves not merely as Roman, but as very particularly Roman. They stoutly protested their devotion to Roman traditions, and they faced the barbarian assailants of the Empire with the resolute courage of true patriotism. The pretenders also claimed to be thoroughly Roman. A challenger of the reigning emperor normally justified his revolt by damning the ruler as un-Roman: he, the pretender, would get the Empire back on to a sound Roman path. Even the rebels, who broke away from Rome in the third century AD to set up a kingdom of their own in Gaul, claimed that theirs was the true Roman society, the authentic Roman state, rather than the debased and corrupt thing from which they had shaken loose.

Late in the century emperors appeared who succeeded in restoring some kind of order. They were men from the Danubian region who, subjected more than others to barbarian assaults, were galvanized into making fierce resistance and they prolonged in some fashion the life of the Empire. They themselves regularly laid claim to the title of "Restorer of the Roman Empire." But, like the lady in Hamlet, they were protesting too much. What they restored was no longer a Roman empire.

Undoubtedly emperors styling themselves Roman continued to reign until late in the fifth century, and in the east for even longer. Indeed they established gorgeous and ceremonious courts where their subjects, also styled Romans, prostrated themselves before the person of the sacred emperors. True Romans would have stared, wide-eyed, in scorn and disbelief, for, as Tacitus records,[53] they prized only the essentials of sovereignty and ignored its vanities. But by that time there was little left that was really Roman. By the fourth century Rome herself had ceased to be the capital or centre of the empire, or even the focal point of its loyalties, despite the continuing magnetism of the name of Rome. The only practical, significant loyalties that there were were of the narrow and parochial kind that made one's own immediate neighbourhood the only thing worth defending. Despite the use of some ancient names and titles, the armed forces and the administrative arrangements had been changed beyond recognition. It was a world of dwindling towns but bloated cities, of crushing taxation and a widening gulf between rich and poor. The few landowners were opulent, the mass of peasants reduced to serfdom. Not only a new art and a new religion, but even a new Latin had emerged. Above all, the geographical unity of the Empire had been destroyed. The once great

Roman Empire after 285 was usually, and after 395 permanently, divided into two or more parts, each under a separate monarch and all liable to be whittled away. The idea of a united empire endured, but the reality was sadly different.

It was not, however, treason or disloyalty that had fatally weakened the Empire. A more potent factor had been the growing carelessness with which the citizenship was extended. The once invigorating and generous policy of admitting new elements from the provinces into the ranks of the Romans got out of hand and brought about a transformation of the citizen body. The imprudent prodigality with which the citizenship was bestowed proved to be the nemesis of empire.

It may well be asked what is the bearing of all this on Britain and her dependencies overseas. The British Empire was not the prey of fifty years of military anarchy over the question of who should rule. The Wars of the Roses belonged to a much earlier period of English history. The dissolution of the British Empire, in fact, was preceded, not by half a century of struggle for the throne, but by half a century and more of a single, glorious reign.

Nevertheless, the story of Rome is by no means irrelevant. The British Empire, too, did not disintegrate because of the uncompromising hostility or active ill-will, much less the treason, of its members; and Britain did not lose her empire through disloyalty any more than Rome did. Even when the parting of the ways came, the Union Jack was not shot down by gunfire. It was struck amid ceremonies of mutual goodwill and understanding, with practically every country, as it became independent, electing to remain closely associated with Britain in the Commonwealth. Burma was the exception to prove the rule, and it probably chose to sever the tie completely because the memory of its wartime experience was still so vivid. The British had been unable to safeguard Burma against the Japanese fury in 1942, and, as Machiavelli remarked centuries ago, a prince who cannot defend his subjects will soon find himself without any.

The disintegration of the British Empire came about with the inevitability of logic. After 1800 especially, the imperial power declared publicly and repeatedly that its first consideration was the interest and the welfare of those whom it governed. A statement made by Lord Macaulay in 1833 when he was secretary of the Board of Control for India has become famous: "We are free, we are civilized, to little purpose, if we grudge to any portion of the human race an equal measure of freedom and civilization." The overseas dependencies were therefore encouraged to study their own histories, preserve their own identities and develop their own institutions, and they did so in the atmosphere of enthusiastic nationalism that the French Revolution, more than any other single agency, had done so much to unloose. Any hope there may have been, that the various countries, as they reached full political maturity, would be content to remain members of an empire, evaporated in the heat of strong national feelings. When the white dominions themselves set the example of preferring full independence to self-government within the empire, it was impossible for countries that had no ethnic link of any kind with Britain, like India, the African territories, and the island colonies, not to follow suit.

In the white dominions the sense of kinship was not nursed and preserved by any policy of integration such as Rome had practised; and in its absence their inhabitants did not go on feeling like Englishmen indefinitely. The children of emigrants from the Old Country had no memories of their own of Britain and could not identify themselves completely with the attitudes and sentiments of their parents. For that matter, emigrants and exiles are hardly likely to be the most effective transmitters of national feeling. In the Empire countries other than the white dominions there was of course no sentimental barrier at all opposing the positive encouragement to particularism forthcoming from Britain herself. In all Empire countries, therefore, nationalism had full scope.

The oft-made assertion that similar nationalism was unknown in antiquity is not entirely true. The war of the Batavians against Rome in AD 69 and 70, to cite but one example, undoubtedly had nationalist overtones.[54] Nevertheless it certainly is true that nationalist feelings did not affect men's outlook, allegiance, and behaviour then in the same way that they do now. It is difficult to see how they could have done so in a world of city-states. In, say, the Roman province of Narbonensis, a man never thought of himself as a Narbonensian, but rather as a burgess of Massilia, or of Forum Julii, or of some other city; and devotion to one's backyard is not the same thing as national feeling.

In the British Empire it was a man's country that engaged his fierce loyalty; and his twentieth-century tendency to make the land where he resided his first concern was reinforced by the self-government that the British had been so liberally willing to grant. The various countries of the Empire were more preoccupied about the success of their own individual societies than about the success of the Empire as a whole. This, in fact, was just as true of Britain as of the others. And it is, of course, something that is entirely natural. For someone who is born and passes his whole life in Canada, the St. Lawrence is bound to have more meaning than the Thames, the more so since the St. Lawrence does not flow into the Thames as the Orontes did into the Tiber.

It has been said that the break-up of the British Empire could have been postponed and perhaps even entirely averted, had the British been willing to grant trade preferences as well as self-government to the overseas countries.[55] Now it is, of course, certain that if the Empire was to be held together, some sort of unifying force was needed. Whether increased imperial trade was the best link was subject to argument, and it was not the only suggestion made to that end. Just after the middle of the nineteenth century (in 1852) a movement advocating full imperial federation was started in New Zealand, but it never made much headway, despite Lord Milner's later revival of the idea (in 1901).[56] In view, however, of the widely held conviction in Britain that trade was the only real purpose of empire, the proposal to set up a system of imperial preferences seemed much more promising. The Australian colonies and Canada were granting tariff concessions to British goods before 1900, and in 1877 South Africa's Cape Colony had advocated a scheme of imperial preferences. In Britain Joseph Chamberlain vigorously supported the notion in 1903, and at the imperial conference in London, four years later, all the overseas statesmen pushed the idea. But it was all to no purpose. Ideas had changed greatly in

Britain since the days of James I in the seventeenth century, when tobacco-growing had been forbidden in the British Isles in order to promote prosperity in the American colonies, or since the eighteenth century, when mercantilism had dominated British policy. By the nineteenth century the free-trade doctrines associated with the names of Adam Smith, Richard Cobden, and the city of Manchester held sway. The Corn Laws were repealed in 1846 and Oliver Cromwell's centuries-old Navigation Act a few years later; and the utilitarian determinists were soon proclaiming that, so far as trade was concerned, the Empire was irrelevant.[57] No matter how ardently Canada, or Australia, or the other overseas countries thought that mutual preferential tariffs by increasing the trade would also strengthen the ties between Empire countries, nothing of the kind really materialized. Late Victorian and Edwardian Britain adhered to its free trade and the colonies, as the dominions were then called, persisted with protectionism, even erecting tariffs against Britain herself.

It was not until 1933, and even then in most gingerly fashion, that the Ottawa agreements introduced imperial preferences over a fairly wide range of products. And by then it was too late. The Balfour Report and the Statute of Westminster had been proclaimed some years previously and W. E. Forster's prediction of 1875 had come true: dependence had been replaced by association. What was once an empire had become a commonwealth.

It may well be doubted, however, whether tinkering with customs duties would really have made much difference. Trade pacts have never yet proved stronger than nationalism. It was not the refusal to practise a kind of closed-shop imperialism, any more than it was active disloyalty, that ended the British Empire. It was the paradoxical nature of the Empire itself. In it visions of imperial greatness faded before strong regional attachments. The clarion call of the Declaration of Arbroath, exalting liberty and independence above glory, had been heard far beyond the borders of Scotland. The various parts of the Empire were concerned to stress their own distinctive aspects and their own interests first and foremost. Immediately after World War II when Britain was intent on promoting her own welfare society, while Australia and New Zealand were chiefly concerned about the security of the Pacific, it was hardly surprising that the two last-named countries should sign the Anzus pact with the U.S.A. and that the mother country should remain outside it.

The ruling power's conviction that it owed responsibility to the ruled and that imperial territories were trusts wherein native interests were the overriding consideration, led to the dissolution of the British Empire; and this is in marked contrast with the Roman Empire where such divergent development of its different parts would not have been tolerated. In the Roman Empire disintegration came for a very different reason. Yet in one respect the British break-up does resemble the Roman. In its case, too, the most praiseworthy feature was the one that hastened the end. Nemesis overtook the Empire because liberalism could not be reconciled with imperial rule.

The experiment of empire, whether British or Roman, indicates that the human race is capable of forming large combinations. But it also proves that the human race is no less prone to practise minute fragmentation. Or is atomization a more appropriate word, in view of the recent creation of such minuscule sovereign states as Singapore, Mauritius, and divided Cyprus? One is reminded forcibly of a Roman poet's vision of atoms in the void, fortuitously colliding and coalescing into ever larger organisms, but at other times no less fortuitously splitting up again and going their separate ways. We, however, can hardly share the complacency of Lucretius at the contemplation of such an endlessly repeated cycle of apparently purposeless coalitions and equally purposeless disintegrations. For the formation and dissolution of empires, affecting the lives of myriads of men, are matters of too much consequence. They seem to illustrate man's instinctive lust for power. But in both the Roman and the British Empire much more was involved than the mere lust for power.

The ordered government of the Roman Empire and the civilized security of its romanized cities, the ideal of administrative probity in the British Empire and the political education of its peoples are impressive achievements. For a space each of these two great empires enabled large areas of the world to go about their business in an atmosphere of peace and some prosperity, and they imbued their inhabitants with the feeling that they were participating in a great adventure of human history. And when the adventure ended, bewilderment ensued.

To the Roman Empire there succeeded a welter of contending and competing states and the myriad confusions epitomized in the expression "the dark ages." The British Empire has not, it is true, been followed by a breakdown in civilization, at least not as yet. But it has left behind it a power vacuum in which disruption is very much in evidence. Harold Macmillan's "wind of change" seems not only to have blown away the Empire, but also to have blown in a large measure of discontent, disquiet, and foreboding.

Yet from the ruins of the Roman Empire there finally emerged the vigorous, quarrelsome, but above all brilliant states of Christian Europe; and who can say what may not emerge from the seemingly formless Commonwealth? The sun has indeed set upon the British Empire, but as a Greek poet long ago remarked: "Even in its setting the sun is ever the same." It may very well be that the British championing of the liberal temper will lead the world to Sir Winston Churchill's "broad sunlit uplands."

Man's attempt to reconcile order and liberty is an old and never-ending chapter in his history; and the creation and decay of empires are aspects of it. Today the West uncompromisingly rejects the idea of maintaining order through empire. But this need not mean that each state will corrupt its liberty into licence as it pursues its own interests in total disregard of international wellbeing. It is true, as Bishop Berkeley said,[58] that westward the course of empire takes its way; but with the setting of the sun, there is also the promise of the morrow's dawn.

In fact tomorrow's dawn may be already breaking. New political ideas and novel combinations are in the air, containing within them perhaps the secret of how to combine national liberty with supranational order. The Europe of the nine is not just another of the military alliances of which history knows so many; and it is not just one more empire in which national identities have become submerged. Nor can so heterogeneous a collection of states be thought of as a federal union. The Europe of the nine is an association of states that have agreed to subordinate unfettered sovereignty to mutual welfare. There is freedom of trade and, much more important, freedom of migration between them; and they seek to offer full scope to individual enterprise and creativity. Linked moreover through Britain and France with the more amorphous associations of states left over from yesterday's empires, the nine present some kind of world-wide look.

Where all this will lead no one can foretell. History has no more business with the yet-to-be than with the might-have-been. Hypothetical history is not a worthwhile exercise and can lead only to doubtful prophecies about the future: as one knows, *l'avenir est à Dieu ... le passé est à l'histoire*. But from its study of the past history does derive reassurance as well as information. It is the past that encourages our hopes for the challenge of the future.

Notes

1. The treaty establishing the Irish Free State.
2. See, for instance, C. Barnett, *The Collapse of British Power* (London: Eyre Methuen, 1972); and especially P.A. Brunt, "Reflections on British and Roman Imperialism" in *Comparative Studies in Society and History*, 7 (1965), pp. 267–88.
3. H.A.L. Fisher, *A History of Europe* (London: Edward Arnold & Co., 1936), p. v.
4. For the Roman Empire in the days of the Roman Republic see E. Badian, *Roman Imperialism in the Late Republic* (Pretoria, 1967) and *Publicans and Sinners* (Ithaca, NY: Cornell University Press, 1972), *passim*.
5. Virgil, *Aeneid*, 6. 851–3.
6. See, for example, Pliny, *H.N.*, *Praef.* 16.
7. Tacitus, *Histories*, 4. 72–4.
8. Sir John Seeley, *The Expansion of England* (London: Macmillan, 1883), p. 8.
9. Adam Smith, *The Wealth of Nations* (London: Dent, 1929), p. 408.
10. Plutarch, *Gaius Gracchus*, 2. 10; Aulus Gellius, 15. 12. 4.
11. Dio Cassius, 56. 16. 3.
12. Cicero, *pro lege Manilia*, 65.
13. See, for instance, Cicero, *pro lege Manilia*, 38.
14. T. Drew-Bear in *Historia*, 21 (1972), p. 81.
15. Livy, 45, 18. 3; 45. 29. 11; Diodorus, 31. 8. 7.
16. The most forceful expression of this attitude is probably to be found in J.A. Hobson, *Imperialism: a Study* (London: Allen & Unwin, 1902).
17. Thucydides, 1. 75. 76.
18. Cicero, *de officiis*, 1. 38.
19. J. d'Ormesson, *La Gloire de l'Empire* (Paris: Gallimard, 1971).
20. W. Dittenberger, *Sylloge Inscriptionum Graecarum*, 2⁴. no. 543, p. 20.
21. Pliny, *H.N.*, 9. 117.
22. S.L. Dyson in *Historia*, 20 (1971), pp. 239–74.
23. Dio Cassius, 56. 33. 3.
24. B. Dobson in *Recherches sur les structures sociales dans l'antiquité classique* (Paris: C.N.R.S., 1970), pp. 99–116.
25. Dio Cassius, 79. 20. 3.
26. See A.R. Birley, *Septimius Severus* (London: Eyre & Spottiswoode, 1971), *passim*.
27. Sir Ronald Syme, *Colonial Élites* (London: Oxford University Press, 1958) (Whidden Lectures, Series 3).
28. Cf. Tacitus, *Annals*, 16. 27.
29. See R. MacMullen in *Historia*, 14 (1965), pp. 85f.
30. F.W. Walbank in *Harvard Studies in Classical Philology*, 76 (1972), pp. 145–68.
31. Dio Cassius, 78. 13. 2f.; Flüss in *Realencyclopädie der Alterumswissenschaft*, 14 (1930), s.v. "Marcius, no. 34," cols. 1547–9.
32. E. Gibbon, *The Decline and Fall of the Roman Empire* (4th edition, edited by J.B. Bury. London: Methuen, 1906), 1, p. 78.
33. See C.P. Jones, *Plutarch and Rome* (Oxford: Clarendon Press, 1971), *passim*.
34. For example, Sarmatae in AD 333.
35. J. Robert Oppenheimer in conversation with the author in 1962.
36. See E. Grierson, *The Imperial Dream* (London: Collins, 1972).

37. *Memorandum Relating to Indians in Kenya* (Command Paper 1922 of H.M. Government, 1923), p. 10.

38. W.R. Crocker, *On Governing Colonies* (London: Allen & Unwin, 1947), p. 139.

39. See, for example, G. Leclerc, *Anthropologie et Colonialisme* (Paris: Fayard, 1971), *passim*.

40. Note the prescient remarks of Tacitus, *Annals*, 1. 4.

41. Cicero, *de legibus*, 3. 18; Tacitus, *Annals*, 15. 21. 1.

42. See R.K. Sherk in *Historia*, 20 (1971), pp. 110–21.

43. G.M. Bersanetti, *Studi sull'imperatore Massimino il Trace* (Rome, 1940), p. 17.

44. Plutarch, *de tranquillitate animi*, 470c.

45. See J. Bayet, *Croyances et rites dans la Rome antique* (Paris: Payot, 1971), *passim*.

46. See the Feriale Duranum published by R.O. Fink, A.S. Hoey, and W.F. Snyder in *Yale Classical Studies*, 7 (1940).

47. R. MacMullen, *Enemies of the Roman Order* (Cambridge, MA: Harvard University Press, 1966), pp. 95–127.

48. See A. Magdelain, "Auspicia ad patres redeunt" in *Hommages à Jean Bayet* (Brussels: Collection Latomus, 1964), pp. 427–73.

49. Carus in 283 is the earliest example: Aurelius Victor, *Caesares*, 37. 5; Mommsen, *Römisches Staatsrecht*, 2^3, p. 843.

50. A.H.M. Jones, *Constantine and the Conversion of Europe* (Harmondsworth: Penguin Books, 1972), pp. 96–105.

51. See P. Brown, *The World of Late Antiquity* (London: Thames & Hudson, 1971) and *Religion and Society in the Age of Saint Augustine* (London: Faber & Faber, 1972).

52. AD Nock in *Harvard Theological Review*, 23 (1930), pp. 256–60.

53. Tacitus, *Annals*, 15. 31.

54. See Tacitus, *Histories*, 4. 14.

55. See, for instance, such works as A.P. Thornton, *The Imperial Idea and its Enemies* (London: Macmillan, 1959), and J.D.B. Miller, *Britain and the Old Dominions* (London: Chatto & Windus, 1966).

56. J.E. Wrench, *Alfred Lord Milner* (London: Eyre & Spottiswoode, 1958), p. 229.

57. In conformity with this doctrine, British capital was just as likely to be invested in, and British imports to be obtained from, non-Empire countries. Conversely, foreign countries were freely permitted to exploit the resources of Empire countries.

58. Over two hundred years ago in his poem, *On the Prospects of Planting Arts and Learning in America*.

Acknowledgements

Particular thanks to Jennie Rubio, an excellent editor at Oxford, who envisioned this book and asked me to work on it as she helped to shape it. This book is a testament to Jennie's creative and intellectual engagement and powers of persuasion. Thanks to Oxford University Press and all those who worked on the idea and the making of the book, which are always collective endeavours. My gratitude also to the Social Science and Humanities Council, which has generously supported my research past and present, and to the University of Alberta, which has long given me support, flexibility, and scope for teaching and writing. My thanks to Anne Barton, Lolita Cayanan, Philip Ford, Luis Galván, Bill Harris, Roland Le Huenen, Anthony Pagden, Andrew Taylor and Gordon Teskey. To the Master and fellows of Churchill College, Cambridge, where I wrote the Introduction and edited this book, I give thanks for welcoming me into such a stimulating community. To Charles, Gwendolyn, Deborah, Alan, and Jennifer, my gratitude. To my father, George, and my wife, Mary Marshall, many thanks and also to our twins, Julia and James.

I remember with thanks my mother, Jean Jackman Hart, as well as Terry Butler, Milan Dimić, G. Blakemore Evans, Harry and Elena Levin, and Northrop Frye. It is my hope that the reader will find these great figures and their lectures as interesting as I did.